Vika and Linda Bull have been singing together their whole lives: in church with their mother; as iconic members of the Black Sorrows; on their own 1994 double-platinum debut, *Vika and Linda*, and on number-one albums by Paul Kelly, Kasey Chambers and John Farnham. Their seven studio albums traverse rock, country, gospel, reggae, R&B, soul and blues, as well as their rich Tongan heritage. They've played gigs for Nelson Mandela and the King of Tonga as well as 100,000 fans at the AFL Grand Final, been nominated for five ARIA Awards, were inducted into the Music Victoria Hall of Fame in 2019, and received the medal of the Order of Australia (OAM) in 2022.

After decades in which they were mostly known for backing up major Australian artists, they hit 2020 with a bang when their career anthology, *'Akilotoa*, topped Australian charts – the first by an Australian female duo to do so. It was quickly followed up by another chart-topper: *Sunday (The Gospel According to Iso)*, recorded during the lockdowns of 2020. And in 2021, with the release of the first Vika and Linda original album in nineteen years – aptly titled *The Wait* – they have well and truly taken centre stage. *No Bull* is their first book and will coincide with the release of their new album, *Gee Whiz, it's Christmas!*

VIKA & LINDA

NO BULL

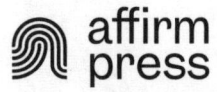

We'd like to dedicate No Bull *to our loyal fans, old and new – we'd still be singing to each other in our lounge room if it weren't for you.*

First published by Affirm Press in 2022
Boon Wurrung Country
28 Thistlethwaite Street
South Melbourne VIC 3205
affirmpress.com.au

10 9 8 7 6 5 4 3 2 1

Text copyright © Vika and Linda Bull, 2022
All rights reserved. No part of this publication may be reproduced without prior written permission from the publisher.

 A catalogue record for this book is available from the National Library of Australia

ISBN: 9781922848260 (paperback)

Cover design by Andy Warren © Affirm Press
Front-cover image by Tania Jovanovic
Back-cover image by Lisa Businovski
Typeset in Adobe Garamond Pro by J&M Typesetting
Proudly printed and bound in Australia by McPherson's Printing Group

CONTENTS

Prologue	1
My Sister	5
Roots	13
Growing up in Doncaster	25
Visiting the Kingdom of Tonga	51
The Things You Learn	81
Bands	125
Changes: Act I	175
Changes: Act II	217
Changes: Act III	249
Epilogue	307
Acknowledgements	313

PROLOGUE

VIKA

I am a pain in the arse to be around on show day. I am quiet, moody, snappy, tense, worried, nervous, sick and excited! The show consumes my every thought from the moment I wake up and check my voice (Can I sing a high note? Yes, phew!), and then I won't talk much, keeping my utterances to a dull growl until around 4pm.

I need to exercise, stay on the move. Motion is lotion and the old body ain't what it used to be. I like a long sound check because it makes the gig better. After sound check I duck back to the hotel for a little power nap before gathering my thoughts and trying to figure out what the fuck I am going to wear. This usually involves about fifteen texts back and forth with Linda, discussing what colour, until I give up and let her decide. Not too much makeup these days because it seems to make me look older, so just the bare minimum – and, anyway, I don't know how to put that gunk on.

I arrive at the gig about forty-five minutes before a show and sit in the dressing-room with the band, shooting the breeze and enjoying their company. Musicians are very funny people and I try not to wet my pants.

LINDA

I used to get really nervous before I sang and had a routine to calm my nerves – ciggie, beer, a shot of Drambuie, a nervous wee, then I'd walk on stage and hope for the best.

I'm much better prepared these days. I will make sure I'm properly hydrated and physically fit. I'll do a vocal warm-up with Vik and I definitely won't smoke anything, but I might have a half glass of wine or a sip of beer beforehand. I still have a nervous wee and it drives Vik crazy because I have to take my costume off five minutes before we walk on. It stresses her out. But we are always together, and it soothes me to have her close by (unless she's really tense; then I'll keep my distance).

The same things always go through my mind moments before stepping out in front of a crowd, so mental preparation is key. It's not the big stuff like the actual singing that bothers me because I have trust in myself and Vik. It's other things, like, How did I get here? What can possibly go wrong? Have I worn the right thing? Am I going to be able to hear myself? But if you let those things get to you, they can really throw you off.

Side stage, I'll look Vik in the eye and we always give each other a nod or a little hand squeeze. It's a private moment, tight and quiet. We have never said it aloud to each other, but I reckon we're both reaching for the same thing: the sound we make when we get it right, the one that only comes from blood harmony, from singing together since we were little kids.

It's the sound that takes me back to family holidays practising in the back of the car with Mum as our coach, the sound that's in our bones from listening to the Tongan choir from the church pew, the sound of our favourite singers we mimicked as kids, the sound we got from belting over the shitty PA systems in the pub rock scene in the 80s, and the technique we've honed over thirty years from being tutored as backing singers by the greats. We both know it instantly when it works and that's what I strive for every night at every show. That we get to share it with an audience makes me smile.

VIKA

Last-minute checks are done. Flies, teeth, hair? Check! We cheers one another and say out loud that 'mistakes are great!' just to ease our nerves.

One last sip, one last shot.

It's SHOWTIME!

MY SISTER

VIKA
Chalk and cheese

Linda and I were opposites from the start. She's always been a daddy's girl, but I clung to Mum. Linda is feminine and I'm more masculine. She is stubborn as a mule, while I'm more likely to go with the flow. I was a prem baby, who Mum said was 'no bigger than a pound of butter'. Linda came out seventeen months later, nine pounds, breech, nearly killing our mum.

My sister and I were chalk and cheese in most ways, including how we went to sleep at night. We'd always shared a room, and after we graduated from cots to beds, Linda's bedtime routine became such a drawn-out affair that it drove me wild. Every night, the two of us would kneel beside our respective matching single Queen Anne beds and say our prayers, like Mum taught us. After 'Amen', I'd jump straight into bed, bunker down and wait for the Linda Show to begin.

The first act started when Linda finished her prayers. She'd stand up, reach for her dressing-gown, and put it on over her pyjamas. Then she'd make her way around the bed, tucking in every inch of the sheet until it was so tight I wondered how the hell she was gonna get into it. That was the second act. The third and final act was when Linda slid her body into her bed, super slowly and super carefully so she wouldn't upset the sheet and bedspread (a process that took about five minutes), and then she'd lie completely still, staring up at the ceiling, and say another prayer. Out loud.

'For goodness SAKE, Lulu!' I'd yell. 'You already said your prayers!'

But it didn't matter how much I shouted, or how many times I called her 'Miss Perfect', my sister continued to carry out this infuriating routine every single night. I'd lie on my side, staring at my sister, wide-eyed and in total bewilderment, until I finally drifted off to sleep. When I woke the next morning, Linda would be in the same position she was in when I fell asleep the night before. Weird.

One area where we were 100 per cent aligned was in the identical outfits Mum made for us, a feature of the 70s for many young siblings. I couldn't have cared less what I wore or how I looked, but Linda was very particular about her appearance.

I was happy getting around in my jeans and gumboots ensemble, but Linda always roped me into her madcap fashion adventures, like the 'Heidi' phase. The Bulls were big fans of Shirley Temple, the pint-sized Hollywood superstar of the 1930s, and our whole family would gather around the TV to watch her movies. We'd usually end up bawling our eyes out, including Dad. Inspired, Linda asked Mum to make us 'Heidi' outfits, which, of course, she did. It must have been quite the sight to see two young brown chicks walking around Doncaster Shoppingtown dressed like they were about to go and tend a pack of goats in the Swiss Alps.

You name it, Mum and Linda designed it, and their attention to detail was second to none. Mum is a proud Tongan woman who always looked beautiful, and she wanted the same for her girls.

One day, when Linda and I were about seven and playing out in the street, one of the mums in our neighbourhood invited a gang of us to come over for cake for her kid's last-minute birthday party. I heard the word 'cake' so was ready to run straight there, but Linda insisted we go home first and change into our party dresses.

'It's only cake!' I pleaded, salivating.

'No, it's a special event,' she told me. 'I want to look good.'

Even Mum said that a full outfit change to eat cake and sing happy birthday was unnecessary, but Linda wouldn't be swayed, and so we both had to dress up just to shove cake in our faces.

To this day, nothing has changed.

LINDA

High and low

We had no other siblings, so Vika has been my most constant companion from the moment I entered this world. When she was a baby, she got hit with the triple whammy of chicken pox, mumps and measles, all back-to-back, whereas I had much better health because of my robust size. I think kids who get sick at a young age end up fighting harder for everything in life, and this is definitely true of Vika. She's always been the tiny fighter in our family. When I was a kid, I remember feeling guilty that Vika had taken one for the team because it seemed like her early exposure to all those bugs helped my immunity.

We spent our first few years in a glorious bubble, the four of us usually at home; Vika and I would always play together and rarely fought. It's amazing that Vika and I got along as well as we did as kids because we've always been such opposites. While Vika is impulsive, I'm careful. I'm into details and she is not. Where she's fiery, I'm peaceful. Vika has a sweet tooth, while I'm savoury all the way. She's a great driver and I'm woeful. Vika sings high, while I sing low.

But we shared some interests too, especially when we were kids. We both liked nature, animals, the water, sport, eating, television and, of course, music. Mum says Vika came out kicking and singing when she was born, and I can believe it. Vika constantly hummed and sang everywhere she went, and I mean everywhere! The sandpit, the toilet, the breakfast table. I don't think she even realised she was doing it. I used to love listening to my big sister singing her little tunes around the house, because she always had such a beautiful voice, even when she was very young.

Like the angels would sound, I remember thinking to myself.

Sometimes I tried to sing along, or find a harmony to accompany her, but for the most part Vika was the singer and I was the talker. This didn't always work out well for me because when

I was up for a chat (which was most of the time) my sister usually wasn't.

The two of us shared a bedroom right beside Mum and Dad's. My bedtime routine drove Vika bananas, and I'd wake every morning still and calm as an Egyptian mummy while it looked like Cyclone Tracy had whipped through Vik's side of the room overnight. My sister thought she was teasing when she called me 'Miss Perfect', but I liked it; the name had a nice ring to it.

Let's get this straight right now. Vika was (and still is) the Boss. If we played shops, she was the shopkeeper and I was the customer. If we played kings and queens, she was the king and I was the princess. If we put on shows for Mum and Dad, Vika was the director and/or the lead role, while my job was to design the show and give out tickets. It wasn't until we were a bit older and started mimicking our favourite bands that I started to kick up a stink. That's when we'd fight. I wanted to be Cher, so needed her to be Sonny, and if I wanted to be Agnetha, I insisted she be Frida. If she was Donny Osmond, then I wanted to be Marie. As it turned out, I was a little bit country and she was a little bit rock'n'roll, so we actually got that one right from the start.

Vika might have been a quiet and gentle little kid when we were around other people, but she was way more outgoing in private. My sister had a hot Tongan temper, and as we got older there were days when the two of us would end up in loud screaming matches at home. But we were always on our best behaviour in public. Our parents taught us to be dutiful and quiet when we were out and told us that speaking over adults was very bad manners. Vika and I were both shit-scared of our mum, so we did what we were told.

We were both drawn to the outdoors and being Dad's helpers, but I also enjoyed being inside, drawing and playing dress-ups with my dolls. I loved dressing up and designing outfits for us to wear, which Mum then made on her Husqvarna sewing machine. My first design, at three, was a flannelette dress with long sleeves. I drew it on a piece of paper and explained to Mum that it had to be made from the same fabric as Dad's flannel work shirts. I planned to wear it on weekends while helping Dad in the garden.

Vika didn't share my love of fashion and would go silent whenever she could see that I was hatching an idea for a new outfit. I think she hoped I'd give up, but once I got fashion inspiration, that was it, and she knew it. So she'd grimace and wear it. I was always happy to be measured and sized up by Mum, but Vika hated the whole process and how long it took. I remember a time when she was a huge pain in the arse, it was the day of our Aunty Moana's wedding and we were flower girls. Vik hated the pink floral dress she had to wear, and, boy, did we hear about it. I'd helped design it so was a bit hurt that she hated it so much. I didn't see her problem. The dresses were a beautiful pink floral chiffon, with Singapore sleeves and a bow at the back. What's not to love? I'd never heard Vika whinge so much, and there were even tears, but Mum wasn't going to let her sister down so Vik had to do as she was told. Vik isn't smiling in a single photo from that day. The grumpy flower girl, that was her.

There's one in every family.

I had an outfit for every occasion, and it used to drive Vika bonkers, but she's accepted that's just how it is. Even now, she texts me before every gig:

What colour are we wearing tonight?

I usually respond with a range of options. Red, blue, white, or black on black on black? It takes about ten texts back and forth before we settle on a colour, which is when Vika signs off with an *ok*. But I know she's screaming into her pillow in the hotel room.

ROOTS

VIKA

Early life in White Australia

Our mother, Siniva, was born in Tonga and came to Australia as a nursing student in 1959. At that time, immigration to Australia was strictly limited to Europeans under the White Australia policy, which prohibited 'alien-coloured immigrants', and Mum had to get special permission from the Australian and Tongan authorities to come here and study. Mum planned to finish her nursing qualification and head back to Tonga to work, but that plan was dropped when she met Dad at the Sandringham Yacht Club in 1965.

Mum and her best friend were there on a group blind date, but Mum's friend soon abandoned her. Dad spotted Mum and could see this young woman was out of her depth. He offered to drive her home, and on the way asked if she'd mind if they stopped to look at the sea. How could an island girl resist a man like that? She couldn't, and married Austen 'Aussie' Bull three months later.

Mixed-race couples like our parents were not the norm in the 60s so Mum and Dad had to deal with a lot of racism when they were out in public in the early days of their marriage. But none of it ever made them doubt or question their love for each other. They've now been married for almost sixty years and are still going strong.

After living in a few flats, Mum and Dad bought their first house in Ayr Street, Doncaster. Linda and I are fourth-generation Donnie chicks and feel a real connection to the suburb. It's the land our dad's parents lived and worked on as orchardists when they first came to Australia from England, before he was born, and we still feel that connection today, even though we moved out of the suburb many years ago. My memories of Ayr Street are vague, but I do remember being concerned about Mum's safety.

She worked nights at Donvale Private Hospital, which was a geriatric hospital back then. Mum used to say that the only people she liked on this earth were babies and old people, and she loved her job. But I was always worried when Mum worked night shifts, scared that she'd be killed in a car crash on her way home. Not just because she'd be tired, but also because she was such a terrible driver. Every Saturday and Sunday morning after Mum had done a night shift, Linda and I would wake early and rush outside to wait anxiously for her to get home. There we'd sit, side by side on our Laserlite veranda, starting every time we heard a car in the distance, and then finally relaxing when we saw our Austin A40 turn in and roll down the driveway.

Dad stuck to Mum's parenting rules when she was around but relaxed them a little when she was at work. He always had one eye on us and one eye on his hobbies, which included gardening, building a wooden catamaran and, like many true 70s Aussie dads, creating a unique crazy-paving patio.

Dad worked for the Department of Agriculture, which involved testing cows for brucellosis in the Yarra Valley. Standing in cold paddocks, testing, tagging and caring for animals all day, must have been hard work in winter, but Dad has always been an outdoors man and wouldn't have coped with a desk job. Sometimes we'd accompany him to those beautiful Yarra Valley farms while he worked. It's a stunning part of the country, with fog rolling off the hills and cattle as far as you can see. He would take us to the local bakery for a meat pie and a chocolate milk, and then we'd all have a little nap before heading to the next farm. If we were extra lucky, the farmer's wife would offer us fresh scones with jam and cream and a cup of tea. Heaven!

My very first school was Doncaster Park Primary School. It was about a 1-kilometre walk from our Ayr Street home, and I walked it there and back alone at four years of age. I was excited about starting school, but it wasn't long before I experienced racism for the first time. I didn't understand why I was being teased because of the colour of my skin. I had a lovely teacher at that school, and I remember her clear as day even now. Mrs Gorski was pregnant and would come looking for me at recess and lunchtimes and plonk me on her lap. I think she knew I was copping it and was trying to protect me. I was her favourite.

One day, on that long walk home after school, I was followed by a couple of horrible little boys not much older than me. They teased me all the way home because I was dark. I was crying my eyes out, trying to hide the snot that was pouring out of my nose and onto my raincoat.

When I finally arrived at our driveway, Dad was there waiting for me. I was relieved. Thank God, I thought. Now these stupid boys are gonna get it!

But Dad didn't say a word to them.

'Don't worry about those boys,' he said, wiping my snot and tears away.

I was so pissed off! I'd wanted my dad to beat the crap out of them, but I should have known that wasn't my dad's way at all. I could tell he was upset for me, but our father is a peacemaker.

When I told Mum, she said, 'Boys who say stuff like that are bloody stupid!'

I was only at Doncaster Park for a year when Ayr Street Primary, a brand-new school, opened on our street. Mum and Dad moved me there because it was closer. I was happy to be moving away from a school where the kids were so mean to me, thinking the new school would be better. But the kids at Ayr Street Primary were the same, and again I was teased for being dark.

Here we go again, I thought.

Before I started school, I didn't know I was different from the other kids in our neighbourhood. I thought I was the same. No one had ever called me names before. No one had ever called me black! Once I went to primary school, though, I spent most of my time trying to convince the kids in Ayr Street that I wasn't a 'darkie'. That was until my Tongan grandparents, Mele and Sione Tuiniua, arrived in town for their very first visit.

Mum's parents had never met their Australian granddaughters, or their son-in-law. The only communication with Dad had been the letter my father wrote my grandfather asking for Mum's hand in marriage. Mum insisted he do this out of love and respect for her father, and of course Dad was happy to oblige. A few years later, my grandparents finally travelled all the way to Doncaster to meet their daughter's husband and children, and to stay with us for three months.

My grandmother was a beautiful, elegant, half-French, half-Tongan woman who was very quiet and didn't speak much English. Before our grandparents arrived, Mum told us how Grandma had constantly scolded her when she was a little girl and made her do the laundry on an old-fashioned washboard until her fingers bled. Linda and I decided to ignore our grandmother as much as possible, as punishment for her being so horrible to our beloved mum. It wasn't until we were older that we thought about the reality of the situation in those days, when our grandma was constantly pregnant – she'd had eight children – and having to deal with a rebellious second-eldest daughter (aka Mum) and that the poor woman was probably stressed and exhausted from having all those babies. My mother says she is sure her mum had undiagnosed postnatal depression.

On one particular day, soon after they arrived, my grandfather decided to pick me up and walk me home from school. A nice surprise, he thought. That day, I walked out of the school gate to see him standing there in all his Tongan splendour, waving and smiling at me.

Grandpa was a very handsome man and always impeccably dressed, and on this occasion he was wearing his Sunday best: a crisp white shirt, lovely leather sandals and a tupenu – a kind of sarong. Over this was a ta'ovala, which is a woven Tongan mat, held in place with a kafa – a belt made from our hair that Mum had made especially for their arrival. A kafa is a Tongan tradition and is woven together with hair from a first haircut and beautiful pearl beads. Not exactly your standard Donnie grandpa uniform. Not only that, but now all the kids would know that I was indeed a black girl because my grandfather looked like Ray Charles. There I was, trying to make a new start and not wanting to be teased because of the colour of my skin, and now everyone knew for certain.

I put my head down, stomped over to him and my temper kicked into fourth gear.

'How dare you!' I screamed at him once we were far enough away from the school and other kids. 'How dare you turn up here! I can walk home by myself!'

I cussed the poor man all the way home, walking five paces ahead and stopping every so often to turn and give my bewildered, and probably deeply hurt, grandfather a piece of my mind. As soon as I got home, I stormed through the front door and proceeded to scream at my startled mother for allowing her father to make an appearance at the school gate.

Of course, now I am horrified by my behaviour that day. My poor grandpa must have been so upset. My only comfort is that once we were home, away from other kids' eyes, he knew how much I loved him, and adored sitting on his lap and playing with his soft earlobes. Years later we wrote 'Grandpa's Song' about the incident.

We took our grandparents to check out Doncaster Shoppingtown while they were here, and it was a real eye-opener for them. They had never seen anything like it. The escalators were mystifying. They were so scared when they first stepped on that they gripped each other's hands, turned and sat down. I clearly remember seeing Mum pulling them back onto their feet as quickly as she could, worried that her parents would scrape their bums when we got to the top. We still laugh, and cry, about that today.

Despite our respective reservations about our grandparents at the start of their visit, Linda and I grew to adore them both, and it was very sad saying goodbye to them at the end of the three months. I would even miss seeing my handsome grandfather, in all his Tongan splendour, waiting for me at the school gate.

LINDA

Tongan church
Mum and Dad always felt it was important to raise us evenly between our two cultural backgrounds. I reckon they did a great job because in my heart I feel that I'm equal parts Tongan and Aussie.

Dad feels like he's part Tongan too, after so many years with Mum. For a typical Aussie bloke from Doncaster, Dad really embraced the Tongan culture, specifically the beautiful singing, a love of family and, of course, the delicious food. It was all so different to what he'd grown up with, especially the food. I think the Tongans also gave Dad something he felt had been missing in his Australian upbringing. Tongans are loud; they laugh a lot, eat heaps of food and stay up all night talking. This lifestyle was very different to the approach of meat and three veg then go to bed after dessert that Dad was brought up in. His family gave him love and security, but the Tongans come in such big numbers with such big hearts, and this was something he wasn't accustomed to in his smaller and quieter family life. Dad loves the Tongan people as much as they love him.

For the most part, we had a pretty Aussie upbringing, but Sundays were always spent with the Tongans. Mum wanted us to be brought up the Australian way because it was our home, but she held on to a lot of Tongan beliefs and ways, including being strict about us attending church. It was a big deal for Mum, so we started going to Tongan church as soon as we could walk. Mum was a founding member of the first Tongan church in our area. She got involved not only because she had such a strong faith, like most Tongans, but also because it was a way to stay connected to her community. The church was her lifeline in a way, because she'd had to adjust to Australian life so quickly and would have missed her home much more without it.

I think the only reason Dad came along with us every Sunday

was that he enjoyed the singing at Tongan church so much. Vika and I didn't love having to go either, but the heavenly harmonies made it bearable for all three of us. Dad adored hearing the Tongans sing. The harmonies are layered and full, and the Tongans can really belt it when they're singing for Jesus. It's the only time during the whole church service when Dad looked vaguely happy. The rest of the time he looked like he was dying of boredom.

Vika and I felt the same way. We'd have to sit for hours on end beside our parents on the bum-numbingly hard church pews, pretending to listen to the sermon, which was entirely in Tongan and we mostly didn't understand. But the beautiful singing made it all worthwhile. As soon as the choir started up, all that pain and boredom would be forgotten. We couldn't have known it then, but all those years of listening to perfect, beautiful harmonies were sinking into our young minds and hearts.

Tongan isn't a difficult language to pick up, and I learned a lot of words and phrases from the Tongans when they all poured into our house after church on Sundays. But it was Grandpa who taught me my first swear word. 'Ta'e' means 'shit', but there were other phrases I loved, like 'Si'i me'a fakahela mo'oni', which sounds a lot like 'Shit, fucking hell, I'm horny' but means 'Oh dear, oh dear'. But the best one in my opinion is 'Faka'ofo'ofa'. When pronounced in English, this sounds like 'Fucka offa offa', but it actually means 'beautiful'. I loved it because it sounded naughty.

Tongans are islanders, so are never in a hurry. 'Tongan time, anytime but the right time' or 'Island time' were phrases we'd all grown accustomed to hearing over the years. Every Sunday, Dad would wait patiently after church for hours and hours, while Vika and I learned different dancing styles from all the Pacific Nations. This weekly routine started when we were four or five. It involved all the half- as well as full-Tongan kids dribbling into our Aunty Kalo and Uncle Doug's living room in Blackburn, where there was lots of giggling and games of Scarecrow Tiggy until it was time to dance.

Pesi, a beautiful Tongan dancer, taught us all the cultural dances of Tahiti, Tonga, Samoa, New Zealand and Rarotonga. She showed Vika and me how to perfect the graceful hand movements that we would later come to rely on in our singing performances. We still use them.

We had all the costumes to go with the dances that we learned too, and all of them were handmade by the mums in their spare time. Mum made ours on her trusty sewing machine, and I can still remember how skilfully she sewed shells onto our grass skirts and made dresses from her rare Tongan fabrics. That was the first time I realised that Mum had an artistic side. She has great creative vision and can make any outfit she sees from scratch without using a pattern. Mum is a perfectionist, so she'd unpick and resew our outfits until they fitted us like gloves. I was always amazed at her refusal to quit, even when her eyes were hanging out of her head and she was completely exhausted. She'd keep sewing, for hours and hours. I used to try and stay up with her, to keep her company, mainly because I was worried she'd fall asleep and sew her hand to the dress.

Mum was also competitive, so it was important that her daughters look the best. (Vika and I are both competitive, like our mother, but only I am a perfectionist and it does Vika's head in.) There was more than a little healthy competition across the board between all the mums, but it was all for a good cause – the yearly Tongan dinner dance.

The Tongan dinner dances were designed to raise money for the church as well as to bring the Tongan–Australian communities together. They were held in the Tongan church hall, which would be filled with big round tables of ten or so, covered in white tablecloths. Loads of families from the community would attend and there was an abundance of kava – a drink made from the ground roots of the kava plant, which has the same effect as weed and tastes awful – and delicious Tongan food to feast on, followed by dancing and entertainment. That was where we came in.

The kids were the entertainment, and the Tongan dinner dance was where we got the chance to bust out our best cultural dance moves, in our best handmade outfits. The Tongan band would play, and we would all file out and perform as a group to the music. The band consisted of a bread box bass, a guitar, a ukulele, a cheesy keyboard, Lali drums and singers. We all looked beautiful, but if you were shy like I was, you could hide behind one of the bigger, more outgoing, kids.

The audience showed their appreciation for our brilliant performance by approaching us with fistfuls of dollars and sticking them on us. Yes, sticking them *on* us. Our skin had been heavily oiled in coconut before the performance, not only to make us glisten and shine, but to make it easier for the notes to stick. This was one of the fundraising elements of the evening, and I always found this custom a little peculiar and confronting.

When the dance was over, the aunties would pick the money off our bodies and the ground, and hand it over to the church. If you were lucky, and nobody was looking, you could sneak a wayward fiver down your top or inside your grass skirt, which was an upside to the whole weird tradition. I did it loads of times and never got caught, figuring it was my pay for all the practice I'd done. Five bucks would go a long way at my local milk bar. It could buy me lots of five-cent bags of my favourite lollies – Eucalyptus Drops and Redskins. Anyway, why should the church get it all? I knew Jesus wouldn't mind.

GROWING UP IN DONCASTER

LINDA
Bottoms

I've always thought Vik is pretty – much prettier than me. My sister has finer bones, lighter skin, bigger eyes, beautiful hair and a good set of pins, while I was always called the 'Heffalump' when we were young kids. I didn't mind Dad's nickname for me because I knew I was chunkier than most kids, and I was happy to be chunky. That is, until I started kindergarten and everything changed.

From day one, my kindergarten teacher made it clear that she didn't like me very much. This woman was a real nasty piece of work and the first person in my life who made me feel like maybe there was something wrong with me. She didn't muck around when it came to letting everyone else know I was different.

Everything in my life took a turn during our first show-and-tell. I was naturally very shy then, which is hard to believe now because I'm so outgoing, but I remember I felt nervous as I got up in front of the whole class. As I stood there, I remember looking at the other little girls sitting on the floor – all fair, pretty and white – and realising for the first time how different I looked to them. Before kindy, I'd had no idea that I was dark-skinned, or that this was even a point of difference, but standing there in that moment it was obvious to me.

'Tell the class about your family,' the teacher said, with obvious disdain.

I took a deep breath then said the first words I ever spoke in front of an audience. I felt like this description of my family was a good way of explaining why I looked the way I did.

'My mummy has a black bottom, and my daddy has a white bottom.'

I regretted the words the second they came out of my mouth. The teacher sneered and the kids rocked back and forth with laughter. Mum was in the kitchen out the back, helping make snacks, and I remember seeing her rush in with a look on her face like, 'I can't believe you said that!' She wasn't angry with me, but the teacher was. I could tell by the way she pursed her thin red lips that she was disgusted by what I'd said. She told me to sit down and, as I did, I hoped the floor would open so I could sink down into it.

I couldn't seem to do anything right. I tried so hard to be good, putting my hand up in question time, waiting my turn, not grabbing the instruments I wanted first, hanging my bag on the right hook and cleaning up after myself, but the better behaved I was, the more horrible the teacher became. She had no reason to tell me off so instead she mocked my drawings, and if the other kids left me out of games, she didn't say anything and just let them.

Hell, I think she enjoyed it.

Every photo I have of myself at that kindy is hard for me to look at, even today, because of the fake smile plastered across my face. I can see straight through that happy expression to the desperately sad little girl underneath. I hated everything about that place: the small chairs and tables, the miniature toilets that seemed ridiculous to me, the smell of the lino, our name tags and those stupid hooks we had to hang our bags on. Day after day, every second I was at kindergarten, I couldn't wait to get out of there. All I wanted was to be home with my mum. My mum was kind, and she didn't treat me like an imbecile. She also smelled a lot nicer than my old battle-axe of a kindergarten teacher.

I can't remember how long I kept going to kindergarten, but I think I only lasted a few weeks. Mum came to pick me up one afternoon and I whispered in her ear, 'Can I stay home from now on? I don't want to come back here.'

I remember Mum leaning down and nodding. 'Yes,' she said. 'You can stay home.'

In that moment I felt a massive rush of love for my mother because I knew she was on my side. Mum had been to the kindy enough times to know that my teacher was a small-minded, sadistic racist, so her attitude was pretty much 'Hell, yeah! I'm not sending you back here!'

She grabbed my hand, walked me out, and we never returned.

Instead, I got to ride in the back seat of our car while Mum learned to drive. Even at that young age I could tell that she wasn't the best driver because I'd be rolling all over the back seat, trying to sleep, as she hit the corners and kerbs of every quiet street in Doncaster. Still, it was more fun than being made to stand facing the wall after I'd peed my pants, with my wet little legs and shoes full of urine, while the whole class laughed at me. The humiliation and sadness I felt in that moment is still potent all these years later. I realise now that the effect of being made to feel like I wasn't good enough was to make me want to prove to everyone that I was. I did this by being nice to everybody and working really hard in school and at everything I tried, and I was careful never, ever to belittle or degrade others the way I had been.

Dad had no idea that any of this had happened. Mum always dealt with anything racism-related because she knew it would hurt him too much. To this day, if we accidentally let a bad memory slip out in front of him, he'll say, 'What? When did that happen? Why didn't you tell me?'

'Because you didn't need to know,' Mum will say. 'Don't worry, I sorted it out.'

And she always did. As one of my daughters has always said, 'We're all playing checkers, and Nan's playing chess.'

VIKA

New house, new school, new friends (again!)
Mum and Dad have always been great renovators, gardeners and homemakers, and after living in Ayr Street for five years, they sold

it for a profit and upgraded to a bigger house in Botanic Drive, Doncaster. We would live there for the next five years.

Linda and I were five and six when we moved into our new house at the end of a court, at the bottom of a very steep hill. It was a 70s modernist-inspired Glenville dream home, with a slanted façade, three windows at the front, a pigeon coop out the back, crazy paving (of course!) and a carport. It had a heavily carved dark-wood front door that was flanked by beer bottle–coloured glass panels. We loved our new home from the moment we laid eyes on it.

Mum had worked hard to save for the three-piece gold velvet lounge suite, which sat atop our red, orange and brown shag pile rug in the lounge room. In the nice room that was only used when we had guests, we had an extendable dark mahogany dining table – which we still use for family dinners today – that could seat four, eight, or ten at a stretch. Mum made all the curtains in our house from lace so they would let the light in during the day while still providing a bit of privacy. She also made linen black-out brocade curtains to keep us cool in summer.

The move meant changing schools again. This time to Doncaster Primary School, the one our father and our grandmother had gone to. The original building is still standing today. Dad lost his father, Claude, to liver cancer when he was just seven years old, so his memories of our grandfather are sketchy at best. Claude met a local Doncaster girl named Gladys Whitten, got married and four years later our father, Austen 'Aussie' Bull, was born. When Claude died, Gladys moved to our great-grandparents' house on Doncaster Road, where Shoppingtown now sits. Gladys's parents had helped to build various structures in the local community, including Doncaster's historic sandstone church, made famous by Scott and Charlene's wedding on *Neighbours* many years later.

Linda and I loved the fact that our father and grandma went to the same school, and Doncaster Primary is also where I met my best friend, Lyn Talbot. Lyn was a beautiful blonde girl, and we hit it off straight away. Unfortunately, I only stayed there for two years because, guess what? Another new school – Botanic Park Primary – opened and so I had to up and move again.

Bloody hell!

Four schools in five years wasn't exactly ideal, but my parents couldn't do a thing because of zoning. I was sorry to leave Lyn, but, luckily, she lived only half a kilometre's walk from us so I continued to see her after school and stayed over at hers most weekends. The Talbots were well-off and had a big house with a pool. Mum and Lyn's mother really liked each other too and were great friends. They liked the fact that I dragged Lyn along to Sunday school at the Church of England on Doncaster Road every Sunday morning. Lyn hated going but I won big brownie points with her mum for taking her with me.

My fourth school, Botanic Park Primary, was newly constructed, and kids came from everywhere around our area. I didn't know a soul there but soon became friends with a beautiful girl named Sally Roxon, and Linda became friends with Sally's sister Nicola, who went on to become the first female Attorney-General of Australia, in 2011.

'Advance Australia Fair' had been chosen as our country's new national anthem so all of us kids at Botanic Park Primary were made to learn it by reciting it word for word in class every day. I thank the Lord for this because those words became part of my DNA, which came in handy many years later.

I didn't encounter much racism at all at my final primary school and remember all the kids in my class at Botanic Park Primary fondly.

LINDA
Botanic Drive
It was 1972 and our mixed-race family stood out in our new, very white, neighbourhood. There was always so much drama going on that we often thought someone should make a TV soap opera called *Botanic Drive*. It would have given *Neighbours* a run for its money, that's for sure. Divorces, marital scandals, gossiping over the fence and family disputes were a daily occurrence in our street. Domestic arguments would cross the bitumen and travel straight through the open windows of every house on the street, so our small ears were permanently cocked for the latest instalment in a neighbour's family drama. It was early training for our excellent eavesdropping and resulted in my family branding me with the nickname 'Gladys', after the nosy neighbour Gladys Kravitz in the

TV show *Bewitched*. As Gladys was also the name of our Australian grandmother, the nickname suited me well. If we weren't listening to the goings-on in our neighbourhood, we were watching. Our eyes were constantly peeping through parted lace curtains.

Mum became a mediator of sorts in our street. Some neighbours used to drink and end up on our doorstep in tears. Mum took care of everyone and was always a shoulder to cry on. It was in her nature to do this, which is why these old boozers were attracted to her. They must have got that vibe from her because she isn't a nosy person, but rather a friendly problem solver. That said, there were a couple of mums in our street who gave our mum the cold shoulder. These women took turns hosting afternoon teas after school, for both the kids and the other mums, but never invited our mum. They also never came to our house when it was our turn to host. Personally, I reckon our mum was just too hot and exotic for those women.

The Palmer family was a mixed blessing. They were all very good-looking, and one of the daughters, Cynthia, was the most beautiful girl we had ever seen. She had long blonde hair and bright blue eyes, but she also had a slightly sad quality about her. This didn't make sense to us at all. How could anyone who had been born into such a super-glamorous family be unhappy? Cynthia's dad was a pilot who was never home, and her mother, Mrs Palmer, looked like the Baroness from *The Sound of Music* and worked at Myer. I was fascinated by Mrs Palmer's amazing fake boobs that stood straight up in the air when she sunbaked on her back deck on hot days.

The second-eldest Palmer child, Lisa, was Vika's archenemy. They were both wild and spirited and hated each other with a passion. They would regularly pull each other's hair out and Mum would have to step in to break them up, before sending Lisa home and Vika to practise piano. The eldest boy, Patrick, was Mum's favourite. He was tall, blond and handsome, and Mum felt sorry for him.

Mum only let us invite girls to our house for playdates (the only exception being her favourite, Patrick) and if she was in the garden when boys from the neighbourhood came around asking if we could play, she'd squirt them with the hose and tell them to go away. Dad was embarrassed by Mum's behaviour. He couldn't see the harm in boys wanting to hang out with us, but Mum never allowed it. Boys were taboo, in her opinion, because as far as she was concerned there was only one thing on their minds, no matter what age we all were.

Mrs McNaughton and Mum took turns driving us and Mrs McNaughton's kids Jodie and Kylie to school. We loved those mornings when it was Mrs McNaughton's turn, and not just because our mum's driving was so bad. It was always embarrassing when Mum dropped us off because our family had such shitty cars. Dad didn't believe in wasting money on flash cars, so he always bought second-hand English bombs.

Jodie and Kylie's older brother, Paul, played guitar, was into music and had posters of David Bowie all over his bedroom wall.

We'd never seen an artist like Bowie before and were instantly smitten by this exotic blue- and green-eyed creature, although the tight red pants and bulging crotch made us blush. Paul McNaughton was so cool. He was the first rock musician we ever met.

Fridays after school, all of us kids would meet out on the street, then migrate from one house to another, grabbing balls, roller skates, skipping ropes, long elastic bands and food, making up games as we went along. On Saturdays, after our respective sports were over, we'd regroup and do the same. Weekends were spent playing cricket, making mud pies, riding our bikes or competing. But we didn't have as much freedom as the other kids and were always on a tight leash. Mum was zealous about our safety, influenced by her conservative Tongan upbringing, which didn't allow girls to go anywhere without a chaperone. We always had to tell Mum and Dad exactly where we were going and had to be home before dark. When we were out, Mum always held our hands because she had a terror of losing us in Doncaster Shoppingtown – a scenario that would haunt anyone.

But Mum's fear for our safety wasn't enough to stop Vika and me from getting in among the action. We played cricket on the street in the summers and footy in the winters, and all the Botanic Drive dads would join in to make up the teams. Dad was a good all-rounder, and what he lacked in skill, he made up for in enthusiasm. Swimming was encouraged in our neighbourhood – we were Aussie kids after all and Aussie kids need to know how to swim – so we'd regularly traipse off to Doncaster swimming pool in a big group. Dad taught us both to swim freestyle, and because he's a lefty we now only breathe on the left.

From the age of ten I started to become really into footy, and Carlton was my team. I was a member of the VFL Junior Supporters Club, which had its own TV show that came on every Sunday morning before *World of Sport*. The show was hosted by Peter Landy and included appearances by footy greats like Lou Richards, and I loved it. Every Sunday morning, I'd pull on my Carlton footy jumper, beanie and matching socks, grab my Weet-Bix and hot milk, then plonk myself down in front of the telly to watch great segments like the play of the day and the handball challenge. I loved Alex Jesaulenko (Jezza) and Bruce Doull (the Flying Doormat), and I'd spend hours drawing the Carlton football logo.

Vika and I were both good at sports, and, growing up, our dad constantly encouraged us and told us we were strong. As I mentioned, Dad's nickname for me was the 'Heffalump', but also 'Lolly Legs' because he said I was built like a rugby player, which he meant as a compliment, of course. There were many times over the years when boys tried to beat us in sports, but they always ended up getting more than they bargained for with the Bull sisters. From early on in life, winning was important to me.

VIKA

Up the creek

There was a mixed bunch of dags we hung out with a lot after school and on weekends in Botanic Drive. We were together so often that we started calling ourselves the Botanic Drive Gang, and Linda and I felt like we had really found our crew. We'd climb over our back fences to venture off into the Botanic Gardens, climb the big pine trees right to the very top and venture down to the creek to retrieve any stray cricket balls that had disappeared down the drain during a game.

One Saturday afternoon, when Linda and I were about seven and eight, we decided to head down to the creek by ourselves to get our cricket balls back. Mum was asleep, having worked night duty the night before, and Dad was busy in the garden, so the two of us slipped away without telling him where we were going. The creek was a slimy, disgusting place; it was where everyone's waste ended up. It stank to high heaven and was full of grey, foamy water. The embankment down to the water was a little slippery, so we had to half-slide, half-walk down it, then use long sticks to try to reach our balls, which were floating on the gross surface.

We were holding hands as we started making our way down to the water, me in front, when I slipped. I lost hold of Linda's hand and slid all the way down the embankment, ending up fully submerged in the disgusting water. I panicked, knowing I would be up shit creek when Dad saw the state of me. Linda, a huge germaphobe, was stressed too, worried that I was going to get some awful infection and that my ears or toes would go green and drop off.

We desperately tried to think of what we were going to say, and arrived home to see Dad standing in the driveway talking to some of our Botanic Drive Gang mates. His happy expression changed when he saw how wet I was.

'What happened?' he asked, looking me up and down.

Linda and I glanced at each other. We didn't want to tell Dad the truth in front of our mates. It would be so embarrassing.

'What happened, girls?' he asked again, but still we refused to fess up.

Only after our friends got the hint and left did we tell Dad what we had done and how I'd fallen into the creek.

'WHAT?!' he yelled. 'You WHAT? You bloody stupid kids, you bloody idiots!'

He was so angry, stomping his feet, scratching his head, yelling and swearing, that he didn't hear the roar of laughter come from behind the nearby fence. But I did. Our mates had only pretended to leave, then hid behind the nearest fence so they could hear everything. I was more furious that they were spying on us than I was about falling into that disgusting creek. But Dad didn't even notice. He just kept saying, 'You bloody idiots!' over and over as he hosed me down. Linda was giving me silent moral support, but I could tell she was trying hard not to laugh.

'Now I've gotta wake your mother!' Dad roared. 'You stupid kids!'

If Dad was going to the extreme of waking Mum after a night shift, I knew I was in real trouble. Mum was the disciplinarian in the house, and I knew what was coming would not be good. She stripped me off and put me straight into a bath full of Dettol, but I don't remember getting the wooden spoon that time, my usual punishment for being naughty. Instead, Mum made me practise piano for the rest of the day, which was absolute torture as far as I was concerned. I'd much rather have had a few whacks with the wooden spoon.

Worse of all, word that 'Vika had fallen in the creek' spread quickly around the 'hood, and the whole gang got a great kick out of teasing me.

Luckily, I didn't get sick after my encounter with the most unhygienic body of water in Doncaster. This was kind of a shame because there were some great perks to getting sick in our family. If Linda or I ever got ill we were allowed to sleep in our parents' big comfy bed with Mum, who is so soft and cuddly, and Dad was sent to sleep in our room. We'd be spoiled with love, affection and presents, even if only one of us was sick. Dad always brought two presents home so the other wouldn't feel left out. One time I had the mumps and was excited, thinking about the awesome present Dad would bring home for me. But when Dad arrived with crappy plastic flowers for me and a drawing set for Linda, I was outraged. My temper reared its ugly head, and I tore Dad a new one, yelling blue murder at him from my sickbed. Another time, a little while after that, I had a bad stack on my bike, and wound up in Mum's bed again. When Dad came home with a beautiful, green toy frog that did backflips and a rubber snake, I was sure the frog would be for me. After all, I was the one who had had the accident, and surely he'd learned from the last time. But no. Dad handed me the rubber snake and Linda the frog. Dad really had no idea and thought that the rubber snake was the better gift.

Despite my swollen head, I still managed to give him a good telling off, but he was unfazed. Now I blame my bad behaviour on not being in my right mind because of ill health. Not making excuses or anything, but that bike stack was full on. So full on that my memories of the whole thing are a bit hazy.

LINDA
The bike stack

Every kid on our street wanted a Malvern Star bike in the 70s, and Vika and I were no exception. We were desperate to have one each, and as Christmas of 1973 got closer, we hoped Santa would come through for us. When the big morning arrived, we unwrapped a flat present addressed to both of us. It turned out to be a map for a treasure hunt. After solving a series of clever clues, we eventually discovered two shiny new Malvern Star bikes in the middle of the lounge room, hidden under a bedsheet.

Mine was red, Vika's was blue, and they were both totally awesome.

The bikes weighed a tonne so it took a bit of practice before the two of us could get a start-up on them, but once we did, we were off and riding! Our new shiny bikes went so fast that they were almost impossible to bring to a sudden stop. A bit of a design flaw, since thousands of little kids all over Melbourne were buying and riding them at the time. Vika and I convinced Dad that we could ride down the hill, very slowly, all on our own. We practised so much, and for so long, that soon we even felt confident enough to dink each other down the hill.

One day during the summer holidays, soon after getting the bikes, our cousins Diane and Heather Froomes came to visit. Being the generous people we were, Vika and I offered to share our brand-new bikes with them, so they hopped on mine, and I climbed on the back of Vika's.

We were all playing outside, riding up and down Botanic Drive, while Mum and Dad were inside getting tea ready. After a couple of hours of nonstop riding, we decided to go down the hill one last time before calling it a day. It was a warm night, so we were all wearing light clothing. Vik had on her shorts, thongs and a T-shirt – most likely her favourite ABBA transfer tee, or perhaps Sherbet. The bike wobbled slightly when we took off, as Vika tried to get her balance with me (the Heffalump) on the back. I shuffled my weight around and tucked my feet up on the back spokes in an effort to help, but I was much heavier than Vika, so finding balance was a challenge from the get-go.

We'd taken off down the hill, gathering more speed than usual due to our heft, when I spotted a few of our Botanic Drive Gang mates watching from the bottom of the hill. This was perfect! It was our final, glorious ride of the day, and the whole gang was there to witness our triumphant descent from the top of the hill. Unable to stop myself, I started waving my arms around and yahooing at them all, showing off.

'STOP!' Vika shouted.

Vika was a good dinker, but with me carrying on behind her it was a struggle to steer the bike and get us safely down the hill. The members of our captivated audience had started waving back when I felt the bike start to shudder and wobble beneath us. The wobble turned into a critical sideways lurch, which morphed into violent shaking as we hit the steepest part of the hill.

We both screamed.

One of our neighbours had swept a huge pile of gravel into the middle of the road that day (no idea why) and this was what we were careening towards, both of us screaming our lungs out. We ploughed straight into it and the bike came to a sharp and sudden stop. But we didn't.

Vika went first, flying straight up into the air and over the handlebars, her skinny little legs dangling in the air as her thongs flew off in two separate directions. Her head was the first thing to hit the road, followed by her face. There was a terrible smacking sound that echoed around the neighbourhood as Vika hit the road and slid along the rough bitumen, facedown.

Meanwhile, I flew up over the gravel pile, high into the air, and landed directly on top of Vika, whose body acted as a superb cushioning pad. There was a moment of horrified silence, followed by the ear-piercing screams of the Botanic Drive Gang, and then everyone came running.

A neighbour, hosing his garden at the time, saw it all happen and was so shocked that he turned his hose directly onto the two of us as we lay on the road. The cold water immediately roused me but failed to wake Vika. My sister was unconscious and in a very bad way; she was barely recognisable. Rice-sized bits of tar and gravel were embedded in her face and legs and had taken off all the skin, almost to the bone in places. The surface of the bitumen had acted like a giant cheese grater on my poor sister's face, which was starting to swell at an alarming rate. Her two front teeth were smashed, and another was missing. She had a terrible gash on her forehead, her lips were swollen, her clothes were ripped, and she was covered in blood and twisted into an unnatural position. She wasn't moving. I thought I'd killed her. I ran as fast as my little legs could carry me into our house to raise the alarm.

Mum went straight into action, and as soon as she saw Vika she knew that she had to get my sister to a hospital. Mum and Dad rushed her to Box Hill Hospital, where the news wasn't good. My sister had fractured her skull, which was now the size of a watermelon, and she was covered in so many other terrible cuts, grazes and bruises. The doctors and nurses tended to her wounds, wrapped her in bandages and gave her something to help her sleep.

When Vika came home from the hospital a few days later, she was allowed to sleep in Mum's bed while she recovered. Dad comforted me by singing me to sleep every night in his best Bing

Crosby voice and told me spooky stories that he made up as he went. They were both scary and funny, and I loved the way he told them. I still love a spooky story, as do our kids, but nobody tells them as well as Dad.

A few days after the accident, Dad came home with a big bag, looking very pleased with himself. He'd decided that a major accident like ours called for some special presents, but his pride and joy was short-lived. He'd thought Vika, a known lover of animals, would love the toy snake he'd bought her, but my sister clearly had a different idea about what she wanted. Vika can't really remember the bike accident but does remember the snake, and the toy frog that I got instead of her – a lack of judgement on Dad's part that still causes issues between us.

Seeing my sister lying on the ground like that was one of the worst moments of my young life. Not only had I been worried for her, but I also felt enormous guilt. I knew in my heart of hearts that it was my fault we had wobbled and crashed. It was my fault Vika had been taken to hospital with a fractured skull, dozens of cuts and grazes, and missing teeth. I had been the one who was showing off, and I had made Vika's injuries even worse by landing on her.

I didn't cry at the time, because I knew there was no time for tears. Mum did not encourage crying in our household. She just wanted to know the facts and if I'd been a blithering mess, I would have been no help. I told Dad it was my fault, but he said it was an accident and not to worry.

'She'll be fine,' he said.

Neither of my parents ever laid any of the blame at my feet. Instead, they very diplomatically held the neighbour's pile of gravel accountable for the whole incident.

VIKA
Musical beginnings

Singing is my thing and I am very passionate about it. I was always singing when I was a kid; it made me feel good and it came very naturally. I sang night and day. I loved singing along to Elvis's *Blue Hawaii* and Bill Haley & His Comets' *Rock Around the Clock* – they were my favourite records in Mum and Dad's collection. When I overheard Dad say to Mum that perhaps one day I would become a singer, I was secretly delighted and thought, Yes! This is what I am gonna do when I grow up; I am going to be a singer.

Mum and Dad said I started singing the moment I learned to talk, and as a little kid I remember doing it all the time. At the top of my voice. When we lived in Botanic Drive, I sang so much and so loudly that everyone in the street could hear me. One day I was sitting on the loo, belting out 'Kookaburra Sits in the Old Gum Tree', and when I got to the end of the song I heard a huge round of applause, followed by a roar of laughter. I looked out the window and saw every kid from our street perched on the fence outside our bathroom, laughing and having a grand old time. My archenemy, Lisa, was laughing the loudest and I found out later that she was the one who'd rounded up all the kids to come and listen when she heard me singing. Mortified, I ran to our bedroom, dived straight under the bed and wouldn't come out for ages. Linda joined me under the bed and finally coaxed me out after about an hour.

'I swear I'm gonna *kill* Lisa,' I sobbed.

But not even a humiliating episode like that was enough to stop me from singing for long. Whenever our cousins from Wollongong came to visit, we would put on concerts for our parents, which for them was tedious and boring, I am sure, but they put on a good act once the performance was underway. The boys were the same age as Linda and me, so they often came to Melbourne, or we drove up the Hume to visit them. In these concerts, Linda and I always did a Tongan dance, sang a song or made up a terrible play, while our cousin David sang 'Moon River'. David had buck teeth, so it came out sounding more like 'Moon Wiver', which was hilarious. Linda and I would struggle to keep a straight face during this performance, but it was always too much for us and we'd end up crying with laughter, literally wetting our daks. His mum, Aunty Barb, was furious but we didn't care.

LINDA
The family that sings together
The first time I sang in public with Vika was in the old sandstone church our great-grandparents had built at Doncaster. We were

around four and five years old, and Mum taught us a catchy church song called the 'Rise and Shine' song to perform at Sunday school. I'd been singing with Vika around the house for ages by then, but this time we were going to sing in front of other people. It was a big deal. We wore matching outfits and Mum had included a hand clap and thumbs-up move in the performance – the costumes and choreography gave it that extra bit of pizzazz. Mum obviously understood how to work an audience before we did. We sang in unison and concentrated hard on getting the melody right because we knew Mum wanted us to sound good in front of her beloved church congregation. I was disappointed that Mum didn't get us to sing any harmony at all because when we got the harmony right it felt good. It was my favourite thing to do.

The performance went off without a hitch because our mum had prepared us so well for our first public gig and left nothing to chance. During the performance, Mum kneeled in front of us, holding up the microphone with one hand and conducting us with the other. The song was a success, and we were officially hooked.

Mum was our first singing teacher (and free!) and we trusted her. She has a powerful and strident voice, like Vika's, and we had heard that voice singing in church every Sunday since we were born. Mum has the kind of voice that could cut through sheet metal, which is an advantage in a choir because everybody wants to stand out, and so we trusted her judgement. Even if we hadn't, we would never have dared to question her because our mum was the Boss.

Mum knew early on that I had a naturally low voice and that Vika's was high, and that's where the early harmonies came in. She taught us to sing each part on our own first, then put the two bits together and, hey presto, ready-made harmony. Our mother was a hard taskmaster and a perfectionist. If she thought we were off or could make the song better, she'd say so with no sugar-coating, and we learned early on that we needed to have a thick skin when she was around.

There we'd be, lying on the lounge room floor singing along to the TV ads, or trying to mimic our favourite singers on *Countdown*, while Mum yelled out instructions on how to make it sound better while she cooked dinner.

'Hold your notes longer, Linda!'

'Vika, you're using too much vibrato!'

'Both of you need to sing louder. I can't hear you!'

'Hey! You need to start and finish at the same time!'

Whenever we got excited and sang along to Split Enz on the radio, she'd burst in with, 'Who is singing off? I can hear one of you is off!'

Newsflash: it was always me.

But all that nagging was worth it for those moments when we got it right. I can still see Mum's beautiful face turning around to look at us in the back seat as we sang along with the radio when we drove to Wollongong to visit our cousins. As we sang, she'd chime in and direct our voices, guiding us with her hand and gesturing as to when we should cut off the note and when to hold it, when to slip down to the low note for me, or the high note for Vika. I got such a kick out of seeing Mum's face light up when we got the sound right. She wasn't naturally a smiley person and seeing her beam like that was a beautiful sight to behold.

Vika and I always tried hard to get it right. This might have been because we were desperate to please our mum, but I think we also wanted to please ourselves and find that beautiful resonating blend that only siblings can achieve. 'Blood harmony', Vika calls it. We always knew we had that, and even though it's partly genetics, we've also worked very hard for over thirty years to perfect it.

A love for music was encouraged in our house but never pushed on us. It was just part of the landscape. Whenever I went over to a friend's house, I was surprised to find that their parents didn't have music blaring like ours did.

Dad has a deep love of music, and always sings while gardening or tinkering in his garage. He sings loudly too and couldn't care less if the neighbours hear him. He has eclectic taste. When we were growing up he surprised us because he fancied the popular music of the time like ABBA, but also Mum's Tongan music and the classical greats like Brahms, Schubert and Handel. Country and western artists like Willie Nelson and Linda Ronstadt also got a great run in our house, as did Peggy Lee.

Vika was taught piano at the age of ten. I followed suit, but I loathed practising and much preferred listening to Vika play. My sister had to practise every day, and if she ever got in trouble her punishment was more piano practice – never a good way to get your kid to love an instrument. I hated my lessons and begged Mum to let me quit. She did, but Vika kept going with it and became a beautiful piano player.

My instrument of choice was percussion, which isn't exactly the coolest thing in the music room. I remember in Grade 1 our teacher dumped a large pile of instruments onto the floor one morning.

'Pick one,' she said.

I made a beeline for the triangle. I loved the triangle, the feel of it in my hands, and if you ever got one or two opportunities to play it during a song, it made a loud and weird sound, which always attracted attention – minimal effort with maximum effect. So, yeah, the triangle was my instrument, closely followed by the tambourine, maracas, and the recorder. Clearly, I was trying to avoid being voted most popular girl in the class.

VISITING THE KINGDOM OF TONGA

VIKA

Meeting our Tongan family

Mum and Dad had been scrimping and saving for years to take us on a trip to Tonga. It had been almost twenty years since Mum had been home and she missed her family terribly, especially her father and her sisters. By 1975, Dad had been working for the government for over ten years and his long service leave was due. Mum and Dad decided this was the perfect time for the four of us to head off for a three-month adventure in the Kingdom of Tonga.

The trip meant that Linda and I would have to miss a couple of months of school in the new year – Grade 5 for me and Grade 3 for Linda – which may not have seemed like a big deal for our parents but was for us. It was my fourth school and Linda's second, and to go away as we were both starting to get settled again was a big risk, especially from a social point of view.

There was an upside, of course. We might not have to attend school at all in Tonga.

'Do we have to go to school over there?' was the first question I asked when Mum told us we would be going.

'No,' Mum said. 'You'll be free to swim and play with your cousins every day.'

Excellent!

'Do we have to go to church?' Linda asked.

'Yes,' Mum said. 'And a lot more than you do here too.'

This was not so excellent and almost enough to make the two of us kick up a stink about going, but the whole getting out of school for three months and swimming every day idea made up for it so we decided to suck it up.

There was a lot to organise for the trip. Not only passports and paperwork, but also injections. A *lot* of injections. Mum started packing three months before our departure date, and I reckon she ironed, packed, unpacked and repacked on repeat for the entire time. She knew better than us what to expect over there and she was determined not to leave anything behind, especially the first aid kit. Tonga was a Third World country and, being a nurse, she knew about the tropical diseases we could potentially be exposed to over there. Of course, all we thought about were the beautiful beaches, coconut trees and tropical fruit.

The day of our departure finally arrived, and Linda and I were so excited. Mum, the alpha female boss that she is, oversaw everything, and, even though we all wanted to help, she was reluctant to give us any jobs that we might stuff up.

'I have everything under control,' she told us. 'All you have to do is get in the car when I say so we can get to the airport early.'

By early, Mum didn't mean two hours prior to departure, which was the requisite time for all international flights. Oh no. Mum wanted to be there four hours before our flight. Every Tongan on the planet likes to get to the airport at least three, maybe four, hours before their flight.

'Just in case there are any problems,' she said.

I begged her to let me help, refusing to accept no for an answer.

'Can I *please* be in charge of the beauty case?' I pleaded.

The beauty case was Mum's only carry-on and held a few actual beauty products, as well as the keys to the suitcases and, most importantly, our four passports.

'I want to be in charge of the beauty case!' Linda complained loudly.

The two of us began to fight over who was the more suitable candidate for such an important job, but Mum shook her head.

'No!' she said. 'Neither of you is going to be in charge of it, okay?'

All day long I begged and begged, promising my mother that at nine years old, I could be trusted. I would be a responsible keeper of the keys and the passports in the case.

Finally, to Linda's outrage, Mum relented and said I could take charge of the all-important case. I was rapt and spent the next few hours lording it over my sister. YES! I was reigning Queen of the Beauty Case!

The lead-up to leaving the house was hectic, and Mum kept at us all morning.

'Have you got this? Have you got that? Have you packed this? Have you packed that?'

'Yes! Yes! Yes!'

'Vika, do you have the beauty case?'

'Yes! I have the beauty case! I told you, you can TRUST ME!'

Finally, it was time to leave for the airport (four hours before our flight) and the four of us piled into our orange Austin Kimberley, along with our four huge suitcases. I've since learned that Tongans always overpack and usually end up paying for excess baggage at the airport, but not my parents! They must have weighed our suitcases a million times before we left to make sure they were bang on the money. There was no way our father was going to part with a cent of his money for a few extra clothes.

Doncaster was a bit of a hike from Tullamarine Airport, so Mum and Dad allowed two hours for the drive there. There we were, driving down Bell Street when Mum decided to do one of her periodic checks.

'Vika,' she said, turning to look at me in the back seat, 'do you have the beauty case?'

My stomach gave a sickening lurch and the blood drained from my face.

I'd forgotten the beauty case! I was so excited to get to the airport that I ran out of my room and left it sitting on my bed. Linda read my horrified expression and her eyes widened. She couldn't believe it.

I couldn't believe it.

No one could believe it.

Dad was furious, of course. He did a U-turn and drove back home like a maniac while Mum glared at both of us from the front seat. I felt like throwing up, and wanted to say sorry but Dad was so angry that none of us dared say a single word. What a monumental stuff-up – thank God Mum had allowed so many hours for the drive!

The beauty case was sitting on my bed, exactly where I'd left it. Mum marched into the room, picked it up and announced that she would be keeping it in her possession until we landed safely in Tonga. I knew I'd blown any chance of being given a skerrick of responsibility for the next twenty years, but at least we were soon back in the car and off to the airport with plenty of time to spare. We have four hours, I thought, what's everyone panicking about! But, yeah, I did feel like a bit of a dickhead.

Luckily, we arrived at the airport just in time to check in and get on the plane.

As we began our descent into Tonga, I looked out of the window, and it was like nothing I'd seen before. There were hundreds of tiny islands, dotted across the ocean as far as the eye could see, a sight my young eyes had never seen before. The ocean was a thousand shades of blue, not green like in Australia. I wanted to jump straight out of the window and into that clear blue water.

As we got closer to land, I could see so many coconut trees that it seemed as if the earth was covered with them. I could also see beautiful little Tongan houses – some weatherboard, some concrete, some scraped together with whatever they could find to make a house or, in many cases, one-room huts – scattered in and among the trees. There were tall palm trees everywhere, and I couldn't wait to get off our stuffy plane full of overweight, wheezing chain-smokers all puffing away on their cigarettes in the recycled air conditioning.

But when I stepped off the plane, the humidity hit me like a tonne of bricks. It was so intense that it felt like I was being punched in the face and I got the shock of my life. We had arrived in Tonga's wet season, and I had never in my life experienced a climate like it. Where was the fresh air I was dreaming of when I looked out the plane window? This felt hotter than it was inside that stuffy plane, and it was harder to breathe. Not only that, but within seconds I was dripping with sweat. Now I understood why the poor Tongans were so cold when they came to Melbourne and wore big fake-fur coats on a beautiful, 24-degree Celsius day. Nope, I did not like this weather at all, and wondered how I was gonna cope here for three whole months.

Getting through customs didn't take long, thanks to Mum. It's not what you know, it's who you know, and the customs official wasn't going to mess with our mum, who just naturally exudes a born-to-rule boss attitude.

We walked out into the airport and I forgot about my sweaty

discomfort when I saw the colourful sight of Mum's whole family waiting for us; and I mean the *whole* family. Tongans love a trip to the airport, and it doesn't matter if someone is coming or going: they will all pile into the car and head to the airport for a family day out. Mum has seven brothers and sisters. Her eldest sister, Tupou, has six kids, her sister Mafi has four, her brothers Pota and Dan have three and two kids respectively, David has three and Moana's two kids were yet to arrive. Mum did have another brother, Totai, but he sadly died from septicaemia when he was eight. There was the same number of aunties, uncles and cousins on her mum's side, and there were rumours that there might have been a few spares around the island, as our uncles were quite popular with the ladies!

This is Mum's immediate family? I thought, looking at them all. Bloody hell, how am I going to remember all their names?

These beautiful brown-skinned people, with their jet-black hair and fresh, brightly coloured, flowered leis around their necks, were wearing traditional Tongan dress – ta'ovala for the men, kiekie for the women, as well as hibiscus and frangipanis in their hair. They were all smiling, laughing and singing when we walked out into the airport. Yep! The guitars and ukeleles were out in full force, and everyone was singing. Some of them were crying too because it had been so long since they'd seen Mum. I'm gonna love this place, I thought. I've just gotta learn how to deal with this shit weather.

Mum started gabbling away in Tongan and hugging everyone straight away. Our relatives weren't shy with the kisses and the hugs, especially because for most of them it was the first time they'd seen me and Linda. We were showered in love by our chubby aunties, who all smelled of coconut. After all the hugging, kissing and weeping at the airport, we climbed into Aunty Mafi's car, with her husband Sinipata behind the wheel, to head to the capital of Nuku'alofa, where she and her family lived. The plan was for us to stay with Aunty Mafi for a couple of weeks before heading to Mum's family home in Vava'u, Tonga's northernmost group of islands – an hour's plane ride away or an overnight ferry trip.

The drive to Aunty Mafi's village was memorable for both me and Linda. Firstly, there were no seatbelts in the car and no traffic lights on the unsealed roads, which were full of potholes, making it a very bumpy ride. Sinipata was weaving all over the place, dodging the holes and the wild dogs that would occasionally sprint across the road in front of our car. There were heaps of these dogs, and they were all skinny, not the pampered pooches we were used to in Melbourne. There were also pigs of all shapes and sizes on the side of the roads too, who looked better cared for than the dogs, and chickens running across the road in every direction. Linda and I were both a bit shocked by the poverty in Tonga, and the sight of so many gorgeous little kids running around with no shoes on.

Aunty Mafi's family had prepared a feast for our arrival, which included a suckling pig, raw fish, yams, taro, sweet potato and all other kinds of exotic foods I'd never tasted. But it was so hot that the only thing I was able to manage was the juiciest, sweetest pineapple and watermelon I'd ever eaten. I showered three times the day we arrived because I couldn't take the humidity and was happy to note that my aunty had no hot tap in her shower, only cold, which suited me fine.

Aunty Mafi's house was gorgeous, and the moment I stepped inside I felt completely at home. Tongan houses are decorated so beautifully. They love to hang pictures of their family all over the walls, and often these pictures are decorated with leis made from fake flowers. They also love lace curtains, and there are always doilies laid out on their tables, and the chairs are placed around the room against the walls. I initially wondered why this was but quickly learned it was because the Tongans love to gather in rooms together and talk. With the chairs against the walls, they could sit and see one another, and there was still plenty of room to sit on the floor if they ran out of chairs. I also noticed that my aunt's skin glowed with health, as did most of the Tongan women – a result of all the coconut oil she smothered on her skin and in her hair.

That first night at Aunty Mafi's house, Linda, Dad and I slept in the rooms our aunt had prepared for us, where big silk bedspreads with loud colourful designs adorned the beds, while Mum sat up and talked with her relatives all night. Dad could never last the distance and doesn't speak Tongan, so he left Mum to it. The Tongans love to talk, and this was the first of many times during our stay when Mum would be up all night, laughing and reminiscing about the old days with her family and friends. Linda and I woke the next morning to find all the adults asleep on the veranda, flat out and snoring their heads off. There'd been no alcohol consumed the night before, just Fanta, but their all-night chitchat had worn them out. Linda and I had four cousins to keep us busy, so we left 'em to their snoring and got on with our first fun-filled day in Tonga.

LINDA

What do you mean there's no TV?
Aunty Mafi's kids were the same age as me and Vika, and from that first day, hanging out with our new cousins, as well as all the family and neighbourhood kids, was very exciting. We spent every day going to the beach, hanging around the shops, going to the market or lazing about. They all taught us Tongan and we taught them English, even though we didn't really need to as most of them spoke better English than we did. Tongan kids learn English as soon as they start school.

Before we went to Tonga, the limited language skills I'd picked up were from the preacher's sermons in church or by eavesdropping on Mum talking on the blower to her family back home. Mum had no idea, but my comprehension was becoming quite good. I had to concentrate hard on the repeated words to learn because how else would I find out the good swear words and gossip from the coconut wireless? Of course, all the juicy stuff was in Tongan so I couldn't wait to expand my growing repertoire, because whenever Mum wanted to hide anything from us, she'd say it in her mother tongue.

I was also curious about how the Tongans lived. I knew the

'Tongan way', otherwise known as 'anga fakatonga', was much stricter, but I was interested to see how much stricter. I'd always thought our upbringing was pretty strict already, especially compared to those of our friends.

The Tongan people are brutally honest and don't hold back on their opinions. Over those first few days there was a lot of squeezing and pinching going on. My fat cheeks were constantly being squeezed and pinched by my aunties and uncles, and they also loved stroking my hair because it was so long. I heard 'faka'ofo'ofa' more than once, which means 'beautiful'. My aunties called me 'Siapani', which means 'Japanese', because they thought I looked more Asian than Tongan. I didn't look Aussie enough to be called Australian, and I looked too Asian to be called Tongan. I couldn't bloody win. I soon stopped caring. I am who I am, I thought. A faka'ofo'ofa Siapani, or a beautiful Japanese kid!

Tonga didn't have a lot of the creature comforts I'd always taken for granted in Melbourne, which is why I now believe travel is so good for kids. It makes them appreciate what they have. I hadn't even been off the plane for an hour when I worked out how very lucky and spoiled I was. Tonga was, and in many ways still is, a Third World country even though it's the same distance from Melbourne as Perth is, and those differences were a huge eye-opener for me.

Aunty Mafi's house had no hot tap in the shower, only cold, and it was the worst water pressure I'd ever experienced. It was more of a trickle than a spray, and the shower-head was so wonky that the drips of water went in all directions when you turned it on. You ended up having to dodge all over the place to try to get the different parts of your body wet. There was no fresh milk on the island either, because they didn't have cows. I loved milk, but all we could get was condensed milk, which tasted great, but Mum wouldn't let me drink it because it was too sweet.

Most shocking of all was the discovery that there was no television, a detail Mum had suspiciously forgotten to tell us before we left. Vika and I loved watching TV. It was one of our favourite pastimes and one of the ways in which Vika and I learned to sing. We'd sing along with the theme songs of our favourite shows, like *Skippy the Bush Kangaroo*, *The Partridge Family*, *The Benny Hill Show*, *Laverne & Shirley*, *Donny & Marie*, *Happy Days*, *Lost in Space*, *Green Acres*, *Petticoat Junction* and *Mister Ed*.

But now, here we were with NO TELEVISION! How would we survive? What would we do after dinner? This was a mini crisis!

After we got over the initial shock, we realised that we would have to make do and not complain because we didn't want to come across as the Aussie spoiled brats. We soon learned that our relatives played cards after dinner instead of watching TV, but it took at least a week for the look of betrayal and disappointment to disappear from our pampered little faces.

The arrival of the bakery truck stacked full of piping hot, freshly baked bread every morning made up for the missing TV, and I loved to meet it at the gate with Aunty Mafi. She taught me how to choose the hottest loaf by hovering my hand in front of the rows of bread to feel which one was giving off the most heat. The last loaf out of the oven was always the one we picked, and first one in our mouths, and we got to have a whole loaf each!

VIKA

Boats, bathers, bratty behaviour and bones

The reason I took to Tonga so strongly was that it was so unspoiled and unaffected, and I remember thinking this even as a young kid. It was just so beautiful, even though the people didn't have much. They were poor but were happy to share what little they had; they were so friendly and generous. Aunty Mafi was a great cook, and I remember she always left food and little snacks out on the table for us to eat, like fried fish, pineapple, fried eggs, fresh bread and butter. I adored it all. Aunty Mafi owned a little blue shop in the village, which was very popular with the locals, and I remember how she would bust open packets of cigarettes and sell them one by one to Tongans if that was all they could afford. At nine years old I thought this was brilliant and wondered why they didn't do the same thing in Australia.

Even though Vava'u was only an hour away by plane, Dad decided that we were going to take the overnight boat trip instead because he loves being out on the ocean. Dad especially wanted to sail into Vava'u, which has one of the most stunning harbours in the world and is a popular destination for many yachties who sail around the South Pacific. Our father has sailed and owned yachts all his life, and Linda and I love the ocean too. But Mum doesn't share his love of the sea – she missed out on the Tongan sailing gene, for some reason, and gets horribly seasick, even though Polynesians are some of the best sailors in the world. For centuries they had to rely on their knowledge and expertise to cover the vast expanse of the Pacific Ocean. They'd watch the birds overhead, feel the temperature of the ocean, pay attention to the winds and the stars so they could navigate long distances without maps. They mapped out the Pacific long before Captain Cook ever turned up, sailing the oceans in their huge handmade wooden canoes. It would have been quite the sight to see these canoes, full of men who all looked like The Rock, circling a fleet of ships. A white, scurvy-ridden English sailor aboard the *Endeavour* might have been more than a little worried.

There was only one boat in the whole area, the *Olovaha*, that took islanders back and forth between the capital of Nuku'alofa and the other islands up north – the Ha'apai and the Vava'u groups. By now it was the end of December, and a lot of the Tongan kids were leaving Nuku'alofa to head home for Christmas. The *Olovaha* was licensed to carry around one hundred passengers but on this night, I reckon they managed to cram at least three hundred and fifty people on board. There were kids and adults everywhere – lying, standing and sitting wherever they could find a spot on the deck. Dad had booked the four of us a little cabin below deck, and when we arrived at the wharf to board the *Olovaha*, we were a little unsettled at the sight of so many people getting onto the boat.

'Don't worry,' Dad told us, grinning. 'It will be okay!'

When we were all on board, we found our cabin and waited for the boat to set sail for Vava'u. Soon after we left Nuku'alofa, the boat made a stop at Ha'apai to take on even more passengers.

This can't be right, I thought, when I felt the boat go literally lopsided as everyone boarded. This bloody boat is jam-packed!

Every single seat on the *Olovaha* was taken, and there were people lying all over the deck. Where were these new Tongan passengers and their luggage going to fit? The boat was leaning so far to one side now that I was convinced we were going to tip over. Mum was already in the cabin being sick so she was no help.

But somehow everyone found a spot on the boat and we set off again for Vava'u.

As we made our way across the water, the sea started to get rougher, and the boat began rising, then plummeting again, over and over, on the gigantic ocean waves. Everyone on that boat, including the captain, got seasick and started vomiting. Mum was spewing her guts out, like at least a hundred other passengers. It got so bad that Dad and Linda started calling it the 'Chuck it Bucket'. Tongans, mainly women, were hurling all over the deck, as the boat rocked and rolled its way to Vava'u. Linda and I loved every second of it, but most people were sick as a dog on that journey. But guess who wasn't?

Dad.

He was up on the deck, clinging to the rails as the ocean spray hit his face and having the time of his life. Dad was in his element, the salty old dog. Live it up, Dad, I thought, knowing there was absolutely no way we'd be catching the boat back. No way in hell. Mum would make sure of that!

Vava'u is a volcanic area, and very beautiful, so when we finally arrived it was like we'd landed in paradise. As the boat got closer, we could see Grandpa Tuiniua and Grandma Mele, dressed in their beautiful traditional Tongan outfits, standing on the wharf to greet us, along with every other member of Mum's family. The aunties were all waving hankies in the air, and the second we stepped off the boat we were swamped, and everyone started crying, which explained the handkerchiefs.

Mum's home was a family compound that was a short walk from the centre of town. It covered about two acres of land and all the families' homes were built around the edges. Our grandparents' home faced the street and was a large two-bedroom weatherboard house with a beautiful wide veranda. This veranda was so solid that it was also used as a shelter for the locals during cyclones. The back of the house faced a huge lawn, which is where the real family life happened. In the middle of the lush grass was an outdoor weatherboard kitchen, where a lot of the food prep took place. The Umu was up the back of the garden. An Umu is a big hole in the ground used to cook food. Hot rocks are placed inside the hole, and the food is placed on top and then covered with banana leaves and wet hessian cloths. It's then covered in dirt, and more hot rocks go on top. The food is left there to cook for a few hours, while a suckling pig is roasted over the coals. The men do all this work and take turns rotating the pig. It is a ritual they enjoy because they love to cook, drink and talk while all this is being done – much like here but more intense work!

Individual fales, Tongan huts, surrounded the kitchen. The houses in the compound belonged mainly to Mum's brothers Pota, Dan and David because the women in the family go to live elsewhere with their husbands when they marry. The women did the washing in big tubs on old-fashioned washboards on that lawn too, and there were long clothes lines held up by sugar cane poles.

Linda and I were to stay in the original home, which used to be a large old homestead but had been destroyed by cyclones. Only a couple of rooms remained, so the two of us slept in there with a bunch of our cousins. We had so many cousins there were usually four of us in one bed. We had so much fun telling ghost stories and mucking about all night long. Grandpa had put in a brand-new toilet and shower in anticipation of our arrival. Before that, everyone did their business in an old-fashioned loo that sat on top of a big hole in the ground. I was very grateful that Grandpa had put in a proper toilet. I don't think I could have coped with the alternative.

Every morning, one of the aunties would get up early and head down to the bakery to buy the hottest, freshest loaves of bread. Linda and I had hot, buttered bread and a hot cup of tea every day and it was heaven. It was real butter too, and if there was no butter my grandma would apologise.

'Sorry,' she would say. 'I only have avocado for you today.'

Avocado? What was this exotic fruit? we wondered. We'd never seen or eaten avocado before that, but Grandma ate it on her bread most mornings. No wonder she looked fifty when she was eighty!

Grandma only spoke in Tongan and was very religious. She read her Bible every day and fasted on Sundays. I'm sorry I didn't get to know her better when I had the chance. Grandpa wasn't quiet. He and Mum got on like a house on fire because he understood her wild nature. We heard more stories about Mum from the aunties while we were in Tonga and got more of an understanding of why she was always being told off by our grandma when she was young.

Linda and I hit it off with our cousins from the get-go. We loved them all to bits and felt completely at home. We were with our people, and the family were glad to have Mum home with her new family, including the 'blond fella with the beautiful blue eyes'. There were so many children on the compound that it was like kid heaven for me and Linda. We were one huge gang and loved getting up to all sorts of adventures together. There was a big mango tree on the property, like huge, and it was full of fruit, and we would love to sit under that tree and wait for the mangos to drop; then we would all scramble to see who would get there first. Our cousin, Mele, would wake before dawn and collect the mangos that had fallen during the night. She would eat the split ones and keep the good ones for Mum and Dad, leaving them on their doorstep every morning, without fail. She was only six years old, and this melted Dad's heart. He nicknamed her Mango Mele.

We quickly learned that Tongan kids don't wear bathers. They swim in shorts and t-shirts and wouldn't ever wear anything as revealing as bikinis. Bikinis were considered outfits for 'loose girls' only. Okay for tourists but taboo for Tongan girls. I think this may have been a leftover attitude from the missionaries, who stuffed up a lot of things for the islanders when they set up their first mission in 1916. Before they arrived, the islanders were a free, loving people who got around with barely anything on at all, but these missionaries turned the Tongan people into prudes, teaching them that they should be ashamed of their naked bodies and needed to cover up. Now, all these years later, the Tongans frowned down upon the whities (or 'palangi', as they would say) for exposing too much flesh. Linda and I had both packed bathers for this trip, but when we got ready to go to the beach and saw that none of the other kids were wearing togs, we were a little perplexed as to why Mum hadn't warned us. In actual fact, she had warned us but we either didn't listen or ignored her. How can you go swimming in your clothes? we thought.

It was also interesting for us to learn that the Tongan kids didn't really like to swim. Sure, they loved the ocean, but sunbaking and swimming weren't really their thing. I vaguely remember learning that the lighter shade of brown skin was considered more beautiful and that they didn't want to get any darker than they already were.

Tonga is made up of about one hundred and seventy islands, but only about thirty-six are inhabited. Some days, for a trip to one of the beaches, we would all pile into the back of Uncle

Dan's early 60s Ford flatbed truck, which had rails and two long benches for us to sit on. It was fire-engine red and, oh boy, riding on the back of that truck was always an adventure, especially when he floored it at top speed through a particular village where people used to chuck rocks at any strange cars that dared pass through.

On one of our first outings of this kind, Dad packed a whole stack of snorkels and goggles for the kids. He knew the snorkelling would be good because the ocean was so clean and visibility would be perfect. When we arrived at the beach, Dad handed the snorkels out to all the kids, but he was a couple short, so Linda and I missed out. This didn't go down well with me. I burst into tears and cracked it big time, like the spoiled brat I sometimes was. Dad just stared at me, disappointment all over his face, but he still wouldn't give me a snorkel. I stormed off back to the truck and sat there on my own, crying like a baby, hoping Dad would hear me crying and feel so sorry for me that he'd come and give me the goddamn goggles, but no luck. He left me to stew in my own juices and didn't come near me. No one came over at all. I was completely ignored. Eventually I got bored, got out of the truck and went back to join the family, my tail tucked firmly between my legs. It was a valuable lesson.

A day spent sailing around the islands, stopping for the occasional swim, was akin to living the rockstar life. The Vava'u harbour is something to behold. The land is lush and green and the water is as blue as the sky on a clear sunny day. There are yachts and little boats scattered everywhere, and islanders in their little dinghies chugging into the mainland for supplies. The harbour seems to go for miles, and you can sail around it for hours, soaking up the beautiful view and feeling at peace, and at one with island life. At night, our uncles would go right out onto the Pacific Ocean on all-night fishing expeditions and return the following morning with a huge catch of all kinds of marine delicacies.

We learned a lot about the Tongan culture while we were there, including the fact that Tongans eat seasonally, and that each Tongan man is given a piece of land to grow crops and feed his family. This land is passed from eldest son to eldest son and is called the plantation. We visited a few while we were there and saw what they grow, including kava.

Our grandfather has an island called Tapana. This is also the place where our great-great-great-great-grandfather used to live, a man who, rumour has it, was a cannibal. The story goes that he would kidnap the fishermen who came to fish around Tapana, then kill and eat them. One year, my uncle decided to find out if this was true. My uncle knew that his ancestor had apparently lived in a cave, so he spent a long time searching for it. One day he finally stumbled upon a hidden underground cave, and what did he find inside? Quite a few human skeletons. When my uncle relayed this story to Linda, Dad and me one night at the compound, our jaws almost hit the ground.

LINDA
A very different lifestyle

Getting the chance to experience traditional Tongan village life, just like Mum did, was fun. Every morning we would wake up to the sound of church bells and roosters and find freshly picked mangos lined up on our doorstep. It was much nicer than waking up to the sound of my Casio digital alarm clock and finding burnt toast on my plate.

The pace in Tonga was so much slower too. Tonga seemed almost frozen in time, like some sort of tropical snow globe, where the colours were dialled up to eleven and the air seemed sweeter. I couldn't have been happier that we would be spending the majority of our time in Tonga in the beautiful paradise of Vava'u.

The family house in Vava'u had kerosene lamps and loads of mozzie coils and candles, so there was always a beautiful ambient glow, mixed with the toxic smell of burn-offs out in the street. There were no billboards on the streets; in fact, I don't remember any commercial advertising on display at all. The only advertising was devoted to the church of whatever denomination the parish could afford. There was one bank and one grocery store per village, and the Lali drum (a wooden slit drum) was still used to signal major events in town. I loved hearing the choirs practising their hymns in the early hours of the morning and drifting off to sleep listening to local firemen singing love songs around the kava bowl after a long day putting out fires. Their high-pitched falsetto voices sang in harmony and would make any woman swoon and every father reach for the nearest shotgun or club.

Mum had already warned us that Christmas in Vava'u would be different to what we were used to in Melbourne. Tongans don't put up Christmas trees or buy each other presents, instead they devote Christmas Day to church and feasting. Vika and I were not impressed when we heard this. No presents! No Santa! What were we going to do? But all thoughts of presents and the big fat man with the beard were quickly forgotten once the day got underway. It was a ripper! Our cousins and the local boys from the village made homemade cannons that they would light with kerosene, making huge explosions that ended with a massive puff of smoke. It was loud and dangerous, and we absolutely loved it.

Best Christmas ever!

Vika and I got tropical fever a few times and it felt like a mixture of the worst fever you've ever had while simultaneously tripping out on drugs. Grandma's bush medicine kept us alive. She'd go off to the plantation, pick a bunch of herbs, grind them into a paste in her mortar and pestle, and then brew this into a potion and get us to drink it. It tasted disgusting, like bitter pond and bong water, but after a full night of the sweats we started feeling better. There weren't many doctors around, and when Vika cut her leg while carving a Lali drum with a piece of glass, we went to the hospital, where there were chickens running around all over the wards. They served as a handy distraction for Vika when it came to getting stitches. The size of the needle alone would have scared Frankenstein's monster himself.

VIKA

Cyclones, kava and choirs

We visited during the wet season, and experienced a cyclone while we were there. I was scared listening to the howling strong wind, but everyone around me seemed to know what to do, which made me feel better. We all hunkered down until the storm was over, and afterwards the rain bucketed down like I'd never seen. Everyone came out of hiding and took a shower in it. The rain was so heavy that we were even able to shampoo our hair – it would have made a great ad!

The whales come to breed and have their babies in Vava'u, and when they do, you can get in the water and swim with them. When we first visited Tonga, the tourists hadn't caught on but now it's big business and people come from all over the world for it. The humpbacks' song sends tingles down your spine. The male sings to attract the female, which is interesting because one of the great traditions in Tonga is the kava ceremony, known in Tonga as faikava, where the men meet to talk, sing and drink kava. In kava clubs, groups of men sit around large bowls, and a young woman, traditionally a virgin, mixes the kava and serves it to them in coconut shell cups. They are passed around and once everyone has finished, they're passed back and the men start singing. They get all fuzzy and sing romantic songs to woo the young beauties in the village. I tell you, a Tongan man's singing can make you weak at the knees. These are big strong men, but when they open their mouths, they sound like heavenly angels.

Tonga is famous for its kava clubs. The kava is made from the root of the plant, which is crushed into a fine powder, then mixed with water. Tongan men can disappear for days after drinking kava. Our uncle used to disappear into the bush for the whole weekend after a kava session and no one seemed bothered that he was gone. They knew he'd turn up on Sunday morning in time for church.

Tongans grow up surrounded by music and singing from the moment they are born. No matter what day of the week it is, or what time of day, there is always a choir practising somewhere. When we were there on that first trip, the singing never stopped. Even at midnight, you could hear a choir practising or praising somewhere nearby.

The Tongans are great singers and harmonisers, and the Tongan choir in Melbourne was nothing compared to what we heard at Grandpa's church in Vava'u. He was part of the Free Church of Tonga, and while we were there we had to go along with him every Sunday. Grandpa and the rest of the elders sat up the front and the choir all sat together. Everyone seemed to have their regular spot. We'd sit there for hours, listening to the preacher go on, while the old men replied in unison, 'Yes' and 'True' and 'Thank you', depending on what the appropriate response was. This was new to me. I'd never seen this in Tongan church in Melbourne. I liked it, even though I had no clue what any of them were talking about.

When the choir fired up, it was like a sonic explosion in my ears. The women sang high, the men low and everything in-between, and when it all came together it was the most spiritual emotional experience I'd ever had. It had all the parts of a mass choir combined with the power of a gospel choir. Since that trip, we've taken heaps of friends to church in Tonga and love watching their reactions when the choir kicks into action. They sit bolt upright, their eyes wide, and then the tears start to flow. It's such a spiritual experience that people can't help but be moved. It was one of the true highlights of that first visit for me.

The Tongan trip was one of the best gifts our parents ever gave us. Having the opportunity to learn about, and immerse ourselves in, our mother's culture and its customs was an amazing education for Linda and me. Everything over there is so different to the Australian way of life. Tongans live in an extended family situation where everyone helps out with raising each other's kids. Tongans love to share. They share their food, their stories and their love for each other, and I love this about them. Kids are never lonely and benefit from growing up in an extended family environment. Tongan adults are strict, and kids are taught to respect their elders. The highest status in the family belongs to the father's oldest sister, and at family celebrations she is offered the best part of the cake, usually the top tier, and the best mats and tapa cloths. In return, she is generous and supports all her family members.

Over the years I have witnessed Mum and Dad's generosity towards the Tongan people. They've sponsored and supported so many who have come to Australia to find work. Tonga is a small country with a population of only around 100,000 people, so a lot of Tongans come here to work so they can send money home to support their families. Linda and I were always excited when a new family member or relative arrived on our doorstep. We always learned something from whoever it was that came to stay, and it was a lot of fun growing up in a house where there were lots of different people coming and going.

When we returned from our trip, Mum brought her youngest sister, Moana, with us. She was heartbroken to leave her family behind and everyone was howling, especially Moana. We hated to see our beloved Aunty so upset, but we knew she was coming to Australia to find the same wonderful opportunities our mother had been given. We were also secretly happy because she was our favourite, but let's keep that between us!

LINDA

Sharks and totems

The highlight of every day was going down to the wharf. Vika and I were strong swimmers and divers, so if it was siesta time for Mum and Dad, we were allowed to go jump off the wharf on our own. Unthinkable to me now, but it was the 70s and rules for kids were different then. The wharf was a massive rustic concrete relic with a crude rusted ladder on the side covered in barnacles that we regularly shredded our little legs on. The water was clear, and we could see right to the bottom to where the sharks were. We'd jump in and see them circling underneath us, seemingly too full of tropical fish to take a bite out of our tasty little Aussie-Tongan legs. Growing up, I had been taught that sharks were creatures to be feared, but I was never afraid when I was diving over them in Tonga. Grandpa told me the reason I wasn't afraid was that sharks are our family's totem, which meant they are tapu (sacred) and are our ancestors and protectors. This made sense to me. The reason they were circling under us was that they were protecting us. Our job, therefore, was to do the same.

We have two family totems, the shark and the gecko, and both originate from our grandfather's side of the family. The shark is from his maternal side and the gecko from his paternal. I've never eaten shark or gecko and don't intend to. For me it's akin to cannibalism. Also, I've seen first-hand the effect eating shark had on one of our family and it was not good. Mum was once carried out of a Polynesian-themed restaurant with severe food poisoning when they accidentally served her shark.

Like many ancient cultures, Tonga has a rich oral tradition of elders passing down family stories to the younger generations. My imagination ran wild as a kid when Mum told me some of the myths and legends of Polynesia. These were not just her own stories, but her country's as well, all woven into intoxicating bedtime tales, and I couldn't get enough of them. My interest ramped up in

Tonga because being home seemed to reignite Mum's memory of the stories she'd heard from her father and grandmother. Stories about the white bat who only appeared when there was sad news on the horizon for a member of Tonga's beloved royal family; or those about the crying owls flying out of the sea at dusk, foreshadowing a funeral. But my favourite stories relate back to our family totems, the shark and the gecko.

One story starts when our great-great-great-great-grandmother was promised to an older man who she definitely didn't want to marry. To escape the marriage, she ran away, and kept running, until she reached the water's edge. She dived into the sea and turned into a shark so she could keep swimming and get far away from her arranged marriage.

The geckos are ancient guardians of our grandfather's house, usually appearing in pairs. Every night when Vika and I slept in our grandfather's house, two geckos would appear. They were huge and looked pretty scary to two suburban kids as they crawled all over the beams above us at night. We complained to Mum, and Grandpa removed them from our room. It wasn't until much later that we learned that he had known it was bad luck to move them like that but had wanted us to feel safe and be able to sleep. I recently found out that his house, the family home in Vava'u, was the site of the meeting place between all the warring chiefs during the first civil war in Tonga and apparently the geckos watched on the whole time. I wish I'd known this at the time as I would never have complained. I might have thought of them as four-legged angels, which would have comforted me as I drifted off to sleep. Every time we've returned to our grandfather's house since then, the geckos appear in pairs to welcome us, then again later when we're leaving to say goodbye.

THE THINGS YOU LEARN

LINDA

School swaps

I changed primary schools three times, and even though I hated it, it ultimately turned out to be a good thing. Switching schools just when I was getting into the swing of things forced me out of my comfort zone and taught me a lot about resilience and adaptability. I learned how to adapt quickly to new environments, and this stood me in good stead when I became a singer later and had to deal with change all the time.

When Mum and Dad told us I'd be missing the first full term of Grade 3 at Botanic Park Primary because we were going to Tonga, it sent me into a panic. I'd started making friends at my second school. What if they forgot about me because I was away too long? The idea of having to start all over again and find new friends kept me up at night as I lay staring at the ceiling in my perfectly made bed.

On my last day of Grade 2 – the week before we left for Tonga – my class threw me a little going-away party. It was my beautiful teacher, Sue Quentin, who organised it all and I loved my oversized card signed by the whole class and the yummy sponge cake. I was touched that Miss Quentin had gone to all that trouble, and it only made me adore her more than I already did. She was so groovy, with her long blonde hair, blue eyes, high-waisted denim flares, tight divvy cardies and wedge heels. To top it off, her favourite band was the Ted Mulry Gang, so she was alright by me. (I'm friends with her still, and she and my other favourite primary-school teacher, Jenny Watson, regularly come to our shows and loudly cheer us on.)

Unfortunately, my going-away party didn't go as smoothly as I would have liked, thanks to a boy named Simon. He was sporty, tall for his age, with tanned skin and cool green eyes, and he always wore shorts, no matter the weather. Simon also had an unhealthy obsession with me. The first time something happened had been earlier in the year, when we were sitting opposite each another at our low shared table. I was busy writing in my exercise book when I heard a noise and looked up to see Simon staring at me and tapping the desk with his pencil. He was pointing at the ground and had an unusual look on his face. This intrigued me, and of course I couldn't resist the urge to look under the table to see what he was pointing at. I regretted this decision the second I took a peep and saw that he had pulled his pants down and had his penis out.

Even though I was totally grossed out, I didn't want to give Simon the satisfaction of knowing I was shocked. So, without changing my expression, I sat back up and continued with my work, all the while thinking that I wouldn't be so silly as to fall for his tapping pencil trick again. I didn't want to see *that* twice.

Simon went beetroot red, visibly hurt and annoyed at my non-reaction to his tiny willy. From that moment on, this kid made it his mission in life to try to shock me into some kind of a reaction. He'd do awful things like cut off the ends of my pigtails, or pull a chair out from under me so I'd crash to the ground in front of everybody. In the playground, he'd jump out from behind a tree, or corner me and grab at me. Before long, I found myself constantly looking over my shoulder, worried that Simon was going to appear from nowhere to either bash or kiss me, never sure which of the two it might be. But on that last day of Grade 2, soon after my going-away party, he went too far.

I was standing in the hallway when he suddenly ran up, pushed me against the wall and unzipped my uniform, exposing my chest, then yelled, 'See ya later, darkie!'

I was only seven years old so there was nothing to see, but I was still horrified, and most definitely shocked. Simon had finally got the reaction he'd been seeking. Unfortunately for him I'd stuffed the oversized card down the front of my uniform (I'm not sure why I did that) so he was unable to perve on my non-existent chest anyway. He was obviously disappointed, but he was soon going to have much more to worry about than not seeing my naked flesh.

After the initial shock wore off, I pushed Simon off me and did exactly what Mum had told me to do if I needed help at school.

I ran straight to Vika.

I burst into her Grade 4 classroom and ran over to her, crying my eyes out and explaining what had happened. All hell broke loose. Vika has a full-on hot Tongan temper, like Mum, but, unlike Mum, my nine-year-old sister hadn't yet learned how to control it. She got up, marched across the corridor, and threw the door of my classroom open so violently that it hit the plaster and made the room bounce. This got everyone's attention and I was reminded of those scenes in spaghetti westerns when the bad cowboy enters the saloon, and everybody freezes. My sister had made quite the entrance, and her look of fury told everyone that she was about to do some serious damage.

She turned to me, trembling beside her. 'Where is he?'

'There,' I said, stupidly pointing him out to my raging sister.

Simon suddenly looked very small and very scared, as he should have.

Vika stormed over to him, grabbed him by the scruff of the neck with one hand, and by the back of his shorts with the other, and threw him across the room. I remember noticing his socks as he was catapulted through the air – one was up, and one was down – before he hit the wall and slid down it like a sack of potatoes.

We were both sent to the principal's office, of course. I'd never been in trouble before, so it was my first visit, but Vika had already been there after she gave a kid a bloody nose. Anyone who valued their life, and their nose, at Botanic Park Primary quickly learned not to call Vika Bull names. (Her first nickname was 'Coke' and she hated it.) That was my last day of Grade 2 at Botanic Park

Primary School and a going-away party I'd never forget.

My third primary school was in Mont Albert, and I started there when Mum and Dad sold the house at Botanic Drive and we moved to Box Hill. At ten years old it felt like my world was caving in, and I couldn't believe I had to start at yet another school as I'd only hit double digits. It was worse too because Vik had gone off to high school, so I'd lost my mate and protector.

I didn't love our new house in Box Hill North either. It was no Botanic Drive. There was a lot to adjust to: a new house, a new school, a new suburb and my sister-slash-protector off at high school. I couldn't see how I was going to get through the next two years without Vika. Fending for myself had never been my strong point, mainly because I'd always had Vik to do it for me. I was always the friendly, laid-back sister at school. My way of dealing with conflict or confrontation was to smile and talk my way out of it, while Vik's way of dealing with conflict was to fight her way out. My sister is quiet by nature, but fierce when she is crossed, and especially when trouble came in the form of racism. She learned early on in life that a good punch in the nose usually shut the shitheads up.

I figured that the popular kids were only popular because they were good at everything. They were good-looking, rich, smart, sporty and competitive, while I was a dork who wore my hair the same way every day – two plaits glued to my head – and dressed in my raglan tee, denim skirt and trusty Le Coq Sportif hoodie. On top of all that, I wasn't white. I knew I had to beat these kids at their own game.

My Grade 5 teacher, Mr Hobby, was so kind to me. He was a tall, handsome man, balding, with piercing blue eyes, who drove a brown sports car. He was cool. Not only that but he introduced me to the concept of competitive times tables using a puppet named Monty. Mr Hobby made the puppet out of a stick and a recycled piece of polystyrene for a head, drew a crude face on it and dressed it in his old shirt and pants.

Every week in maths class, everyone had to get up and compete against each other. Whoever got the most sums correct in the shortest amount of time was declared the winner, and they would then be given the honour of competing against Monty in a times-table challenge. This competition totally changed my life.

I won a bunch of times and so would stand at the front of the class, facing off against Monty (aka Mr Hobby) while another kid shouted times table equations at me. It was my way of showing the class what I was good at and Mr Hobby knew it. I became so obsessed with times tables that I would make my poor mum test me for hours on end after her long and punishing shifts at the hospital. Mum had retrieved an old piece of cardboard from some packaging and handwritten the entire times tables on it in blue sharpie. She'd stand at the foot of my bed with a ruler and point to the times tables as I recited them. Feel free to quiz me on any times table equation and I'll fire the answer straight back at you, thanks to my beautiful mum.

In Mr Hobby's class I beat all the popular kids by a mile, and I slowly started to rise higher in the social ranks. But one of the popular girls (I'll call her Samantha) was very smart and hated the fact that I beat her in the times table comp every week. She decided she was going to do everything she could to destroy my life.

Samantha made up nasty stories about me and poked fun at my 'poor people' clothes and lunches. Little did she know I wore the same clothes to school every day because I liked them, not because I had no other clothes to wear. It was my uniform and I was okay with it. It was true I didn't have the budget for a tuckshop lunch every day and that I had stinky sandwiches, like every other kid, but Samantha got a weird kick out of telling everyone that my parents were so poor we couldn't afford good food or good clothes. My parents weren't the financial norm in any way, shape or form. Mum earned the bigger pay packet in the private sector, and Dad made a public servant's salary. We weren't rich by any stretch of the imagination, but we certainly weren't as poor as Samantha made us out to be. I was in a tomboy phase and proud of it.

The more success I had in the classroom and in the playground, at sports, the nastier Samantha became. Also, she was dark-skinned like me, which was a real kick in the guts. I assumed we dark-skinned girls would stick together, but I couldn't have been more wrong. Maybe she resented the fact that I was drawing attention away from her, like there was only room for one dark girl in the village. But this only made me want to piss her off even more. What choice did I have? I could either bow down and let her dominate me or beat her at everything she cared about. I chose to fight.

As Samantha's nastiness increased, so did my competitive streak.

In fact, I can probably thank her for lighting a match to it. It was full-on war. Anyone could see that this wasn't going to end well, and this time I didn't have my sister to step in and throw Samantha across the room by the back of her pants. I had to fight my own battles. I set about getting myself onto every sports team and passing every test with flying colours, just to shut Samantha up.

Eventually the most popular boys in school, Peter and Matthew, chose me over her for their footy team, and she stopped harassing me. I was no longer sidelined. In fact, I had leapfrogged right over the top of her and she knew it. I had officially made it to the ranks of 'popular' kids.

School wasn't the only place where I got my sports fix. I stayed active on weekends too, playing tennis and basketball. I remember the distinctive smell of the Bulleen basketball stadium, where I loved training and doing drills. I also loved our white and red uniform. I was a big kid and not afraid to throw myself into the action.

Life became a lot easier after I became popular, and that awful knot in my stomach every morning went away. Finally, I could relax, knowing I wasn't the new kid anymore. But the knot soon came back a few months later when I was running in a race at school. A boy I liked was running behind me, and when I turned to grin at him, he yelled, 'Fat bum!'

That was it. Every bit of self-confidence eked out of me in that moment. I was devastated. I felt so embarrassed about my 'fat bum' that I set about starving myself. In a short amount of time, I went from a healthy kid who ate pretty much everything to a health-conscious exercise fanatic. Mum noticed I wasn't eating my lunch and raised it at the dinner table in front of Dad and Vik one night.

'I'm a nurse,' she said. 'You can't survive on one Salada biscuit and an apple all day.'

But I ignored her wise words and continued starving myself. I stayed active at school, and could feel myself getting thinner, and my clothes looser, as the year went on, and by the end of Grade 6 I weighed a very unhealthy 35 kilos. I was only twelve years old, so my bad habits put a complete halt on my physical development. Dad used to comment that I had more curves on my back than my front because my shoulder blades were sticking out.

That's how flat I was in the boob department, and I didn't like the way it looked, but by then it was too late.

VIKA

Fitting in at Camberwell

In 1977, high school was looming, Mum and Dad were planning their next move, and my time at primary school and in Botanic Drive was coming to an end. With their eldest daughter starting secondary school, my parents wanted to be closer to public transport, so they sold our beautiful home in Doncaster and bought a brand-new three-bedroom brick veneer home in Box Hill North that was a 1-kilometre walk to the nearest tram.

This was a big move, the biggest in my life to that point, and

I felt emotional about leaving our mates in Botanic Drive. When the end of year rolled around and the time came to leave primary school behind forever, I was sad to say goodbye to my best friend, Lyn. We were heading off to our separate private schools – Lyn was going to Camberwell Girls Grammar School (CGGS), and I was enrolled in Methodist Ladies College (MLC). Dad would have been happy to send me to the local high school, but Mum was a big believer in education, and felt the private school fees were worth it. She didn't care how expensive MLC was, or if she had to bust a gut paying for both of us to go there. But Dad knew private school probably wouldn't suit me (just me, not Lulu; we all knew my Virgo sister would thrive in a private girls' school) so he suggested ERA, an alternative, progressive co-educational secondary school in Donvale. ERA stood for Education Reform Association. Mum, however, wouldn't hear of it. She wanted both her girls to have the best education possible, and in her Boss Woman opinion, that meant private school.

I had accepted this, knowing there was no way Mum would change her mind, but if I had to go to private school, couldn't it at least be the same one my best friend was going to? I begged and pleaded with Mum to send me to Camberwell instead of MLC, until she finally caved and agreed to check it out.

The principal, Miss Sutton, took Mum on tour around the school.

'Should you decide to send Vika here,' she said, 'do you think she'd mind if the girls called her by her middle name, Susan?'

Linda: Mum came to Australia to study nursing in 1959. Her plan to qualify and return to Tonga got derailed when she met this handsome stranger at Sandringham Yacht Club and he invited her to 'look at the sea'. They've been devoted to one another ever since. Then we came along – Vika first and me the following year.

Happy snaps with Mum and Dad in the 1970s. There were no selfie sticks back then, so someone had to take the photographs! If there is a pic of the four of us together from that time, we can't find it.

Vika: Mum and Linda had a wicked creative partnership in designing and sewing matching outfits – wicked because I was forced to go along with it.

Our Tongan heritage has always been incredibly dear to us.

(*Above*) With our gorgeous grandparents on a trip they took to Australia that didn't start so well …

(*Below and opposite top*) In the 1970s on our first trip to Tonga, pictured here with our cousins. It was an incredible, defining experience for both of us.

(*Opposite bottom*) Singing at our Tongan church. A love for music was encouraged by both our parents, but never pushed on us.

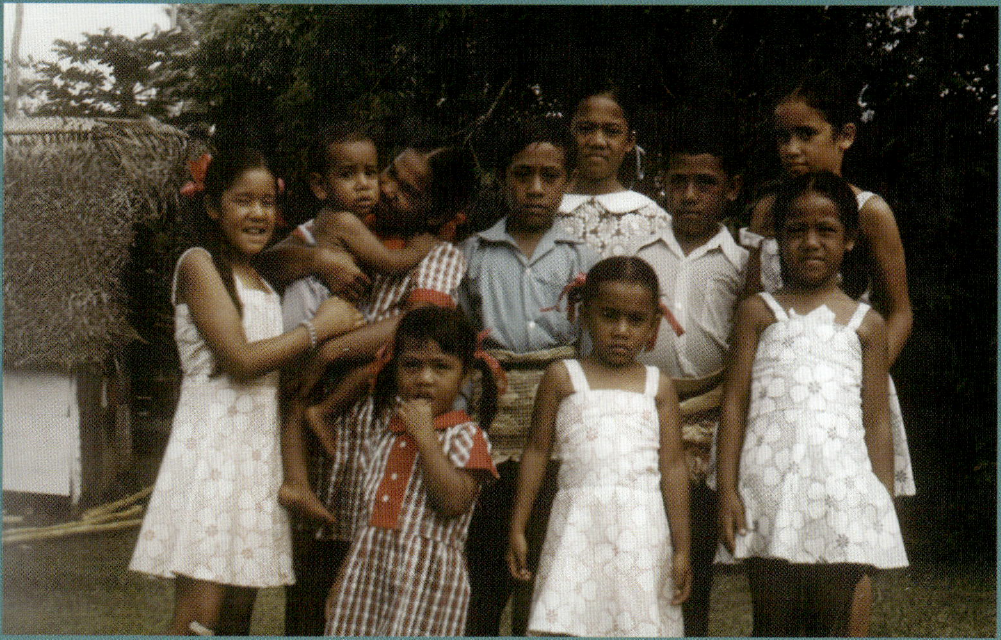

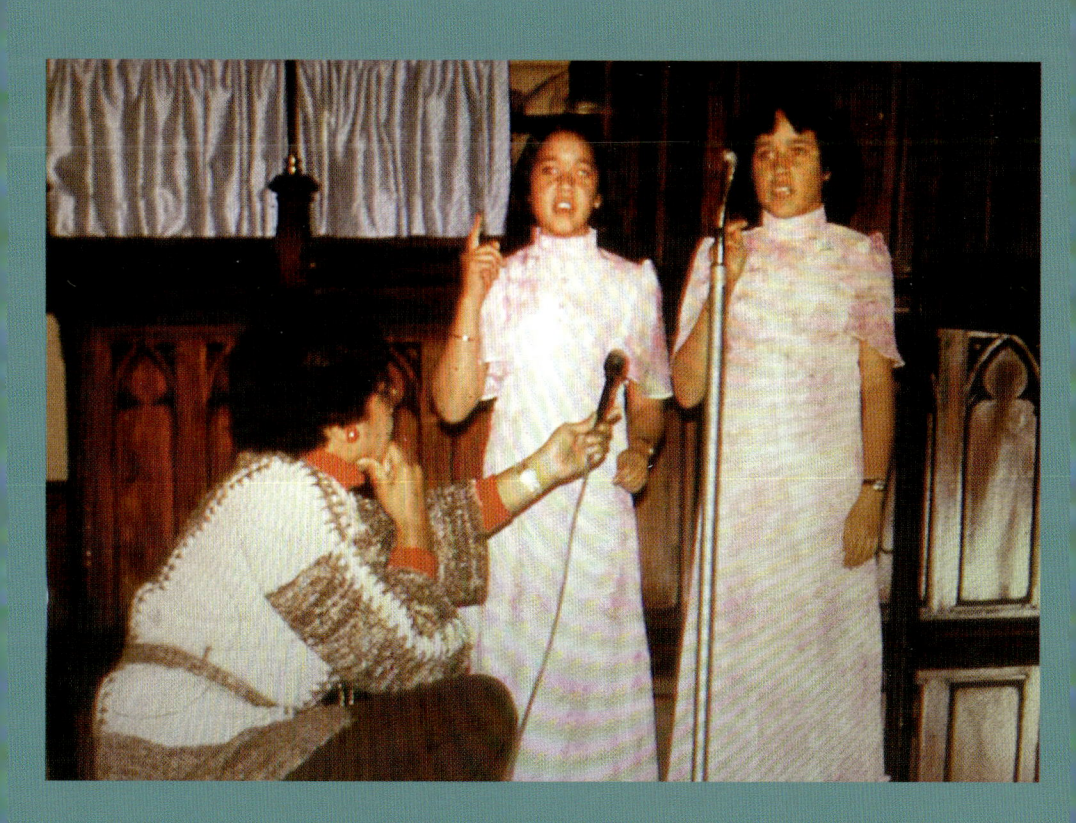

Vika: It was in our high-school years that the differences between Linda and me came into sharp focus. Linda (*above*) was academic, whereas I (*below*) was wild, seen here post-mohawk. By the end of Year 11, Linda was a prefect and I had quit school.

Linda: It's fair to say that a career in music was definitely not what Mum wanted for us. But when my parents (*above with Vika and me*) and I first saw Vika singing in public (*below*) we were in awe. It felt like her destiny.

Vika: When I heard the early-60s girl-band sound of Sophisticated Boom Boom, I was hooked. When I was asked to join the band in 1986, I threw myself into it.

Linda: This might have been the calm before the storm. After we'd both moved out of home (nudged by Dad on both counts), we always caught up for Sunday lunch, and it was at one of these gatherings that Vika suggested I sing with her. Mum hit the roof at the prospect of both of us committing to music.

'Her name is Vika,' Mum said in a steely tone. 'It's two syllables. VI / KA. Is that going to be too hard for your students to pronounce?'

Miss Sutton had met her match in Mum, another strong-willed career woman. After zero negotiation, Vika (not Susan) commenced a secondary education at Camberwell Girls Grammar School in 1978.

Happy days!

As if the fees alone weren't bad enough, Mum also had to fork out for a school blazer, summer, winter and sports uniforms, and matching undies, socks and shoes. I kind of dug Camberwell's uniform. It was a lovely navy blue, and the school motto – *Utilis in Ministerium* (Useful in Service) – was stitched on the blazer pocket. Not a bad motto to have on display five days a week, I thought.

The school was strict about how the uniform was worn, and if we didn't adhere to the rules we got order marks. Order marks were given for all kinds of bad behaviour, and prefects, as well as teachers, had the power to dish them out. Who'd wanna be a prefect? I thought when I heard this. If you received six order marks, you got detention. After three detentions, you were suspended. This was serious stuff.

To get to school I had to walk to the tram terminus on Whitehorse Road, then take a tram all the way to Burke Road. There, I'd switch to the tram that stopped right out front of Camberwell Grammar. A lot of kids from other schools caught the same tram, and it was a great way for girls to check out fellas from the neighbouring boys' schools. I cringe now to think about how silly we acted on that tram sometimes. God, the teenage mating ritual is so embarrassing.

My best friend Lyn, with her gorgeous blue eyes and blonde hair, became popular with the girls straight away, but I felt all at sea in my new school. It was so different, and intimidating, as was our homeroom teacher. The first time she strode into our classroom, looking like a boss woman in a corporate-style suit dress and shiny black high heels, I thought, My God! What the hell is going on here?

I wasn't used to teachers who looked like this.

'Take notes, please!' she said in a sharp, crisp voice that first morning.

Everyone around me immediately started scribbling notes in their folders, but I just sat there staring at them and wondering what 'taking notes' meant. The teacher sure didn't bother to let me know and so I instantly hated her. It's fair to say my first Camberwell Grammar class didn't go well. I spent the whole time trying to take everything in while also trying to come to terms with the fact that I was in a room full of girls. It just didn't feel natural. I missed the boys, not because I wanted a boyfriend but because I liked hanging out and playing sport with the boys in Botanic Drive.

My first tuckshop experience wasn't that great either. I was standing in line for the canteen. Two very gorgeous girls from a grade two years above were standing in front of me, and one of them turned to look at me and said, 'Oh, you're a boong!'

I was shocked and didn't know what to say. I felt small and embarrassed and thought, Here we go again! What the hell is wrong with people?

'Don't say that!' the other girl said to her friend. 'That's not nice!'

I was grateful to her for saying something but still wondered if I was going to have to put up with this kind of treatment for the rest of my life. And, if so, what could I do about it?

I made a decision then: I wasn't going to let people with ignorant racist comments get to me anymore. If people wanted to call me names, then I was just going to ignore them and get on with my life. From now on, I wouldn't get upset. I couldn't punch that girl in the nose or pick her up by the scruff of her neck and throw her across the canteen, which was my preferred technique of dealing with racists. Now, I had to learn how to walk away. It was hard but I had to be strong and not let these kinds of people get under my skin anymore. Besides, I was now attending a strict, conservative girls' school and if I was suspended, or worse, expelled, for giving this girl exactly what she deserved, my mother would have been proud but also very disappointed. I couldn't do that to her.

I'd watched Mum put up with this kind of shit my entire life and heard her crying in the bath as she told Dad how people in shops told her she 'couldn't afford to buy certain things because of the colour of her skin' or how some racist patients didn't want her 'black hands to touch them'. There was my beautiful mum, the most caring person in the world, trying to take care of these sick, racist old pains in the arse and they were saying shit like that.

Well, I wouldn't let those kinds of racist pigs get me down.

'Be strong,' Mum had always told us. 'Be tough!'

Okay, Mum, I thought, as I stood in the tuckshop line that day, waiting to order my open-toasted cheese roll, I will.

LINDA

You went to private school?

Vika and I had very different experiences at school. While Camberwell Girls Grammar School wasn't the perfect fit for Vik, it was for me. I fell in love with it the first time I saw it, when I tagged along with my family to check it out for Vika.

For this special 'Open Day' outing, I'd worn my favourite high-waisted, tight brown pinstripe pants and my three-tone brown skivvy, and had slicked my hair back into a low ponytail. I thought I looked great, but upon reflection I may have looked more like a brown licorice all-sort. My chosen outfit must have embarrassed the hell out of Vik, who was a lot cooler than me at that point, but my clothes weren't the only thing that would annoy her that day. On arrival, I'd been handed a huge orange balloon at the gate, and for the rest of the day it zigzagged all over the place, constantly hitting my sister in the face and giving her the shits big time.

Embarrassing outfit and wayward balloon aside, my main

memory of that day is falling in love with Camberwell Girls Grammar the second I walked through its gates. How could I not? Not only were the grounds picturesque but there was even a tennis court. The school had acquired some old Edwardian homes surrounding the main building, used for art, home economics and HSC classes, and they were beautiful. Not only that, the uniform was an elegant navy blue and white and very pretty. I immediately felt at home there and couldn't believe I'd most likely be coming here in a couple of years' time. It was clear to all of us by then that Mum was going to let Vika attend Camberwell instead of MLC, and I knew I'd go to the same school as my sister. I couldn't have been happier.

Camberwell was small then, with only around four hundred and fifty students, so nowhere near as big as MLC. It also wasn't as multicultural as MLC. Vika and I would be the only half-Polynesian students on campus. I think this was a big worry for Mum, especially after her first meeting with Miss Sutton.

I had a different experience with Miss Sutton almost two years later, when it was my turn to be interviewed. We locked eyes across her big desk and as she sized me up with her bright blue eyes, I felt an instant connection with her. She looked a lot like the Queen, with her grey hair, big bosom, beautiful brooches and smart suits, and if the British Monarch had been a bit sexy. I liked her straight away and knew I'd be okay at Camberwell.

Vika and I were both aware of the financial sacrifices Mum and Dad were making for us to attend Camberwell, but even knowing this wasn't enough to make Vika embrace it the way I did. My sister was too much of a free spirit and would have been better off in a creative school like ERA, instead of a rules-based institution like Camberwell. It upset me to see her so miserable there. She rebelled against Camberwell and its strict rules. Vika hated homework and being forced to study. My sister is smart as a whip, but school wasn't her thing.

But at that time I loved school and from Year 7 onwards I studied hard and gave it my all. I was the sort of student who planned assignments a long way out from the due date, making sure to give myself enough time to prepare and perfect. I wanted to get A's on everything and mostly did.

Art was my favourite subject, followed by sport. I had a go at all kinds of sport in high school and tried out for every team. I wasn't a runner, but discovered I was quite good at high jump. I used to practise at home on the weekends with a makeshift broom and mattress, and, considering some of the mishaps I had, it's surprising I can still walk. One weekend I dislocated my knee after another broom and mattress session, and it's a recurring injury I still carry.

I also played on the hockey team, which meant training at 7.30am, three days a week. I loved the rough nature of that game. I loved tennis too, and we even had an ex-Wimbledon player as our school coach. The only time I ever wagged school was when I went to Kooyong to watch the English champ Sue Barker play. Unfortunately, the game was televised, and the only seat available for me was on the actual court, right next to the ball boys and girls. Mum and Miss Sutton were surprised to see my face popping up on their televisions throughout the match. Miss Sutton was a lot more understanding than Mum, who was absolutely furious, but I had managed to get Sue Barker's autograph (after banging on her caravan door and annoying the bejesus out of her) so that softened the blow somewhat.

Vika and I used to hang out at the Balwyn Baths a lot then too, so springboard diving became another favourite sport of mine. I never had the guts to go up to the 10-metre tower but loved diving off the 5-metre one. If I was feeling brave, I might even have tried the 7-metre, but mostly I stuck to the 1- and 3-metre springboards down below. I loved the feeling of jumping up high, then diving straight to the bottom of the pool. I'd touch it, then push my way up, holding my breath and imagining I was a mermaid, or Brooke Shields in *Blue Lagoon*. In truth, I probably looked more like a whale venturing up from the deep.

Vika was a beautiful diver and able to enter the water without a splash. She eventually attracted the attention of a diving coach named Mr Walton, who was an ex-champion diver and a very sweet old man. Much to Vik's annoyance, I joined her training sessions with Mr Walton, and we both took up diving at a competitive level. Mr Walton would instruct us both from the side of the pool, yelling at us to twist this way and tumble that. Never once did I see him get in the water to demonstrate. He was that good. We'd just copy his body movements, and voila, off we'd go. My favourite dive was a one and a half forward pike off the 3-metre board. I think Vik's might have been the inward pike, and it was perfect. I remember becoming quite obsessed with diving, but eventually I quit when fear got the better of me.

The school swimming carnival was always a highlight because I was a natural swimmer, and the diving competition was a shoe-in because, let's face it, most kids take up netball, footy or cricket over diving. I had Mr Walton training me three, sometimes four nights a week for three to four hours, so I had a massive advantage over my classmates. Most of the time, the girls would just do a forward dive, but I liked to show off a bit while I was up there, pulling out my favourite one and a half forward pike off the 3 metres. Vika and I always won the diving events at school, and I only wish they'd given out trophies for them. I would have loved that!

I'd always come second in the swimming events, though. I was no match for the girls who trained their arses off in the pool all week, so it gave me a good taste of my own medicine. It must have given them the shits that I came second, though, especially since I had no special swimming gear or ever had to get up at 5am to stare at the bottom of the pool for hours on end. (Instead, our punishment was the bum-breaking church pew on Sundays.) My favourite stroke was backstroke, and being double-jointed and pigeon-toed meant that I was fast. My feet may not have been that attractive out of the water, but in it they acted like natural flippers and were dynamite!

Dad's only instruction when teaching me to swim was 'Don't

panic, don't forget to breathe, swim like hell, don't sink and have fun! See you at the other end!'

The rest was up to me.

I always went into a swimming race with that killer instinct, thinking, I'm gonna beat you Nikki-slash-Karen. Because I had no training, the pressure to succeed was off and that was liberating. I felt sorry for the others when they had so much expectation on them to win. I still love swimming and try to get in the water every day. Even when I'm on tour I'll always search out the local pool in the area to get my laps in.

VIKA

Over and out

I didn't take part in the choir or any of the plays in high school. If anything, I shied away from that stuff because there were other girls who seemed to have those bases covered. Also, I didn't like the songs they sang, or the plays they did. They all seemed square to me. I did loads of sport instead. I did swimming, netball, softball and basketball and was pretty good at all of them. Our sports teacher was a buxom woman who always wore a tiny little netball skirt, in both summer and winter, and was constantly flashing her undies at us. She only paid attention to the kids who were good at sport, couldn't stand the unco ones, and made it obvious who her favourites were. She was a pain in the bum.

Soon after starting Year 7, Lyn and I began to drift apart. It might have made me wonder if I should have gone to MLC after all, but if I had I would never have met the girl who would become my best friend for life. Kerri was as cute as a button and we were both young for our year. Most of the girls in Year 7 were thirteen but we were twelve and it wasn't long before we became best friends I adored her family – still do to this day. We befriended some other great girls, too. One of these girls was George, and we'd meet at the tram terminus in the mornings and travel to school together. When we got a bit older, George and I started going behind the shops for a quick smoke before hopping on the tram.

George was hilarious, and naughty like me, and one day when we were in Year 9 we snuck out of school at lunchtime to the nearby abandoned railway track for a quick fag. It was a big risk because if we'd been sprung, we would have been suspended on the spot, so we must have been full-on addicted by then … or bored.

In Year 9 we started dancing classes with the boys from Camberwell Boys Grammar. Wow! Fantastic! Boys! Kerri and I couldn't wait. The classes were held on a Monday night and we both loathed and looked forward to this weekly event. All of us filed into Camberwell Girls' school hall, girls gathered on one side and boys on the other, silently checking each other out until the boys were told to select their partners. I remember thinking how cruel this system was. Why on earth didn't they just pair us up and save us the embarrassment of not being asked to dance? The boys always chose the prettiest girls first, then there were the ones who were already going out so they automatically paired up. Those of us who hadn't yet blossomed were always left sitting on the sidelines feeling awkward and unattractive. We'd shuffle into a circle around the dancing teacher, so he and his partner could demonstrate the waltz or the cha-cha for us as we tried to smother our giggles and hide our embarrassment.

Our teacher, Mr Haulsman, and his partner were terrific ballroom dancers. I felt bad that they had to put up with students with more interest in hooking up out the back of the hall and pashing their brains out. I met a lovely boy and we went out for about three weeks. He was good-looking, and he had brown skin too, so everyone said we were a good match. I remember thinking that didn't necessarily make us a good match. And it didn't.

Around this time, I got my first job at McDonalds in Balwyn. I was fifteen and excited to be making my own money. The lovely woman who employed me liked me a lot, but she was only standing in for the owner while he was on holidays. When he returned, he was not pleased about the half-Polynesian girl ruining his all-blonde counter. He wanted to sack me but knew it wouldn't go down too well with the rest of the staff. Also, I was a good worker: I could add up and was fast. This was before computers, so we had to take orders manually and add them up on paper right there in front of the customer. If you took over $200 in an hour you were considered a fast worker, and I did this on several occasions. The boss hated that I was so good because he wanted to hide me out the back on fries, but I was making that bastard money, so he kept me up front. I stayed to spite him.

I was good at sport so was made Schofield House Sports captain in Year 11, but this meant I also had to take part in non-sport activities if I wanted our house to win the school cup. Dammit! I'd have to do all that singing, dancing and theatre stuff I'd avoided for four years.

By this time, Linda was at the same school and I decided we would do a performance of 'Summer Nights' in front of the whole assembly. It was our first time singing together at school and I decided to spice things up a bit for my performance as Danny Zuko (Linda played Sandy). Those musicals were so boring! I slicked back my hair, made a big curl down the middle of my forehead, whacked on a leather jacket, and rocked out. The girls all roared with laughter, but the teachers weren't impressed with my raunchy performance. I didn't care. If nothing else, I'd shown them I could sing … and sing LOUD!

Most Sundays, I'd meet Kerri at the end of her street and walk to the Camberwell market. It was the highlight of our week and we were intrigued at the sight of all the young wannabes walking around. There were punks, mods and new romantics, all with their fantastic unique looks. One afternoon, I arrived home from school with my own fantastic and unique look – a Mohawk. The moment I walked out of that hairdresser I panicked. Mum was going to go ballistic.

I put off going home as long as possible, and when I finally walked through our front door Mum freaked out on a level I'd never seen before. She screamed her head off; she even burst into tears and told me I looked bloody stupid, then stormed out of the house. Boom! Just disappeared for two whole days!

I was devastated and didn't know what to do, even though, to be honest, I thought it was a bit of an overreaction on Mum's part. It's only a haircut, I thought. It will grow back!

Dad was always great in those situations. He knew Mum was a hot head (like me) and tended to blow up and go over the top, so he'd always sit me down to talk about what had happened in a calm way.

'You've really upset your mother,' he said. 'I know it's only hair, but you've gone a bit too far this time.'

I cried the whole two days Mum was gone, desperate for her to come home, and when she finally did, she was still very upset with me. Mum didn't like radical things like strange haircuts or tattoos, and I knew that. She was very conservative and would have preferred me to wear three-quarter-length dresses with ribbons in my hair, but I was fifteen years old so that wasn't an option. I wanted to be different, so I was rebelling and being a total pain in the arse, always pushing Mum and Dad to the edge. Dad was able to handle it, but Mum pushed back and was always trying to rein me in. She knew I was wild, just like she'd been at my age, and that if left to my own devices I would go to town and do some damage.

I had to wear a beanie to school for three months after the Mohawk incident because Camberwell Grammar wouldn't accept this haircut on one of their students. As if the haircut wasn't bad enough, soon after this I cut my school tie to make it shorter and thinner. I'd always hated the fat end of the tie and wanted it to be long and thin like the mod look, so out came the scissors – another bad day in the Bull house.

Looking back now, I see what an ungrateful pain in the neck I was. Mum and Dad slaved their guts out to pay for my education, counting every penny, and that was how I repaid them. Dad was constantly telling us we were not well off, and I knew how much they'd sacrificed for me to go to Camberwell Grammar. We never went on flash holidays, Mum made most of our clothes and we only ate out occasionally. When we did go, I always stressed when the bill came because I was sure Dad wouldn't have enough money to pay for our meals. The favourite restaurant for Tongans at that time was the Swagman, and we always went there on special occasions. We even took the King of Tonga there for dinner when he visited Melbourne. The whole Tongan community went along for a great night out, but I remember not being able to enjoy the night as I should have, because I was so worried Dad wouldn't be able to pay our bill.

But school didn't interest me at all and so I rebelled. Instead of studying, I spent most afternoons listening to the radio and smoking out of my bedroom window. School wasn't for me, and I couldn't wait to get the hell out of there. I scraped through Year 11 and knowing I'd probably fail Year 12, I decided to leave. The school gave me a gentle nudge in this direction as well after my terrible end-of-year report, but I'd already made up my mind by then. Enough was enough. I wanted out.

Unfortunately, this all unfolded while Mum had returned to Tonga with her father's headstone. Grandpa died in 1979 but Mum hadn't been able to go back before now. As if that time wasn't upsetting enough, she returned home to discover that I'd quit school with Dad's blessing. He knew school wasn't for me and believed I was making the right decision.

'You know, darl,' he said, 'I'd be proud of you if you decided to go to Tasmania, chain yourself to a log, and get yourself arrested for protesting the damming of the Franklin River.'

He meant it too. Dad is a greenie who loves wildlife and has spent his whole life looking after animals and growing trees, but Mum didn't share this attitude. She was disappointed and wanted to know why I'd decided to leave, but I refused to discuss it. I'd already thrown my report in the bin so she couldn't read it.

After some long discussions, arguments and a few tears, the three of us came to an agreement. Even though I never took part in any music at school, I secretly knew that I could sing because I was always singing at home and listening to music. So I just wanted to get as far away from school as possible and join a band. I had another best friend at Camberwell, Elizabeth, who I spent a lot of time with and she was always saying that we should form a band. Deep down I knew that this was what I was going to do, and although I never expressed it out loud, I just went and did it. But I agreed to enrol in Stotts Secretarial College to get myself skills to use out in the real world, as per Mum's wishes.

'Secretarial college first,' she said. 'And if you pass, then you can go join a stupid band, you bloody idiot!'

LINDA
School, boys

I never had a problem relating to men because Dad and I always got along and spent a lot of time together. Also, I was a bit of a tomboy and was used to hanging out with the Tongan boys at church. I had been able to hold my own against the boys on the football field in Grades 5 and 6, as well as on the cricket pitch and in the pool. I even broke a few bones going up against boys on the footy field when I went in hard, because I hated the idea of losing to them.

So I wasn't intimidated by the boys at all when I started going to Camberwell Grammar's dancing classes every week in Year 9. While I was there, I met two boys who had weirdly similar names: Peter Stephen, aka 'Weenie', and Peter Stephens, aka 'EO', and I loved them both. The dancing classes were so stupid and old-fashioned, but it was the only way for any of us to meet boys who weren't brothers, cousins or neighbours.

When I first met EO we weren't attracted to each other at all, or at least, he wasn't attracted to me. He was way cooler than me, and I soon figured out that we were better as friends. Our friendship also gave me a ready-made date whenever I needed one for our school dances, so the arrangement probably suited me better than it did him. I fell hard for Weenie, and we ended up dating for about six months during Year 9. After he dumped me for another girl, I pushed him off a tram seat then ran to McDonalds and cried into a vanilla thickshake all afternoon.

I dated a few of his mates after that, which involved going to the beach, hanging out at each other's houses on weekends listening to records, or going to see our favourite bands like the Oils. The boys I dated were all very different: the good-looking surfer, the artist, the John Lennon type, the musician and the model. Clearly, I don't have a type.

The private school hierarchy for students includes prefects and house captains, but the top dog position is head prefect. There's a lot of prestige attached to this title, and a lot of pressure, and all students and teachers in the school vote, so when Miss Sutton told me I had been elected to the position at the end of Year 11, I was shocked. In my mind, head prefect was a smart person who was perhaps a little square and conservative, not a cheeky, sporty type like me. Clearly everyone else at school thought I was a square. But Miss Sutton believed in me. She was one of my earliest mentors and had always encouraged me to get up and speak at assembly or take potential new students and their parents on school tours over the years.

As Miss Sutton sat me down in her office to run me through the pros and cons of being head prefect, or head defect as I liked to call it, I started worrying about my exams and how I was going to find time to study. I didn't want to be the first head prefect in the school's history to flunk her VCE; also the responsibilities of the role put me off because I had the authority to punish girls for not wearing their uniform properly, for smoking or wagging, which would make me the biggest dobber in the school. I wasn't up for the idea of bossing people around or telling kids off for doing the kind of stuff I was guilty of whenever I was off school grounds. Things like smoking, not sticking to the uniform rules or leaving school to grab chips and a dim sim from the local fish'n'chip shop.

'It will make me a massive hypocrite,' I told Miss Sutton.

But she wasn't fazed.

'Can I think about it a bit more before accepting?' I asked.

'Of course,' Miss Sutton said.

I still remember her wry smile.

I told Mum as soon as I got home, and she was over the moon. I remember the proud look on her face as she stood in our kitchen, still in her nurse's uniform, leaning against our shitty brown wall oven. This was her reward for all the sacrifices they'd made and all her hard work to get us to Camberwell. It had been a long and difficult journey for my mum, and the fact that her little choc drop of a kid had been given the highest honour any student could get at that school meant so much to her. But I still wasn't sure I could accept. The risk of taking the position would mean possibly failing my exams, but the other risk was failing my mum and dad. I didn't want to do either.

'I'm not sure I can do it,' I said to her.

'Of course you can,' Mum said. 'I believe in you, and think about how much this will help you get into Melbourne University.'

This was a good point, but the deciding factor for me was not wanting to let my mum down. I had to take a punt. I went back to school the next day and told Miss Sutton I would accept the role. She looked very pleased but also unsurprised.

And so, I became the first dark-skinned head prefect at Camberwell Girls, as well as house captain of Schofield, and sports captain. My plate was full, and the pressure was on. All my achievements and positions were embroidered onto my blazer pocket in Year 12 for the whole world to see, and it was completely full.

Mum still has it, wrapped in a plastic dry-cleaning bag and hanging in her wardrobe.

VIKA

Leave school, join a band

When I left school at the end of Year 11, I knew I wanted to be a singer but had absolutely no idea how that was going to happen. I bade farewell to my schoolmates, sad to leave them, as well as feeling a real fear that I'd be missing out. At seventeen I headed out into the big wide world and Stotts Secretarial College.

The college was in the city, which was one long tram ride away from our house. Travelling to the city five days a week was a real adventure. I felt all grown-up and glad to be rid of the school uniform, the school bell and the strictness of the school routine. I was finally free. Stotts was totally different. It was up to me if I attended my lessons, and the school treated us like adults because they knew that in a year's time we'd be joining the workforce, so we had to get hip real quick! If we didn't turn up, we would fail and that was on us.

At Stotts, I learned typing, shorthand, grooming and bookkeeping, and to my surprise I thrived. Secretarial college was a breeze compared to school. I learned to type on an old manual Olivetti typewriter and could eventually manage up to seventy-five words per minute, as well as one hundred words of shorthand a minute. The other students were great too. I met all kinds of girls from all different walks of life at Stotts, and I just adored them all. They came from all over Victoria and there were Italians, Greeks, Chinese, Lebanese and Aussies. A lot of them came from suburbs I'd never heard of, which made me realise how small and protected my life had been up until that point. I'd been living in a bubble! We all learned how to dress like proper secretaries, and lived on cigarettes, pineapple donuts and coffee for a whole year.

I hadn't started seriously partying yet, as I promised my mother I'd get the certificate, so I put my head down and worked, just like my Camberwell friends were doing at school. When I graduated with honours at the end of the course, Mum was very proud and happy.

While I was at Stotts, I went to a party one night and met a gorgeous girl named Kim. She was a free spirit and like no girl I had ever met before. With her long dark brown hair and deep green eyes, Kim looked like a beautiful gypsy as she got up and sang for everyone at the party. Her voice was so powerful, and after a few drinks I found the courage to get up and sing with her. We clicked and she instantly took me under her wing.

Kim sang in a band called Fear of Flying, and after our performance together that night, she asked me to come along to their next band practice and sing backing vocals with her. Of course I said yes. There I was, fresh out of school with no experience in the real world and being asked to join a band! It was exciting.

I went along with Kim to Factory Sound in South Melbourne, which was a grotty rehearsal studio. The place didn't have much of a vibe, but the band members were all cute as hell, although I could see straight away that the lead singer, John, was a troubled soul. He played guitar and wrote all the songs, and I could feel the tension between him and the other band members from the moment I arrived.

I started practising with Fear of Flying every week. We rehearsed a lot. John was very particular about his songs and wanted them to be perfect before he played them for the world, so we were one of those bands that practised more than we played. Even at the ripe old age of seventeen I could see that John wasn't a great front man. Kim would have been much better, with her charisma and good looks – like an Aussie Stevie Nicks. The band was a mixed bunch. Half of them smoked a lot of pot, and the other half were fitness freaks. I didn't know much about drugs or the Australian music scene back then, but I knew I could sing and play piano a bit, so I chucked myself in the deep end from the get-go.

I gotta start somewhere, I thought. Let's see how this goes!

LINDA
Top dog

My final year at Camberwell was one of the most stressful times of my life. It was 1985 and failure wasn't an option for a perfectionist like me. Mum's goal was for me to get into Melbourne University to do law or medicine, but I wanted to be a printmaker. Either way, I wanted to do well in my VCE, and I wasn't one of the lucky kids who get good grades without having to study loads. I knew I'd have to work hard if I wanted to get into those courses.

Back when I'd first started high school, I was still struggling with my self-esteem and was obsessed with my weight. I wasn't eating, and things had become so bad that I could feel my hip bones digging into the bed at night. I'd buy myself bikinis, thinking they were huge when in actual fact they were tiny and the smallest size on the rack. Once, in Year 9 or 10, I went windsurfing with friends from school and when I got home, my hips were covered in bruises from my bones hitting the board. That's when I knew I was in trouble. That, and the fact that my hair had started falling out. I clearly needed help. Mum stepped in at that point and told me that I was doing myself serious permanent damage by not eating, and so I began to slowly introduce larger portions more regularly. My favourite new snack became a coffee scroll from the local bakery after sports practice. But Mum was right, of course. Not eating properly for so long had messed up my body's natural development, and I didn't get my first period until I was nineteen. I didn't tell any of my friends what was happening, which made me feel even more isolated.

But as Year 12 went on and I locked myself in my room after school, studying my arse off, I stopped exercising, started eating and ballooned from 40 kilograms to 70. The days of starving myself were over, and even though there was never any discussion with my parents about my weight gain (I think they were worried I'd starve myself again if they pointed it out) I could tell they were relieved.

Not only was I studying a lot, but my head prefect responsibilities were also taking up a lot of my time. Some of my many duties included running assemblies, public speaking, writing speeches and organising the end of year dance for the entire school (an enormous pain in the arse). I also had to help run the fete, open days and sports days presentations, take potential new students on school tours and listen to students' complaints and concerns.

I was having fun and going out whenever I could and, of course, there was also the Year 12 formal, Camberwell's biggest social event of the year. As head prefect, one of my duties for the night involved standing at the door to the venue alongside my date – and oldest friend to this day, EO – and Miss Sutton, to greet everyone as they arrived.

We did not have enough money to buy a fancy formal dress so, as usual, Mum made my outfit for the big night. I loved the whole process, which involved dragging Mum to the shops, picking out something I liked and then waiting for her to make a perfect copy of it on her Husqvarna. One week later there would be a new dress, exactly like the one I'd chosen, laid out on my bed when I arrived home from school. Mum really was an amazing seamstress.

For this final formal, I'd picked out a lovely yellow, drop-waisted, taffeta dress, which Mum copied to perfection. Unfortunately, I resembled a life-sized banana when I put it on. To make matters worse, at the last minute I decided to wax off my sideburns and the hint of a moustache that was hovering around my lips.

When EO arrived to pick me up for the big night, my sideburns were weeping and there was a sizable rash under my nose, which had started creeping up my face because it turned out I was allergic to the wax product. EO, however, showed no signs of leaving me on the doorstep, and how he kept a straight face the moment he saw me is a mystery. So off we went, a drop-dead handsome young man in Colonel Sanders tie and cool stovepipe tailored suit, and the overripe tropical banana split. Sadly, there's photographic evidence to prove it.

When VCE exams rolled around I managed to pass all of them except for maths (Mr Hobby would have been horrified). I hated maths but would have loved to get over the line and pass. I just couldn't do it. Apart from this, I have no regrets about my last two years at school, and all the extra duties I took on, because I had a wonderful time. I had some amazing experiences over those years at school, including the time I had the honour of meeting and welcoming Princess Diana to St Paul's Cathedral. A real highlight. I also loved hanging out with my friends in the art room, during home economics cooking classes, on sports teams and on the trampoline. My dear principal and friend, Miss Sutton, died in 2012. Vika and I both attended her funeral, and I will always remember her smile, her laugh, her kindness and her willingness to change her mind. She supported and believed in me, and I owe her so much. Hell, she even let me change the school uniform when I introduced a white cotton cable-knit jumper to the summer uniform. What a brilliant woman.

VIKA

Respect

When I turned eighteen, I moved out of home with my beautiful schoolfriend Elizabeth. We moved into a horrible flat in Lennox Street, Richmond, right beside a funeral parlour. Dad helped me move, but Mum wouldn't come to help because she didn't want me leaving home at that age. It was Dad who had given me a gentle nudge. He told me to get out into the real world and learn to fend for myself, which suited me fine. I couldn't wait to fly the coop!

After a few months in the Richmond place, I moved into a block of flats on the corner of Punt Road and Alexander Avenue. Elizabeth and I lived in the bottom flat, Kerri and her mate Cinzia lived in the top one, and a couple of our other friends lived in the middle one. Over the next couple of years, our little gang had the run of the place, partying and having a great time.

I had another schoolfriend, Ria, whose dad, Jim Mountford, owned Platinum Recording Studios in Chapel Street, South Yarra.

Kerri worked at Platinum full time and Elizabeth, Ria and I all got jobs there working night reception. We'd all gone to school together, and not only were we still hanging out but now we were all working together too. What a great job – we were right there in the thick of the action, watching all the aspiring musicians make their beautiful music.

One afternoon the singer Rebecca Barnard came in for a vocal session. She was supposed to be doing it with another singer, but the girl had lost her voice, so they needed a fill-in. Ria, Elizabeth and Kerri all happened to be there this particular afternoon, and they all piped up.

'Vika can sing!'

It was true that I could sing but I'd never sung in a studio before and wasn't sure I'd be able to do it.

'Do you want to come in and have a go at singing with me, Vika?' Rebecca asked.

I was nervous and unsure, but my friends all encouraged me to give it a go, so into the studio I stepped, with Rebecca coaching me through the whole thing. She was fantastic, and so patient, and she had a beautiful voice with a gorgeous tone. I want to thank Rebecca for that day. Not only for giving me my first break, but for holding my hand and being so supportive and nice to me. I'll never forget that.

Another day I met the boys from Cattletruck when they came in to do some recording. I got on well with their bass player, Tony Dennis. He invited me to move into the South Yarra house his family owned and which he shared with his girlfriend. The drummer from Cattletruck, Bruce – an absolutely top bloke – lived there as well with his girlfriend, and a gorgeous gal, Tanya, moved in too.

Tanya was wild like me, so the two of us were like peas in a pod. We'd party all night, come home and Tanya would cook an exotic breakfast like leek and potato soup. Then we's sleep all day and get back on it again at night. Sometimes, after we'd snorted coke, we'd drink Jack and have all-night cleaning sessions! God it was fun, except when I'd wake up to the sound of someone sucking on a bong. I drew the line at bongs. Dope wasn't my thing but partying with my buddy Tanya was. She was funny and fun, and I became known as Morty, as in, 'More tea, Vicar?' Tanya was my party pal, and we partied until our heads almost caved in. One time, after pulling an all-nighter at Inflation nightclub, we drove to Sydney on a whim, still in our little black dresses and bright red lipstick, our hair teased to the nines, blasting Billie Holiday in the car, then drove back again. But we always managed to show up for work. After all, we had to be able to pay for all our shenanigans.

It was the 80s, life was good, and we were reckless as hell. I lived in that gorgeous South Yarra share house for a couple of years, and when I was twenty-one, I met my other best friend for life, Samantha Gowing. I was waiting for the bus at St Kilda Junction one day when I noticed a striking girl. She had a walking stick and was wearing leather pants, a Rolling Stones T-shirt and a suede brown jacket with tassels, and her blonde 80s hair was shaved at the back and sides and long on the top. She was groovy as hell and on a mission. I couldn't stop staring at her and desperately wanted her to stare back so I could talk to her, but she wouldn't engage. We got on the bus and at Bridge Road she hopped off. I thought, Well that's that, I'll never see her again, and off I went on my merry way.

That night I was invited to a party in Muir Street, Richmond. I walked in and, lo and behold, there was the striking girl from the bus! This was my opportunity.

'Hey!' I yelled over the music. 'I saw you on the bus this afternoon.'

'Really?' she said. 'I didn't see you.'

How rude!

'Yeah, I saw you,' I said. 'I'm Vika.'

That night, we struck up a friendship and discovered that we were born on the same day. No wonder I found this gal intriguing. I ended up moving into another share house in South Yarra with her and her best buddy, Brett Kingman (aka Burger) who played guitar for James Reyne. That three-bedroom Victorian house in South Yarra was perfect for us. Many wild, hilarious nights were spent there with all sorts of characters coming and going.

I was still working at Platinum, and another great opportunity came my way when the band Noiseworks recorded their debut album. Jon Stevens, the lead singer, got wind that I could sing a bit, so he invited me to come sing some backups on the single 'Love Somebody'. I'm not sure if they ever used them, but having an incredibly powerful singer like Jon encouraging me to give it a go was a huge boost to my confidence and self-esteem.

While I was working nights at Platinum, I also worked for a super accountant during the days. So there I was, making money, paying rent, buying clothes, singing in bands, going out and living the life! The drinking had begun, and my friends and I were partying seven nights a week. The biggest night of the week was Wednesday at the nightclub Inflation. We would drink this horrible white wine there, which was pure poison, but because it was so cheap we took full advantage and got completely legless most nights. Friday nights we'd go to the club Razor, where we'd stay until the sun came up, drinking and doing drugs.

I spent a lot of my weekends rehearsing with Fear of Flying at Factory Sound and sometimes we'd hear Australian Crawl, one of my favourite bands, practising in the next room. I couldn't believe it! Sometimes when they were there, I'd sneak out of our room to listen to them. I'd wanted to see them in concert when I was sixteen but had got such a bad school report that Mum and Dad grounded me for three months and I couldn't go. Now, here they were, rehearsing in the room next door to me with their two ripper backing singers. I felt a bit embarrassed to be singing in such close quarters to those gals. Little did I know that my future husband was playing drums in that room as well … but more on that later.

When Fear of Flying had their first gig, at the Central Club in Richmond, I invited Mum, Dad and Linda along. I was nervous about them coming, especially since they'd never been in a place like the Central Club, but they all came along to show their support. I think they were secretly thinking Vika just needed to get this band thing out of her system and then life could go back to normal.

The show that night was great, and John even let Kim and me have a solo each. I did Aretha Franklin's 'Respect', which was ambitious. Now, as an experienced singer, I know better, and like Renée Geyer says, 'Never touch Aretha. Just don't go there!' But at seventeen I was very green and very cocky. I wanna belt out a tune, I thought. I know I can!

I'd never sung anything like 'Respect' at home or at school, but now that I was on a stage with a band, I wanted to do it. This was my way in, so I was gonna go for it.

The song wasn't perfect, but it went over a storm and the audience showed their appreciation by applauding loudly. From the looks on their faces, my family seemed to be in a bit of shock. They were not used to rock venues and were unsure about this new world I had entered. I think they liked the fact that I could sing but were also worried sick they were about to lose me to rock'n'roll. They weren't wrong either.

But I felt so at home up there on that stage, and to this day I'm grateful to John and Kim for giving me that opportunity, because my performance that night was the beginning of my career.

LINDA
She can sing!
Mum, Dad and I went along to watch Vika's first singing gig with

Fear of Flying, at the Central Club, when I was in Year 12. The three of us must have been quite the sight, standing there watching Vika sing, with our mouths open and our eyes popping out of our heads. None of us had any idea that my sister could belt it out like that before that night. We knew she could sing, of course – Vika had always sung – but this was next level. She was belting out Aretha up on that stage, in front of a crowd, and it was incredible. I thought our family concerts, the singing we did in church or along with the telly were for fun, and I had no clue she had serious aspirations until I saw her perform that night. But if I think about it, the signs were always there.

I still remember the day when the kids in our neighbourhood all laughed when they heard Vika singing 'Kookaburra Sits in the Old Gum Tree' on the toilet, and how embarrassed she was. I spent that night lying in bed and wondering why the kids would make fun of something that sounded so good. Early lessons in rejection aren't the worst things for kids with ambition. For the kids waiting for a little flicker of a flame or spark, they act as kindling for the fires within. And maybe that's what that day did for Vik.

But that night at the Central Club no one was laughing at my sister's singing anymore. She sounded amazing and looked so at ease in front of the audience too. I was shocked by the way she was dressed, and how she stood and presented herself on stage. Vika was dressed head to toe in Bettina Liano, wearing a short green skirt with a ruffle down the back and a matching jacket that zipped up at the front. She wore bright red lipstick, and her hair was set in a big curly bob, with a short fringe, and a scarf was wrapped around her head. She had large hoops in her ears and was wearing six-inch heels. It was a total transformation from the Vika I knew. Her whole demeanour was different when she had that microphone in her hand.

At that stage, my sister and I were living very different lives. I was eighteen and focused on passing my VCE, while Vika was totally immersed in the live music and nightclub scene. I was a self-described surfie chick who wore bright colours like watermelon-pink and emerald-green, three-quarter pants and baggy belted tops, and a lot of cheesecloth, because I was into Stevie Nicks. Vik was more into the alternative scene and liked artists like Malcolm McClaren and Depeche Mode. I thought this was a bit ironic, since those artists were so influenced by fashion and Vika had never been interested in fashion or clothes in her life, but she seemed to suddenly have a whole new group of very cool friends, many of whom I slowly got to know at her gigs.

It was the mid-80s and there were all kinds of things going on. There were the New Romantics, with their eyeliner and frilly shirts, big pants and belts and asymmetrical haircuts; the Buffalo Girls in their long, full skirts with baggy tops and belted jackets, headscarves under baseball caps and boots on their feet; and the Dexys Midnight Runners look, with their denim overalls. They were all groovy as hell. Vika was mad for that fashion and copied it. They all shared a love of music and looked amazing, but I do remember thinking they were all a bit pale and needed to get some sunshine. It wasn't my kind of scene – I was hanging out with surfers and footy players – but Vika loved it.

When I heard she'd joined a band I was surprised because even though we'd been singing together at home and in church forever, Vika had never taken part in the music program or done any musicals at school. Neither of us had. Instead, Vika had spent most of her time at Camberwell Grammar getting into trouble with my parents. She was a rebellious teenager and, boy oh boy, did she push that envelope.

Now, here she was, standing on a stage in the Central Club, blowing all of us away with her amazing voice and stage presence. Even Mum, who had been coaching us in singing since we were very little, looked completely amazed as she watched Vika on that stage. It was obvious that Mum had no idea her daughter could do *that*.

The crowd went nuts.

Uh oh, I thought. Now she's gonna have to tell Mum she wants to be a singer, not a secretary.

I could not *wait* to see this.

BANDS

VIKA

Boom Boom

When I was twenty, I got a job at the Black Cat Cafe in Brunswick Street, Fitzroy. It was a retro style cafe that served onion burgers and coffee. I looked forward to starting each shift because the owners, Henry Maas and Toni Edwards, were a very hip couple with a very big and tasteful record collection. The best part of working there was hearing the music they chose to play. Henry had a band called the Bachelors from Prague and got wind of the fact that I could sing. Soon after that he was always encouraging me to get up and sing with them. I would also go see Phil Ceberano play at different clubs around Melbourne and he got me up to sing with him and his band. My favourite song to perform with them was 'Devil Gate Drive'. Dad loved this song because he absolutely adored Suzi Quatro and had always dreamed of running away with her on the back of her motorbike.

Henry Maas also opened a cool club in North Melbourne called the Batchbox, which had big round tables, heavy velvet curtains and no stage, so bands played on the floor. This place was like something out of the 50s. The kind of place where girls wore beautiful dresses and smoked their cigarettes through cigarette holders while sipping champagne out of coupes, and boys wore stovepipe pants, black jackets and thin black ties with their hair slicked back.

I stayed in Fear of Flying for around a year, then joined John Justin and the Thunderwings as a backing singer. John was really into Marc Bolan and his band T.Rex. I absolutely adored Marc Bolan. I thought he was such an exotic creature and had a bit of a crush on him and his music. But I soon realised that I was only ever going to be the backing singer in John's band. John was definitely a rock star and the prettier one of the two of us!

Then Toni Edwards formed a band called the Blue Tomatoes and asked me to join. We played at the Batchbox with the Bachelors every week and Toni taught me a lot about music. She had such good taste and a healthy appreciation for all styles, including jazz, soul, R&B and samba. She also played percussion and was hip as hell.

One night, around 1986, I went to the Club to see Paul Kelly and the Dots with a group of friends, including my best friend, Kerri. I and remember it as one of the greatest gigs I've ever been to. We were hanging from the rafters; condensation was dripping from the roof, and we were all gagging for the Dots to come on. The place was packed but first we had to watch the opening act. They were a band by the name of Sophisticated Boom Boom and the minute they started playing I was instantly hooked. Oh my God, I thought. I love this band!

They looked like they were having so much fun, pumping out

that late 50s/early 60s girl-group sound, and I desperately wanted to be a part of it. One of the three female singers, Kerri Simpson, was amazing. I couldn't keep my eyes off her. She was a pocket rocket, and all those girls, as well as the four boys, stole my heart. When the Dots came on afterwards, the place went off and they rocked the house, but I knew I'd never get the chance to sing in a band like that. Those guys were way too cool for me, and besides, there were no girls in that band.

Later in 1986, Kerri Simpson left Sophisticated Boom Boom to go to America and broaden her musical career. The Boom Boom girls had seen me sing with the Blue Tomatoes and asked me to audition. When I found out that I'd been chosen to replace Kerri I was so excited. Playing gigs was this band's bread and butter. The fact that they were pretty much full-time musicians sealed the deal for me; I had met my people. The three of us girls – Jenny Boom Boom, Louise Boom Boom and me – were up front singing girl-group harmonies, while four boys played at the back. It was Jenny's group. She was a real 50s chick who had a passion for the music from that era and she made all our costumes. Jenny could jive, she dressed like a rocker and her flat was completely decked out in 50s decor. The three of us would meet at Jenny's flat to rehearse our harmonies and, although I was the youngest and greenest of the three, I knew immediately that I was the strongest singer. Kerri was a strong singer too, so I had an inkling this was why I got the gig.

We did covers of songs like 'Heatwave', 'Leader of the Pack', 'One Fine Day'. I sometimes think I was born in the wrong decade because I adored this kind of music and that girl-group sound, with its harmonies. It was right up my alley and I loved singing with those girls and that band. I learned so much from them all, like how to write out lyrics properly and how to work out three-part harmonies. We did this by sitting around Jenny's tape player and singing along. We would listen, stop the tape player, sing the harmony, rewind and do it all over again. We sure gave that tape player a run for its money. We all had very different voices, but they seemed to work together. Jenny knew which songs would suit which person, and we all took turns singing lead. She also worked out the dance moves. Louise was a natural mediator and often kept the peace between Jenny and me. Sometimes, when I got a little bit too big for my boots and overstepped the mark, Louise would give me a pep talk and I'd pull my head in. I'm so glad she did.

The boys in Sophisticated Boom Boom were great too. There was Jenny's boyfriend, Steve, on double bass; Mick, an old rocker, on guitar; another Steve, a lover of jazz, on saxophone; and Jeremy on drums. I went out with Jeremy for a minute. He was so sweet, and cute as a button, but I chewed him up and spat him out pretty quickly; I was a total bitch. Those boys were fabulous musicians and very talented, as well as volatile and moody. The whole shebang!

Sophisticated Boom Boom was a popular band, and we got a lot of gigs playing with another band called the Swingin' Sidewalks. Jenny's boyfriend was also their lead singer. He had a great voice too, so the Boom Booms and the Sidewalks were a terrific double act.

All the Boom Boom band members had extensive musical

knowledge, and one night Steve introduced me to an artist who would change my life. It was during sound check at Subterrain, a club at the top end of Swanston Street in Melbourne where we played a lot, when Steve walked over and handed me a couple of Etta James records.

'Check this chick out, Vik,' he said. 'I think you're gonna dig her A LOT!'

At home I put Etta on the turntable and immediately fell in love. Oh my God, I thought. Who is this woman? She can *sing*!

I sang along with those records every day, for weeks on end, and copied everything she did – Etta's power, her passion and the way she sang a love song and told a story with that incredibly soulful voice. Not only that but the woman was beautiful too. Etta became my musical inspiration from that day on. Don't get me wrong, Aretha was still one of my favourites, but my knowledge was starting to expand. The members of Sophisticated Boom Boom introduced me to some incredible singers, including Ruth Brown, Dinah Washington, Billie Holiday and Bessie Smith. These guys had great taste in music, and I felt so lucky to receive this kind of musical education. Up until that point I'd only ever listened to Mum and Dad's collection of records, and Top 40 radio.

Sophisticated Boom Boom and the Swingin' Sidewalks played heaps of gigs around Melbourne, and we also travelled to Adelaide many times to play at the Austral Hotel in Rundle Street. We'd travel there, usually five to a car, and I always got lumped with the middle spot in the back seat. Shit, this is uncomfortable, I'd think as we travelled down the highway in the middle of the night. If I ever get my own band, we're gonna fly everywhere!

LINDA
Working girl and sister act
A couple of months after finishing high school, I started a Bachelor of Arts degree at Melbourne University, training to get a Diploma of Education. I would have quite happily stayed living with Mum and Dad, but Dad had given me a gentle push to get out and stand on my own two feet. So, in 1986, after a bit more convincing, I packed up my single bed, my Casio alarm clock and my Blondie poster and off I went, straight into the lion's den of Acland Street, St Kilda, where I moved into a share flat with a girl called Sherine and her boyfriend Robin.

Sherine was a singer in a popular band at the time called BiG PiG and I had met her at a gig one night through Vika. I soon realised that Sherine and Robin were much more worldly than me and that I'd been very protected so far, but I was excited about my new independent life. Now I just needed to find a job to pay for it!

Mum helped get me a job as an assistant chef (glorified kitchen hand) at Donvale Private Hospital, where she was the senior nurse and second in charge. I worked the morning shift on weekends with Olivia, the chef, a beautiful Italian lady. Olivia is the woman responsible for teaching me to cook. I learned to peel, chop, mince, vitamise and season anything and everything she threw at me.

Vika also got a job there as a kitchen hand (dishwasher) and I made sure to use the biggest pots when we were cooking and burn the crap out of them so they'd be harder for her to clean. She hated me for this, but I have no regrets.

The weekly trip from St Kilda to Donvale started to become a bit too long on the bus so I left my kitchen job after about a year. When I was in my first year at uni, my mate Cath McKinney helped me get a job at a pub in Clarendon Street called the Emerald, but unfortunately I was the world's worst waitress. What I loved about that job, though, was the Allan Browne Quintet, who played four sets of jazz standards there every week. Allan was the drummer, cheeky as hell, and, boy, could he play. I looked forward to going to work so I could hear them, and it was because of them that I became a lifelong fan of artists like Billie Holiday, Lena Horne, Ella Fitzgerald and Sarah Vaughan. Allan sang some songs, and the band also did instrumentals from these amazing artists and many more. The first time I heard the song 'All of Me' I swooned. I went home and learned all the words, just in case Allan ever needed a fill-in singer, but the one and only time he asked if I could sing, I was suddenly overcome with shyness.

'No,' I said. 'I can't sing.'

One night, soon after moving to St Kilda, I headed out to see Vika sing with the Blue Tomatoes at the Batchbox. The place was pumping with Fitzroy's bohemian set: musicians, painters, dancers, actors, hairdressers, cafe owners, furniture makers, sculptors, vintage shop owners, poets, sexy door bitches, models and students, and everyone was dressed up and dancing to the Bachelors. Drinks were cheap (bowling club prices) so you could get wasted on about ten bucks and, since I was a tight-arse student, this suited me.

As I was leaving, I fell down the stairs. I've always been a clumsy person – not the graceful kind who falls lightly or politely either. I'm all arms, legs, thumping and swearing. When I fall, I fall hard, and that night I fell right in front of the Bachelor's percussion player, Justin. He laughed and helped me up, and I remember feeling slightly, but not overly, embarrassed as I stared at his happy shoes – Japanese-style black cotton slippers.

I stared up at this guy. From the look on his face, I reckon he was more embarrassed than me.

'Hi,' I said, brushing myself off. 'I'm Linda.'

Soon after that we started going out.

In late 1986, I moved into a share house in South Yarra with my best buddy EO's girlfriend, Jane Kleimeyer, and her bestie, Sarah Murphy (Murph). Jane's mum owned the house and she was the best landlord in the world. I was lucky enough to score a big beautiful room at the front, and knew I'd landed on my feet after the shoebox room I'd had in St Kilda. But the rent was a hefty fifty bucks a week, so I needed a job that paid more money.

Vika told me the Black Cat needed staff, so I went in to meet Henry and Toni and got myself a job. The staff at the Black Cat did everything, including making coffee, prepping and cooking the food, cleaning the toilets and floors, scrubbing down at the end of the day and, most importantly, playing DJ.

Toni and Henry's playlist was next level. Latin, Brasil '66, R&B, 50s and 60s girl groups, Aretha Franklin, Sam Cooke, ska, dancehall, reggae … you name it, they had it, and the best part was you got to choose the music for your shift. I thought I'd died and gone to heaven.

I'm still friends with a lot of the people I met at the Black Cat, including Ros Sultan. Ros and I worked a lot of shifts together and got along from day one. A proud Eastern Arrernte and Gurindji woman, Ros was older than me and took me under her wing. I loved her and I also loved her little boys, Dan and Luke, who she'd sometimes bring to work. When Dan started singing at the top of his voice, I'd throw bagels at him and tell him to be quiet. Thank goodness he took no notice of us and went on to become one of this country's greatest singers.

Vika was working as a receptionist at Platinum Recording Studios and living in South Yarra with her mates Tony Dennis and Tanya at that time. They all partied way more than I did, and Vika was establishing herself as a singer with the Thunderwings and the Blue Tomatoes, and guesting with the Bachelors.

Getting the job at the Black Cat was life-changing for me. It my introduction not only to a whole new world but also to the fantastic music scene. I'd been at Melbourne University for a year by then and had made some beautiful friends, but I was also starting to realise that everybody else was much better at teaching than me. I already felt out of my depth as an artist but doing my student-teacher rounds at Collingwood College was the straw that broke the camel's back.

Collingwood College was rough back then and seemed like it was falling apart at the seams. One of the kids tried to jump out of the second-storey window on my first day, and the principal had a nervous breakdown on my second. Everything went downhill from there.

I was put on yard duty at recess that first day and told to keep an eye out for any shenanigans. I wasn't much older than the Year 12 students and was soon cornered by a group of Year 11 and 12 thugs who tried to jump me. Instinct kicked in and I took off my shoes and belt to fight my way out of it and was luckily unhurt. But I never went back to that school, or to uni, after that day. I'm very superstitious and so I took my experience at Collingwood as a sign that it wasn't meant to be. No one else I knew had had an experience like mine and it spooked me.

The only good thing about those rounds was seeing an already famous Brian Nankervis walking around the halls in his beret and clutching his books. I was starstruck. But other than that, it wasn't a good experience at all.

I didn't want to quit teaching so soon after starting, but I was spending more time at gigs, watching Vik sing with the Boom Booms or the Blue Tomatoes, than concentrating on my studies, which was very out of character for me.

At a family lunch one Sunday, I was whining to Vika about my life and what I was going to do now. Family lunch was always our chance to relax and unwind. We could drop the armour and be ourselves. It was, and still is, an important part of our connection to our parents and for us as sisters. We'd thrash it out – whatever was front and centre in our lives would be on the table, whether it be what was happening in our personal lives, in our jobs, our relationships with our flatmates and friends or boyfriend problems. You name it, we talked about it, because our parents had time to ask and we had to answer – they could tell if we were holding back.

But I think Mum hoped I'd shut my mouth when Vika said, 'Well, why not come sing with me?'

※

It was 1987 when Vika offered me a chance to sing with her. I knew that I sounded okay doing harmonies in the lounge room but didn't know if I was prepared for the stage. But Vika was singing with the Bachelors from Prague at that point and Henry Maas suggested I join her for a duet during their set, and that we do 'Something Stupid' by Frank and Nancy Sinatra. We agreed because the song was in harmony, and we knew we could harmonise well.

'I'll call you up after our first few songs,' Vika told me.

I was excited but also nervous. 'Something Stupid' sounds like an easy song to sing and, like a lot of young singers, I underestimated the expertise needed for it. I was doing Nancy's part, which sounds like a drone, and Vik was doing the heavy lifting by singing the melody, which moved all over the place. I spent ages learning it, and we sounded good at rehearsal, but when I turned up to Subterrain that night for the gig and saw how many people were there, I was terrified.

'Whatever you do, don't drink!' Vika told me beforehand. 'We've just gotta sing this one song and then you can drink as much as you want, okay?'

'Sure,' I said. 'Got it.'

But nerves got the better of me. As soon as Vika was up on stage, I went out to my Datsun 120Y and sculled half a bottle of whisky for courage. By the time I got up with Vika and the band I was more than a little loosey goosey. I sang out of tune and didn't stick to my part, so Vika couldn't harmonise with me at all. She was furious and kept glaring at me. I'll never forget that LOOK. I also remember the band members looking like they were torn between wanting to burst out laughing and wanting to burst into tears. I certainly wanted to cry. 'Something Stupid' has an eight-bar instrumental and it was the longest eight bars of my life then and since.

Basically, we sounded completely shithouse and it was all my fault. This had been my chance, a chance my sister had given me, and I'd embarrassed her, and myself, and let the team down.

Afterwards, Vika didn't tell me off or yell at me, but I got out of there as fast as I could. I left my car there and caught a very expensive cab home. All the way I was thinking, This music thing obviously isn't for me.

Second chance

Necessity soon presented me with an opportunity to redeem myself. Louise was leaving Sophisticated Boom Boom to take up a teaching position and she and the band encouraged me to give it a go. I was so grateful to them and was determined to never let anyone down again.

The songs Sophisticated Boom Boom did were perfect for a young singer like me. They were tough as well as tender, and a shy girl from the suburbs could pretend to be sassy while singing them. I went forensic on the music and the parts I had to learn and can still remember those songs today; they're burned into my brain. The band was already very popular in the underground Melbourne scene, so I got to enjoy the results of all their hard work right from the start.

Although she wasn't technically the lead singer, it was obvious that Vik was the best singer in the group. She sang with such ease and power, so it made sense that she was given more and more lead singer duties and attention. Watching on, I could see the friction that this was starting to cause between her and the other girls.

Meanwhile, I was having a great time. I was making a few hundred bucks a week, cash in hand (cash!), and, because I was nineteen, I blew it all on booze, ciggies, clothes, food and petrol … in that order. It was unreal. If only I'd listened to Dad's advice about saving $20 every week, I'd be set now, but I was young and stupid.

I hadn't fully thought through the whole telling-my-parents-my-plan-to-forget-teaching-for-singing thing but finally found the time, and the guts, to sit them down and tell them I wanted to sing with Vika.

'I don't mind that you're having a crack at singing together,' Dad said, 'as long as you're happy doing it.'

Mum didn't have quite the same positive reaction. She stared at me, disappointment all over her face, as she tried to process what she was hearing. My mum had always suspected Vika was going to join a band, but I was a different story. As far as she was concerned, I'd shown no interest in singing and she'd assumed I'd go into law or teaching art because I always had a book or a paintbrush in my hand. Now, here she was, losing not one kid, but two, to music. It was a double whammy. To be honest, I probably would have felt the same way, realising that all my hard-earned private school education, and fees, was going to go down the drain. For what? A career on stage?

'Well, I am not happy about it,' Mum finally said. 'But whatever you do, remember to stick together, look after one another, don't take drugs and don't get a tattoo.'

Good advice, Mum.

It was the first time I'd gone against what Mum wanted for me, and this hurt her, which hurt me too. Up until then I'd been the easy-going, well-behaved and dutiful kid, so it was a big change for both of us. The last thing I wanted was to let my mum down, but I also needed to give this new thing a go. If for no one else, I had to prove to myself I could do this.

VIKA

Sisters doing it for themselves

I didn't think about starting a band with Linda until she joined the Booms Booms in 1987. We wanted to broaden our repertoire and the idea of going out on our own soon took on its own momentum. One night, when she was working at the Black Cat, Linda asked Henry Maas if he had any ideas for a name and he suggested the Honeymooners, after the 1960s TV show. I hated it, but by the time Linda told me, Henry had already designed our first poster, so it was too late. Linda felt bad afterwards that she hadn't bothered to ask me first, but looking back it was a pretty good name for a band. Henry's poster featured a huge black panther with our names on it in bright orange writing, and the posters went up all over Fitzroy.

Our first ever street poster! Now we just had to put a band together.

Back then a lot of the musicians came out of the Victorian College of the Arts (VCA). They were all very good jazz players who played and practised and read music twenty-three hours a day. If you ever needed a player it was always a friend of a friend who could play this or that, which is how we formed our first band. Decisions were made on the spot, and it was pretty brutal. We'd get together for one rehearsal to check potential band members out, and if our combo worked, they stayed; if they didn't, it was see ya later.

In the end we had ourselves a great band, with Thierry Fossemale on bass; Jack Abeyratne on guitar; Linda's boyfriend, Justin, on drums and percussion; and Steve Sedergreen on piano. It was a soul music band with the whole bit.

Next, we had to sort out our material. We knew we wanted to play soul music, but apart from that we really didn't have a clue what we were doing. We knew we could sing but that was about it. There were some very talented musicians in our band but the songs we wanted to sing were probably a little out of our depth. Songs like Sam and Dave's 'Soul Man', Otis and Carla's 'Tramp', but we wanted to sing them because they were catchy. We decided to do covers of mostly old classics, concentrating on soul, R&B and country singers, including Al Green, Wynona Carr, Ruth Brown, Etta James, Aretha, Ann Peebles, the Staple Singers, Linda Ronstadt and Bonnie Raitt. Linda and I planned to take turns doing lead, while the other did backing vocals or sang harmony.

Vika and I decided to move northside around this time, taking over the lease of a big old Edwardian in Carlton. We rehearsed in the living room of our share house and started mucking around with melodies of classic old soul songs to suit our style. If there was a song that didn't have a harmony on it, we'd make sure it did by the time we were done, so the other wasn't standing there like a shag on a rock.

We each had our roles, which worked smoothly for a while. I wrote the set list and made sure the band was paid before anyone else, Linda designed and organised the poster run, and her boyfriend, Justin, booked us the gigs. We started getting some bookings and it was easy to tell which songs went down well and which ones didn't. We wanted a reaction after every single song, preferably positive, so we massaged our set list to accommodate our audience. The only way we'd get more shows with more people (and therefore bigger pay cheques) was if we gave the people what they wanted. It wasn't rocket science.

The singing itself was a bit of trial and error, but once we learned to trust our gut, it all came together. Linda and I learned how to push the song as far as it would go for our voices, and by playing with the harmony within the melody, we found the perfect key. We were young and excited and wanted to sing everything, and so we gave everything a crack.

Our fees started going up from $50 a show to $100. If we did three shows a week, bingo! Linda and I knew people liked harmonies, and that if we kept doing them, we'd be okay. But we also understood that we needed our own unique sound, so we devoted ourselves to that.

We lived and breathed music, and the lifestyle was exciting too. Unfortunately, I hadn't yet learned how to communicate with band members, so I could be a bit of a shithead, yelling my head off at the band like a complete madwoman. I'm embarrassed about this now. These were trained musicians, while Linda and I had learned by ear and couldn't speak jazz. We didn't know our theory when it came to explaining what we wanted to hear, and my frustration with that, and not liking what I'd hear sometimes, would cause me to scream at them. It wasn't until our sweet piano player, Steve Sedergreen, gave me a look of absolute horror one day that I realised what I was doing and how badly I was behaving. This was a turning point for me. From that moment on I understood that I couldn't, and shouldn't, speak to musicians that way, and that I had to prove myself before I ever spoke up again. It was a very valuable lesson.

The Honeymooners played many gigs, and we got better and better, landing residencies at the Hotel Esplanade (aka the Espy) in St Kilda and the Royal Derby Hotel in Fitzroy, and making a name for ourselves around Melbourne. As we got more popular we were paid better and soon our fees were up to $500 and more.

Linda and I were still working our day jobs, only singing at night, but eventually the singing took over and the day jobs had to go. Back then, you'd do a show, then run off to another venue to see someone else play and would be up until five most mornings. That was normal. We lived hard and played harder, but, ultimately, we never missed a gig. Voice or no voice, we battled through, which was the advantage of being a duet as opposed to a solo act. One could always cover for the other. Our job as singers was the most important thing to us, so we worked hard, often doing two shows in a day on weekends. Neither of us had a voice left come Monday morning but we didn't care because no other bands played on Mondays (except Dianna Kiss). This was our life now, and we were hooked! Yep, sex and drugs and rock'n'roll was the life for us. Yahoo!

We were friends with many other bands, singers and musicians, and the vibe was supportive, friendly, wild and fun, which is how we first crossed paths with Peter Luscombe in 1986.

LINDA

The audition

Peter Luscombe was the drummer in a band called the Black Sorrows, which was Joe Camilleri's new band following his huge success with Jo Jo Zep and the Falcons, and he was a machine – he lived and breathed the drums. Some of the Black Sorrows members were musicians like Jeff Burstin, who had been with Joe since the Falcons days, but Peter 'Lucky' Luscombe, Wayne Burt and Mick Girasole were new crew. Before Vika and I came into their lives, the Black Sorrows had already released popular albums like *Sonola*, *Rockin' Zydeco* and *A Place in the World*.

Peter had seen Vika singing with John Justin in the Thunderwings, but when I first met him he was playing drums in a band with my ex-flatmate Sherine and her brother, Jack, who was our guitarist in the Honeymooners, and so our worlds were already intertwined.

At that time, as Vika and I were cutting our teeth in a small but tight scene in the Honeymooners, the Black Sorrows were in the middle of recording the album *Hold On to Me*. Venetta Fields, a very gifted American singer, was Joe's favourite backing singer, but she was busy singing with John Farnham. Venetta was the real deal. She moved to Australia after touring with Boz Scaggs and had sung and danced with many of the greats. She was an Ikette for Ike and Tina Turner; she sang backing for Aretha, Bob Seger and the Rolling Stones. Heck, she was even a Raylette (backing singer for Ray Charles)! She'd already done most of the singing for *Hold On to Me* but was unavailable to go on the upcoming tour. Peter had started looking around for a couple of backing singers to replace her and came to see us perform one night at the Royal Derby. After the show, he came backstage to say that he was going to talk to Joe about us. We were already fans of Joe's, and so were very excited at the prospect of playing in his band, but we tried to play it cool, especially because the Honeymooners band members were within earshot.

Pete liked what he heard and, being as astute as they come, knew that two sisters would survive better on the road because we'd have each other. He could also hear that we had a natural blend and wouldn't need to manufacture a sound that wasn't already there. They'd save money on accommodation too because we'd share a room. Pete went back to Joe and suggested he give us an audition to go on the six-week national tour, and Joe agreed.

We knew it was a great opportunity but were also torn because if we got the gig, we'd be letting our own band down. A band we adored. We'd have to abandon them and join a completely different group of people for six whole weeks. Vik and I discussed it and decided it was only a short time and that we could just start up again with the Honeymooners when we got back, with more experience and more money. Also, we really liked Joe's music and that was the clincher. The two of us had grown up glued to the TV every Sunday night when *Countdown* was on, so of course we knew who Joe Camilleri was. How could we forget the turban!

We said yes to Pete, got the songs, learned every one of them and went off to audition for the Black Sorrows.

VIKA

Joining the Black Sorrows

Joe tells me I wore a very short skirt to the audition. I really don't remember, but he says I did. I had a good set of pins, so I liked showing them off in miniskirts, but I'm a little embarrassed now that I didn't dress more appropriately. I was a bit wild in those days so that stuff didn't matter to me then, but it does now. Linda and I pretty much nailed the audition, and Joe was impressed that we'd learned the material so quickly. He decided to give us a six-week try-out, and we headed straight into the studio to add some harmonies to the nearly finished album, *Hold On to Me*.

Venetta Fields was in the studio too. I found one of those early sessions with Venetta a bit tricky. I'd been used to taking the top harmony, while Linda always took the low, but on this occasion, I was given the middle part and just couldn't get it. Both Venetta and Linda were very patient with me, but eventually Venetta gave up.

'That's it!' she said. 'I'm going outside for a joint!'

I'd stuffed up and felt like a total failure.

I redeemed myself that week when Joe was recording a song for the album called 'Chained to the Wheel'. The song was almost finished when Linda and I came on board, but Joe thought it might be a good idea for me to sing a verse. Jeff Burstin was producing, and as the 'tuning meister', he made sure I was singing in tune. Both he and Joe were pretty tough, listening closely to every breath, note and phrasing, but it was good for an inexperienced singer like me. I learned fast.

Our first show with the Sorrows was at the Parkview Hotel in North Fitzroy. North Fitzroy in 1987 was nothing like North Fitzroy today. It was still very working class back then, had an active First Nations mob and a vibrant alternative arts community. The Parkview was a great old live music venue and held around three hundred people, and when Linda and I walked onstage for that first gig, we were shocked to see the audience sitting on the floor.

What a bunch of fucking hippies, I thought.

There I was, all of twenty-one years old, judging Joe's loyal longtime fans. What a drongo. By the end of the night, everyone was up and dancing, and it was a fantastic gig. I wish the Parkview was still like that. Now it's full of poker machines and big-screen TVs.

It was pretty obvious from the get-go that Linda and I weren't going to leave the band once our six-week trial was up. Venetta was busy with John Farnham, and we were having way too much fun and got along so well with the boys. We always knew that we wanted to stay, but also knew that the decision was ultimately up to Joe. We never really had a formal conversation about it, and once the six weeks were up the tour kept getting extended, and we stayed with the Black Sorrows.

We knew that our days with our own band, the Honeymooners, were over. It was a tough decision to make because one of our good friends and Linda's boyfriend were both in the band and we were effectively quitting on them. Losing two lead singers doesn't always mean the end of a band, but it did for the Honeymooners. When we sat down to tell them we were leaving, a few of them were pretty pissed off, including Linda's boyfriend. Apart from Justin, we never worked with any of those musicians again because there was too much bad blood. It was our first tough lesson in a tough industry. But we wanted to advance our careers quickly, and we knew that staying with the Sorrows was our golden ticket. We'd have been idiots to knock the opportunity back.

We slogged it out with Joe and the band in the clubs and small pubs of inner Melbourne for about six months, until the album came out. These fellas were all total strangers to us in the beginnings, so those gigs in the lead-up to the *Hold On to Me* release were good practice and gave us a chance to get to know the way Joe and his band worked. The experience was invaluable. We could see that they worked hard and played loud, and quickly figured out that we'd have to get our shit together if we wanted to keep up. Joe liked to change the set regularly too, and was always adding songs, so our knowledge of music started to grow. The audiences were still pretty small at that stage, at least compared to what would come once the album was released.

The first single, released at the end of September 1988, was the title track, 'Hold on to Me'. 'Chained to the Wheel' was released as the third single off the record, a few months later, in January 1989, and was a hit the moment it hit the airwaves. Our lives would never be the same again, and I'd had no idea when I sang it that day in the recording studio that it would be so big, or that they'd still be playing it on the radio today.

LINDA
Bandmates

Most of the guys in our new band were a good ten to twenty years older than Vika and me, which meant that we learned a lot from them. First, there was our fearless leader, Joe Camilleri. Joe was the best-dressed man in show business. Still is. He wore expensive clothes, which he'd buy from his favourite retro stores, and when we were touring he'd appear on stage every night in a different shirt, vest, shoes, scarf, hat or swanky jacket he'd bought that day. He loves playing around with colours, and the lucky dude can wear all of them. I reckon pink suits him best. Joe taught us that presentation is important.

'You gotta entertain, you gotta play and know your instrument well, but you gotta look good too!' he'd say.

Joe is the ultimate salesman. In his early days, we heard, he'd finish a show, then race out to the carpark, covered in sweat, and straight into the throng of his adoring fans, who were always eagerly waiting to meet him. He'd flog his records straight out of his car boot, yelling, 'Get your records here, folks! One for twenty-five or two for fifty!'

How could anyone resist buying from this guy who always made everyone feel like they were getting a bargain? That was until they walked away, dripping in Joe Camilleri's sweat with no change and two vinyl albums in their hands. But they loved it! Joe was always smart with money and ended up sinking all his hard-earned cash into real estate. He didn't get the nickname 'The

Pope of Elwood' for nothing.

Joe is one of the most robust people we've ever met. We've never seen him drunk or high on drugs, and he never overindulges. Joe loves good food and good coffee and, whenever we'd hit a new town, he always had his favourite places for his daily fix of coffee and cake.

He has a great sense of humour and is always up for a laugh. But he can be dark and moody too, which we got to see on the road sometimes. When he was in one of those moods, we'd try and avoid him. We understood that he had the weight of the world on his shoulders as the leader of the band, and sometimes he needed to retreat to his room when he felt like that.

When Joe started becoming successful, he sent televisions, heaters and all sorts of things back to his grandmother in Malta. He had thought they would help make her life more comfortable, only to find out that she'd given them all to the church, for others who needed them. Joe told us his grandmother struggled through cold Maltese winters and stiflingly hot summers for the good of the congregation, which was very similar to the kind of thing Tongans, especially our own mother or Aunty Mafi, would have done.

The Sorrows' drummer, Pete Luscombe, was our closest friend in the band and was instrumental in getting us a leg in the door. Pete is the eldest son in a large Irish-Australian Catholic family, and, like us, understands the importance of strong family connections. Funny as hell, with an encyclopaedic knowledge of music, Pete was not a back-seat drummer in any sense of the word. He always made sure his opinion was heard, both in the rehearsal room and the studio. I admired Pete's willingness to argue his point. He was from a big family where, as the saying goes, 'He who shouts loudest gets heard'. I learned a lot from him. If I'm too shy, I'll be ignored, I remember thinking. I need to speak up like Lucky does.

Pete, along with the rest of the band, gave me the best twenty-first birthday present: a pair of LP bongos I still have. He took the time to teach me different patterns on the tambourine, how to hold it for the best sound, where to come in and, more importantly, where to stay out. When I finally passed my driving test (after four attempts), I went straight over to the terrace in Carlton that he shared with his girlfriend Tania. I felt so happy to share my news with him. He was like a big brother who took us under his wing, looked out for us and was never afraid to tell us off if we stepped out of line. Peter Luscombe is very important to us both. He's been there from day one.

Jeff 'Joffa' Burstin was our no-nonsense lead guitarist, a bear of a man and a solid-as-a-rock musician. The stable foil to Joe's unpredictability, Joffa kept incredible time and had extensive music knowledge so could go anywhere Joe fancied, musically speaking. We were on the back foot in this regard because we didn't grow up on the music they did, so Joffa taught us about sound and the kind of attitude they were chasing when we played. Every sound check involved a lot of Joffa playing guitar, and Joffa liked to play loud. Vika and I were always way down the list when it came to sound-check priority, which used to shit me up the wall, as did trying to hear ourselves over Joffa's guitar. As much as we loved him, he just wouldn't turn himself down, so we had to suck it up and sing. The whole band was incredibly loud, and this was back in the days before in-ear monitoring, so the louder the band got, the more we signalled to our foldback guy to turn us up. But no matter what we did, we could never hear ourselves over a full rocking band like the Sorrows.

Joffa was a huge influence on the Sorrows' sound. He went forensic in the studio. He produced all the vocals alongside Joe and often pulled out his trusty acoustic guitar to help us figure out the more intricate parts of the harmony if we got stuck. Thank God that he had the patience to help two young girls figure out their harmonies, which must have been a very frustrating process, especially when we were harmonising with Joe, who ducked and weaved all over the place. I was always given the tricky middle to lower bit, which made my head spin, but it trained my ear to listen for the hard parts in songs. During late-night sessions, I'd get so tired when we went over and over a particular part and would think, What was wrong with what we just did? I never asked this out loud, though. Joffa knew it wasn't good enough and would push us to get the best take. When Vika sang lead vocals on 'Never Let Me Go', Joe made her sing it so many times that her vocal cords nearly bled. I was in the control room with Joffa at the time and got so worried about my sister that I eventually pleaded with Joffa to tell Joe to stop. He did, and then ended up choosing Vika's second take!

Wayne Burt was the other guitarist in the band and shared

duties with Joffa. He was hilarious, sensitive and a Virgo, like me. Wayne was a mild-mannered, gentle and vague creature, but put him onstage and he transformed into a guitar-shredding rock god. He brought a lot of showbiz to that side of the stage, with his tight skinny jeans, boots, studded belt and country shirt. He had a young family so was frugal whenever we were on tour, and we never did see Wayne party on the road. But he was hilariously funny.

Mick Girasole was our Egyptian bass player who smoked stinky rollies. He had gorgeous long brown hair and clashed big time with Vik. Once, when he was rude to a waitress in a restaurant, Vik told her to pour a jug of water over his head.

There were two phases to the Black Sorrows' career path: the early phase, when we were a small unit playing the infamous pub rock scene, and the second phase, when we became a much larger band playing to much larger audiences in much larger rooms.

As the band became more popular, Joe wanted a bigger show, which meant bringing more people into the band. In 1989 our bass player Mick Girasole left, and a talented young fella, Richard Sega, aka 'Dickie', took his place. Dickie was a quiet riot, but had a few demons so moved on after a few years, and Stephen Hadley, who was playing in Vince Jones's band at the time, took his place. Steve was a VCA graduate, and could make that bass talk, which was a must if you played with Vince. Vince had a reputation for only hiring the best, most skilled jazz players, and Steve was most definitely one of those. He also looked like a movie star and drove an Aston Martin, which didn't hurt, but it was the way he played his instrument that really counted. We loved hanging out with him because he was always up for a drink, a laugh and a bit of mischief. Once, on a night out in Norway, Steve decided to go for a late-night swim. He'd had just the right amount of schnapps to numb the cold and so he jumped in the fjord. It's lucky he didn't die. From that moment on we called him 'Harrison Fjord'.

Joe also added Jen Anderson on violin in 1989. He first saw her when she was playing with Dave Steel, who opened for us at the Harbourside Brasserie. Jen was a beautiful blonde and a wonderful violin player.

In 1991, more members joined, including Robbie Burke on saxophone, Tony Norris on trumpet and Michael Barker on percussion. The horns were a late addition to the line-up, brought in to fatten up the sound and add some extra pizzazz to theatre shows. We liked Robbie and Tony a lot because they were always up for a laugh. Joe referred to them as the 'Tin Men'.

Michael is Maori and, being Pacific Islanders, we naturally gravitated towards him. He was a trained, tuned percussionist and a prodigy. You could feel the good energy radiating from him, so much so that when he did a conga solo, the place went crazy. When he hits that stage, he is always smiling and animated, and his talent shines. It oozes from his pores. Having him in the band really helped Vika and me, because his energy took the pressure off us a bit. We all fed off each other and gave the audience lots to look at and listen to. Both the ladies and the fellas liked to look at Michael.

The Black Sorrows was a motley crew of sorts, as most bands

are, and Vika and I were so lucky to have met and worked with all of them. The knowledge they passed on to us, both individually and as a group, changed our perception of what we could sound like, and opened our eyes to the possibility of a long career rather than a short one. Basically, they taught us to be good at what you do and never quit.

VIKA
Voice trouble

The Sorrows got popular very quickly after we joined them, and we were soon playing six nights a week. Most days were spent recovering from the night before, as Linda and I tried to get our voices back in time for that night's show.

I've been a belter all my life. The term 'belt' in singing means that you sing head-voice range notes, with chest-voice power. Chest voice is where you speak from. It is the most powerful, and when you keep trying to use that power in higher notes your voice will naturally break and go into the head voice. Yodelling is an example of going from chest to head voice. It's great fun because it's a very physical way of singing, but it can also damage your voice big time, and damage it I did.

When I first started singing in bands, I thought I should probably have some proper lessons. Mum had taught us how to sing when we were kids, and gave us a good start, but I decided I needed to learn about breathing techniques so I found a great teacher in Hawthorn named Cynthia McCracken. Cynthia was great. She taught me some handy things like how to strengthen the diaphragm, figuring out where to breathe in songs, how to use expression, and all that kind of stuff. The first song I learned with her was 'Yesterday' by the Beatles. It's a great one to start with for learning where to breathe, and how to sing with feeling.

Cynthia taught me a lot, so now I had my scales and warm-up exercises, and I was off. These were all very useful, but I was a belter; it was my workout!

'Why you gotta shout all the time?' Dad would complain when he heard me singing as a kid. 'Can't you just sing?'

'Shut up, Dad,' I'd say. 'What would you know?'

From the very start, I always sang as loud as I could.

When you're young, you can abuse the crap out of your body and bounce right back. When I first started singing in bands, I'd sing all weekend, drink like a fish, smoke like a chimney, spend one day recovering then bounce right back. I did that for years, and when I eventually quit my day job and became a singer full-time, the partying didn't stop. I stupidly continued to smoke and drink and sing, and then spend the whole next day in silence so I could sing and drink and smoke the next night. What a pain in the arse!

Eventually it all caught up with me and I slowly, gradually, started having voice trouble. The first time I lost my voice was in Sydney in 1990 when we were touring with the Black Sorrows. We used to drink before the show, during the show and after the show, as well as smoke cigarettes. Combining that with singing at the top of my lungs for two hours and trying to compete with a loud band was a recipe for disaster. I went to bed with hardly any voice that night and woke up with no voice at all!

Fuck! I gotta sing tonight! What am I going to do?

It was the first time I'd completely lost my voice. I tried my usual concoction of lemon, garlic, honey and ginger in hot water, drinking the liquid and eating the garlic and ginger. This was always the magic remedy that brought my voice back, but not this time. My vocal cords were swollen and needed rest. So I locked myself in my hotel room, lay on the couch and watched TV all day. I didn't utter a single word to anyone. I kept my mouth completely shut and drank only water. All day long I was in a panic, thinking there was no way I'd be able to sing 'Chained to the Wheel'. No way.

Maybe I'll ask Joe if we can leave that song out of the set tonight, I thought. Linda can do backing vocals on her own and I'll mime and pretend I'm singing. But I knew Joe wouldn't go for that. Joe was always complaining about his voice, but he was tough and managed to sing every night no matter how he felt. But Joe didn't smoke or drink much either, so I knew he wouldn't take pity on a fool like me.

I didn't go to sound check that afternoon and stayed silent right up until the gig. I walked out on stage and BANG! The adrenaline kicked in and, hey presto, the voice came back!

Linda couldn't believe it. I couldn't believe it either, but I learned something very important that day. Total voice rest and hydration will bring your voice back. I was also lucky that I was young.

I should have taken that day as a warning sign, but I didn't. I kept abusing my voice, belting night after night, smashing my vocal cords together, and soon a little lump – a nodule – started to form on my throat, under the skin. Nodules are like calluses that form on the vocal cords and when this happens the air can't pass through for you to make sound, which is why you lose your voice. I was doing serious damage, but like a true idiot I kept it up.

Most singers worry about their voices a lot. On tour, the first thing we think about each morning is: can I sing today? When you're feeling a little raspy it can be very stressful, and all you can think about all day is if you'll be able to sing that night. No one wants to sing just enough to get by. You want to be at your best and sing all those beautiful high notes you know you can reach because you don't want to let your audience down.

The first thing I did when I woke up every morning was to have a little sing. If I couldn't reach the high notes in my head voice, I knew I was in trouble. The head voice puts less strain on the vocal cords and allows you to reach the higher notes with ease. It's not as powerful as the chest voice, but it's very useful and effective. If I couldn't even do that it meant I had to remain silent for the rest of the day or talk at a low volume to allow the swelling to go down so I could sing that night.

When we were touring with the Black Sorrows, I was constantly losing my voice, getting it back, then losing it again. I got away with it for years. I abused the hell out of my poor voice, but it always managed to bounce back. It's amazing what the human body can do and how it can repair itself, but letting it rip every night eventually takes its toll.

Touring

The band was booked to play one night at Expo 88 in Brisbane, an international exhibition that people still talk about. Whenever Linda and I mention it, so many people say, 'Oh, I was there!' Expo 88 is also where we met Paul Kelly for the first time. There's a photo of the three of us at a Japanese restaurant together.

This was a huge event, and we were one of the headline acts, along with John Farnham and the Divinyls. It was a great atmosphere, and our performance was televised live to a national audience. Unfortunately, there was a foldback wedge behind us on the stage and at one point Linda stepped back and fell flat on her back with her legs in the air, mid-song, flashing her undies to the entire country. Mum was horrified, but what a TV debut!

I was lucky enough to witness up close the brilliance of Chrissy Amphlett, the Divinyls' lead singer, from behind one of the road cases on the side of the stage. I felt like a little kid in the presence of greatness. Back at the hotel bar later that night, Chrissy and her band walked in for a nightcap. I was about to be in the presence of greatness once again, but this time I was a post-gig, partially pissed kid. The Sorrows and the Divinyls got shitfaced together, and the inevitable competitive 'old guard meets new guard' sparks began to fly. Long story short, I had to defend Linda, it ended in tears, and flowers arrived from Chrissy the next morning. We became friends from that day on.

Queensland was still struggling to get its head around the rock'n'roll culture at that time, which we found out after a gig in the Valley one night. We were all sitting backstage having a few beers when two guys lobbed up and crashed our party. I could tell straight off they weren't our kind of people, but after a gig most bands are full of love – and half full of booze – so we let them stay. The party continued and ... fast forward to 5am, when there was a loud banging on our hotel room door. It was an early morning raid by Queensland's finest.

The same two fellas who'd crashed our backstage party the night before burst into our hotel rooms, along with a host of their uniformed associates. They dragged us all out of our beds to search our rooms. Linda and I sat on the ends of our beds in T-shirts and undies, scared, perplexed and embarrassed, while one of the cops apologised to us.

It was the 80s and life was good. We were touring, partying and playing in a different pub every night. The Australian pub rock scene in the 80s was a great atmosphere for people in our industry to grow up in, and those gigs toughened up a couple of protected private school girls very quickly. Singing a two-hour show for six nights a week was hard, but great training. When we first started with the band we stood up the back, but Joe quickly brought us down to stand on his left, up the front.

The Sorrows were loud, so most nights we'd walk offstage hoarse from trying to sing over them. We smoked too. God, we were idiots, but it was the 80s and lots of singers smoked. The best remedy for a hoarse voice is rest, silence and to stop smoking! But our voices soon became more resilient and were able to withstand the strenuous workout they got each night. Joe always gave 110 per cent on stage and we learned to sing like it was our last ever gig. He was a very good teacher in that respect. Joe didn't care if there were two or two thousand people in the room, he always put on the same show, with the same level of passion and enthusiasm. It was a great thing to witness and learn from.

I have a real affection for those old pubs and clubs we played in, and the stench of ciggies mixed with the beer-soaked carpet. I still love the smell, and when I walk into an old venue it brings back fond memories, even though it reeks. That familiar scent instantly transports me back to that time when people packed into a venue, all dripping with sweat, as we stood on the stage and belted out a two-hour show.

Linda and I shared a room on tour, which was great because we were very young to be away from home for six weeks at a time, and it meant that we never got lonely. Our favourite motels were the ones with the little holes in the wall where breakfast was delivered in the morning. The simplicity of those little Aussie motel rooms with a kettle, a couple of teacups and a packet of Arnott's biscuits on the bench reminded us of our childhood and the shitty motels we stayed in on our way up to Wollongong.

We played in Darwin, which was a bit wild back then. One of the craziest venues was a place called the Cage, where bands played behind chicken wire because the locals were so wild that they'd chuck their beer cans at you if they hated what they were hearing. At the end of the night, the staff would hose everyone the hell outta there.

My favourite part of touring Australia was driving in a rented Toyota Tarago – also known as the 'Cone of Silence'. The Tarago is an iconic rock bus, and star of many a rock legend's stories. We learned so much about music in the Tarago on that first tour. Everyone had good taste in music, and our new band members introduced us to people like the Band, Little Feat and Robert Johnson.

Joe rode in the Tarago whenever he could. He hated flying; he preferred to drive all day or all night to get to the next gig. He'd get up at the crack of dawn to fang it to the next town, while we all slept in and then jumped on a plane later that morning. Linda used to hate going to the toilet on the plane and once she held it in for so long and was squirming around so much that I cracked it.

'For God's sake, what's wrong with you, Lulu?' I snapped. 'Why are you squirming around like that?'

'I can't go to the toilet,' Linda said. 'I'd feel like I was peeing on Joe somewhere beneath us!'

Mum and Dad were reluctant to let us go on that first tour, scared we'd succumb to the evils of the rock'n'roll lifestyle, especially me. They feared I'd take to it like a duck to water. And I did. I revelled in it. But whenever I'd been hitting it too hard and we got back to Melbourne, I'd retreat to Mum and Dad's house for some good old-fashioned home cooking and lots of sleep.

We copped our fair share of racism in the early days in the Sorrows too. We'd gone from a private girls' school to touring the country, which was a slightly different scene! When you live in your own little bubble it's easy to forget that there's a whole world out there, full of people with completely different views, which are sometimes confronting and disturbing. Linda and I have both been spat at while on stage. There we were, happily singing away with Joe, and the next thing we see a lump of spit coming towards us. This kept happening through a few songs, and though we didn't stop the show, we did signal to the audience mid-song to tell us who was doing the spitting. They happily pointed him out, and we then signalled the bouncers, who came and kicked his sorry racist arse right out the door.

Western Australia was probably our favourite state, even though it's so massive, and we'd spend hours in the Tarago going from town to town. We would always play Perth first and then travel south to Fremantle, Bunbury, Margaret River, Manjimup, Albany and Esperance. Esperance was especially gorgeous and unspoilt back then, with its beautiful beaches and soft white sand. The First Nations people there are so good-looking too. One night, the Sorrows were playing at a hotel in Esperance, and we had to walk through the entrance of the venue, past the bouncers, to get to the band room. Linda and I turned up about thirty minutes before the show, all dressed up in our gig clothes and ready to rock the packed joint, only to see some idiot refusing entry to a group of Nyungar people.

'What's going on here?' we asked the locals.

'This fella won't let us in,' one of them said. 'We paid for our tickets, and he made us all go home and get changed but now he still won't let us in.'

Linda and I were furious.

'What the hell?' we said to the bouncer. 'Let them in.'

'Nah, and youse girls aren't coming in either,' he said.

'What?' I said. 'We're right there on the poster, you idiot!'

But he wouldn't budge. 'Nup, that's not you. You're not coming in and neither are they.'

'You're a fuckwit,' I said, then turned to the group. 'Come with us.'

We took them around the back of the venue and found our way in and around to the band room, where everyone was waiting for us.

'What the hell's happening?' they said, when they saw us walk in with a bunch of people.

We told the band what had happened and that we were sneaking our new friends in through the back. Joe saw red when we told him what the bouncer had done, and he happily let them all in to see the show.

Our parents always worried about us when we were out on

the road, and sometimes they had good reason, like the time we played the Harbourside Brasserie in Sydney. We always packed the joint out. It was ridiculous really, especially in summer. One night it was so jam-packed and so hot that poor Lulu fainted and fell right off the front of the stage. I panicked and didn't know whether to keep singing or stop, but luckily Joe had seen it happen too. He immediately jumped down and picked Linda up off the floor before she was trampled to death. I'm convinced Joe saved my sister's life that night.

We kept travelling with the Black Sorrows, and Joe took us all over the world: England, Germany, France, Italy, Belgium, Norway, Denmark, Sweden, Switzerland, New Zealand, USA, Spain and Malta. What lucky women we were to get paid to travel the world doing what we loved. I don't think we even realised how lucky we were, even though Joe's manager, Doug Hunter, used to remind us every day.

'Aren't we lucky?' he'd say over and over. 'Aren't we *lucky?*'

It used to drive me nuts but, yes indeed, Doug was right. We were very lucky.

LINDA

Success with the Sorrows

When 'Chained to the Wheel' was released as a single in 1989, it went straight into the top ten. Overnight, we went from playing to twenty people at the Star Hotel in South Melbourne to performing for two thousand people at the Palace in St Kilda. Vik and I were more than a little perplexed when we rocked up to play there the first night and saw the long line of people waiting to get in.

'Hang on, what the hell is going on here? Have we got the right night? Is there some other band playing? Why are all these people queueing around the block?'

It was very confronting since the most we'd ever played in front of was a couple of hundred people. This was our first introduction to the power of radio, and it changed our lives.

Audiences kept getting bigger and so management kept adding dates to the tour. We had fewer and fewer days off, rarely saw our partners or friends or family, and lived out of suitcases. We were hardly ever at home, and when we were out in public, people recognised us in the street. When you've been anonymous your whole life it's a very weird thing to suddenly have strangers know your name and come up and talk to you. We were also doing a lot of photo shoots, TV performances and interviews. We had to learn quickly how to do an interview without saying something silly or putting our feet in it, but we managed to pull that off 50 per cent of the time.

When Jen Anderson joined the band it initially caused a bit of tension. Vika and I had enjoyed being the only two gals in the band up until then, so when Joe employed Jen we couldn't help feeling like another female was invading our territory. I felt sorry for Jen as she tried to find her place alongside two sisters who were very tight, and we didn't exactly make it easy for her to fit in at the beginning.

Our first shows with Jen were in Perth, which was the first place to really break the Sorrows in Australia. Perth understood the Sorrows immediately. When we first went there in 1988, we were playing to about twenty people, but by the end of that week word of mouth had got around and we were playing to packed houses. So when we arrived in Perth in 1989 with our new violin player in tow, we all headed to our favourite hotel, the Orchard, to check in. But when Vika, Jen and I all stepped out of the elevator and ended up in front of the same door, we knew something was up. We opened the door and saw three double beds all crammed next to each other, with no room to get in or out of the beds, or even to walk to the loo. Vika and I couldn't believe it. Were we supposed to spend the next week in this room with someone we didn't even know? Poor Jen went white, while Vika and I saw red.

Joe immediately fixed the situation and poor Jen had to share with Wayne. Then, when we got wind that she had gone straight to the same pay scale as the boys, we were not amused. Jen was a beautiful musician, but, gee, we were angry.

When we had first joined the Black Sorrows a couple of years earlier, we knew we were being paid less than the band. It was pretty shit money, but we were happy to be in such an awesome band, so we didn't complain. But now that we knew Jen was getting more than us, we had to say something.

I can be confident when I need to be. Vika is afraid of rejection, but when it comes to us being undervalued, I won't stand for it. Vika was pissed, but no good at asking for more money. I didn't have a problem with that.

'No, fuck that, Vik,' I said. 'I'm going to speak to Joe.'

I went straight to Joe and asked for a pay rise. Of course he said yes and our pay went up that very day. We'd just needed to ask.

Joe had the fantastic idea to turn the Palace in St Kilda from a rock venue into a cabaret venue, and this is when Vika and I fell in love with Jen. Instead of a rock band playing to two thousand people at the Palace, we performed for half as many people in the same venue but with a much more intimate vibe. Round tables and chairs were brought in, and the dinner-and-show vibe was introduced. Joe had such good taste and knew exactly how he wanted the place to look: velvet curtains, candlelit tables and table service transformed the Palace into a beautiful supper club. No one would be battling to see the band from behind some tall dude who was ruining their whole rock'n'roll experience. We had Lucky on drums and Dickie on bass, Joffa and Wayne on guitars, Joe on sax, Vika and me on backing vocals and Jen on violin. And Jen really hit her stride.

Joe had hired a three-piece string section to play with us, and when they started playing Jen's string arrangements, our whole attitude towards her changed. Every night, as we sang that show with Jen's arrangement, Vika wept. We could see that Jen understood Joe's music. She took the music to the next level, and it was the most beautiful thing we had ever heard.

Joe also expanded his management team, adding Andrew Walker, and his partner Michelle Buxton as publicist, to the fold.

On top of that we had our front-of-house guy, Graeme, and crew, consisting of lighting, foldback and stage personnel. The roadies are some of my favourite people, and we learned straight away that these are the people you need to take good care of because they work the hardest. They are the first to arrive at a gig and the last to leave, and they work their butts off. Roadies are very loyal to the band they are working for, and we had some terrific crew in the Black Sorrows. We also witnessed them get up to all sorts of sex, drugs and rock'n'roll shenanigans on tour, but it didn't make us think any more or less of them.

There were now around twenty of us on the road, which is a big group, and sometimes, after we'd been on the road for a while, each member's little idiosyncrasies started to give everyone the shits. We were together for so long and felt tired all the time, but you had to learn to put up with everyone's eccentricities and let them go through to the keeper in order to keep the peace sometimes. We all did that. If you couldn't, then you'd either leave or be replaced, although I can't remember Joe ever having to sack anyone. Joey had a lot of mouths to feed at that point, so I don't blame him for being a bit stressed.

VIKA

Watto

While touring heavily with the Black Sorrows, I was still living in the South Yarra house with my best buddy, Samantha, and our mate Burger. I was touring a lot at that time, always in and out of the house, and came home one day to see a photo of some fella I didn't recognise on the noticeboard in our kitchen.

'Hey, Burger,' I said. 'Who's that guy?'

'That's Watto,' Burger said. 'He plays drums for James and is great. You'll like him.'

John 'Watto' Watson had been living in South Yarra and playing around Melbourne for a while when he and Pete Luscombe had words about how there was only room for one left-handed drummer in this town. So Watto moved to Sydney and now he only came down for gigs. Apparently, he'd been over to our house a few times, but I'd never met him because I was hardly ever home. But, soon after this, I found myself with a night off, and James and his band, including Burger and Watto, were playing at the Palace in St Kilda.

Great! I thought. I like James's songs and the whole gang will be there, so I'll go watch Burger play.

My mates and I all went into the VIP bar upstairs to watch the show. It had a great view of the stage, and even though the glass wall lowered the sound a little, it was still my favourite place to watch a band. I hate standing in a crowd with two thousand other people and have always found it kind of scary. I prefer the view I get from the stage, rather than the other way around. So, that night, we could all still talk and enjoy the music without the sound blowing our heads off. The boys absolutely rocked the Palace that night! We all knew every single song, word for word, note for note, and we drank beers and sang along with the whole show. Afterwards, the band joined us upstairs, and that's when I met Watto for the first time.

I was instantly smitten. He was twenty-seven years old, six foot four, had a goofy smile and was quiet, which I liked. A strong silent type with big blue eyes and thick brown hair, and a gap between his two front teeth so wide that you could park a truck in there. I liked that too. I thought it was cute as. And, apart from all that, he sure could hit them drums. Watto is a wonderful drummer, very powerful, very strong, and great to watch. He drove the band, watching James's every move, and never taking his eyes off him.

We were instantly attracted to each other, but then I discovered that Watto had a girlfriend in Sydney and that they'd been together since they were fifteen years old. Twelve whole years! This was not good. As soon as I found out I should have said, 'Oh my God, you have a girlfriend! Well, piss off, then!' But I didn't. Soon after that night we started seeing each other whenever he was in town, and those stays got longer and longer each time, even though he was still with his girlfriend, who eventually figured out what was going on. I gotta say, I was young, stupid and selfish, but the attraction between us was so strong that I didn't care that he had a girlfriend. It got nasty, and she fought tooth and nail to keep him.

John and I liked to party together, which was one of the reasons we were attracted to each other. One Christmas Eve, we pulled an all-nighter and ended up at Mum and Dad's at 6am. We came crashing in, waking my parents with all our pissed commotion, then immediately fell asleep. Mum and Dad had never met, or even heard of, John before that night, and now here was this drunk stranger waking up in their house on Christmas morning.

'Who the hell is in your room?' Dad said, when I finally emerged later that morning.

'That's my friend,' I said sheepishly. 'He missed his flight to Sydney. Can he stay for Christmas?'

Mum and Dad weren't particularly happy, but they're good, polite people so they said he could stay. But, boy, were they mad. Dad walked over to the Christmas tree, picked up my gift and chucked it in my lap.

'There's your Christmas present, you pain in the arse!' he said.

I didn't see my dad mad very often, so I knew I'd probably gone a bit far this time. My parents were used to my wild ways, but at Christmas? Not cool.

I woke John up and told him to come out and meet my mum and dad. How's that for an introduction to the parents!

At one point, John's girlfriend came to Melbourne to try to get him back, and when he returned to Sydney with her for a couple of months it broke my heart. I was touring with the Sorrows at that time, and he didn't contact me at all for that entire period. I spent most days in bed, crying my eyes out and playing Tetris. It was my first experience with heartbreak, and I didn't like the feeling at all. People shouldn't have to go through it more than once in their lives, as far as I'm concerned.

After a couple of years of kind of hanging out – and kind of not, because of his relationship in Sydney – John finally left his girlfriend and decided to come to Melbourne. When I told Mum I'd fallen in love with someone, she asked who it was. I stared at her and Mum knew immediately.

'Not the guy from Christmas morning?' she said, looking appalled. 'Oh my God, Vika, really?'

LINDA

The Sorrows exit

It's not an unusual story, the one where the lead singer/songwriter falls out with the band over money, but this is what I believe caused the end of the Sorrows. The harder we worked and the more successful we became, the more money was involved, which brought more issues.

We didn't write songs or produce any of the material, but we did believe that we had contributed to the success of the band. We knew there were discussions going on between other, more established members of the group, which was fair enough because they had been in the band for longer, but Vika and I tried to distance ourselves from the heated discussions that had started to happen. All we cared about at that stage was being paid the same as everyone else and receiving fair and equal treatment.

By now we had been with the Black Sorrows for four years and the band was at the height of its fame. I was young and having the time of my life, but even I noticed that more money was coming in. I got an idea of how much money the others were making one morning when I found an old satchel bag that our tour manager had mistakenly left behind at the airline check-in counter.

Band check-ins at airports are a real pain in the arse. They can be chaotic at best, and disastrous at worst. On this day, I was hovering in the background when I noticed the Ansett Airlines bag had been left behind. It was neatly tucked under a shelf at the counter, and I knew it belonged to us because I'd seen our tour manager carrying it around. I quickly grabbed it. When I opened it and saw that it was stuffed with bundles and bundles of cash, I nearly fainted. I had expected it to have tour books and contracts inside but, no, it was full of the most money I'd ever seen in my life. It was obviously show takings because it was all dirty and bundled neatly in rubber bands. I used to collect the money after Honeymooners shows, so I knew it was Joe's gig money and that they'd accidentally left it behind. We were flying from Perth to Adelaide that day, and when I got on the plane, I told Vika what I'd found.

'I'm going to hang on to it, just to see how long it takes them to realise it's missing,' I told her.

We giggled all the way to Adelaide and played the 'How would you spend it?' game with each other.

Two hours into the flight, halfway over the Nullarbor Plain, a hand shot up to hit the call button and I saw our tour manager rummaging around, fussing under her seat and in the overhead locker. It had taken two hours for the penny to drop! The poor girl looked white as a ghost. Her eyes were darting everywhere and she was a hot mess, too scared to tell Joe, who was sitting across the aisle from her, listening to music on his Sony Discman to distract himself from the fact that he was flying, and was oblivious to the drama.

Vik and I were cracking up, but it was evil of me, and I had to put her out of her misery and give the bag back. When I asked for a finder's fee she thought I was joking. I wasn't. But the whole incident got me thinking. If that kind of cash was being made and left at airports, what else was going on?

I never begrudged Joe (or the rest of the older members) any of the money they made because they earned it. Joe was the hardest working guy in the business and always had been, from his early days selling records out of the boot of his car after gigs.

But we could feel a shift starting to happen. As time went on and the band became more successful, the weekly band meetings became longer and more tense, and I loathed them. I'd rather have been left out of the heated negotiations and just told where to be and when, but I did learn a lot at the same time. Listening to all the negotiations, discussions and nitty-gritty was a lesson in business. I watched silently and took note of the interactions between the management and the band.

CHANGES: ACT I

LINDA

The PK factor

Vika and I decided it was time to start thinking about writing and making our own music. Six years down the track with the Black Sorrows and we hadn't bothered to write a single song, but this all changed thanks to our new friend, singer/songwriter Paul Kelly.

In between breaks on the road with the Black Sorrows, Vik and I started getting together with Paul. PK was the first person to encourage us to write our own songs, and in 1991 Vika and I arranged to meet him at our parents' new house in Clifton Hill.

We sat around the kitchen table thinking, How the heck are we going to be good enough to write anything remotely passable?

The pressure was on, but Paul is a gentle and kind man and could see how nervous we were. To break the ice, he pulled out his acoustic guitar and played us a song he'd been working on. It was called 'We've Started a Fire' and I loved it immediately because it had a reggae feel to it, and Paul told us we could record it when we were ready.

He explained the meaning behind his songs, which was lovely

of him, because I was always too shy to ask, and it saved Vika and me the embarrassment of admitting we didn't know.

'"We've Started a Fire" is about waking up next to the wrong person,' Paul said after he played it.

Hello! I thought. Here we go. I guess we're gonna have to be open and honest with this guy. This would be interesting because we didn't know each other at all, but we all liked one another. Paul always made us feel like equals, even though we were nowhere near his level as musicians or performers. He never made us feel inferior as songwriters either, even though we were. We were singers, not songwriters, but Paul pushed Vik and me to be ourselves and wouldn't quit until he had a song in good shape.

We all share a love of food, so we'd make lunch and have cups of tea (followed by beers later in the day) and he'd get us to talk about our week or tell him a funny story. This was how he broke the ice with us, by trying to get us to relax and open up to him. Once we did, he'd write a song about something that had come up in our conversation. This was the process whenever we got together, and it was punishing work, but we always ended up with a tune and words to sing into his old Panasonic cassette recorder. Finding the words was always the hardest part for me. The melodies came more easily.

We decided to try some of these songs out on an audience. In between tours with the Black Sorrows we asked Pete, Steve Hadley and Joffa to come and play with us because we were all free at the same time and could do shows together. We'd pull out whatever we'd written with Paul and slot it into our live set, which was mostly covers, and test them out on crowds at places like the Cherry Tree, the Grace Darling or the Espy.

As much as we got a kick out of singing with the Sorrows, we knew we couldn't be Joe's backing singers forever. The time was coming for us to leave and make our own way, but the difficulty was finding the right reason, and the right time. It was 1990 when we actively began looking for a solo record deal and management. Someone suggested we meet with Chris Murphy. Mr Murphy was a big shot in the industry who was famous for managing the worldwide phenomenon that was INXS. Instead, we decided to ask Joe's manager, Doug Hunter, to manage us.

It was a natural progression because we'd spent so much time with him already, but I should have given some thought to whether it was too close. Joe may have been uneasy about it, but if he was, he didn't let on. Doug was doing a great job with the Black Sorrows but he wasn't your typical rock manager of that time. For starters, he didn't have a ponytail, and he wore baggy trousers, polo shirts and jumpers. He looked like the love child of Jughead from the Archies and an English college professor. Most rock managers in those days were abrasive, and wore black on black on black, with a jacket. They liked to shout and scream a lot if things weren't going their way and were usually men with big handshakes, and big appetites for everything. They were a serious bunch who took 20 per cent commission from gross earnings.

Our father thought this was outrageous and said so on many occasions. He was right too. So, we set about negotiating Doug down. We went back-and-forth a few times and ended up agreeing on a new number. It wasn't a big concession, from his original percentage, but it was better than nothing and that was important to me. It showed him right off the bat that he had to watch himself a bit.

Doug had an odd sort of humour and was softly spoken. I didn't get his jokes at all but liked that he liked to laugh. His company, Unspeakable Acts, represented two other acts: Joe Camilleri and the Doug Anthony Allstars (DAAS). He divided his time between the three of us. His real passion lay in comedy; he was very well connected in that area. Music wasn't something that came naturally to him, and he never talked about other bands or their music, only the business of it. But he always talked about comedy, and I can still remember his favourite comedians: DAAS, Flacco and the Sandman, Wendy Harmer, Anthony Ackroyd, Roy and HG, Mikey Robbins and Greg Fleet.

This should have been a clue.

VIKA

Mushroom

Linda and I played it safe when we asked Joe's manager to manage us. We asked Joe if he was okay with it, and he said yes. I'm not sure if Joe really was happy about it, but he was incredibly supportive. He put us in touch with a good lawyer and advised us what to look out for in recording contracts.

'Keep the term short and your percentages high,' he told us.

'And retain your copyright at all costs.'

He even came along to the early meetings that Doug arranged with Sony and Mushroom Records. Doug had been used to dealing with Sony, which was very different to Mushroom in the way it Mushroom was collaborative and Sony was all 'It's our way or the highway'.

Intense negotiations went on between us, Sony and Mushroom for a while, but when Mushroom said our copyright would be returned to us after twenty-five years, that sealed the deal for us. It meant we could use our own music, in whatever way we wanted.

Doug and Joe were both great at helping us out in those meetings. There we were with Joe Camilleri, a notoriously hard negotiator, coming in to support us while they gave us their pitch. I would have shat my pants if I was a record company guy and saw Joe coming into the meeting.

Holding out for what we wanted was risky because both record companies could have given up and moved on, but, in the end, Mushroom wanted us more, so we signed with them. We also knew that the head at Mushroom, Michael Gudinski, was a good man, which meant the company would care more. It was more of a family vibe at Mushroom, and there were a lot of women in senior and junior roles, and so it was an exciting place to be. They never pushed us to be the kind of artists who could make them a quick buck. They didn't exploit us or make us feel like our Tongan culture was something that could be sold or, worse, that it had no place in the musical landscape. They encouraged us to acknowledge our culture in whatever way we felt comfortable. If we wanted to celebrate being Polynesian by giving every guest at our album launch a flower lei, they were all for it.

Linda and I didn't really have anyone, besides Paul, steering us when it came to deciding on our musical direction. We grew up in Australia, influenced by what we heard on the radio and what we saw on *Countdown*. Polynesian culture wasn't something that was celebrated in this country or in the mainstream media, so how were we to go about this? I wish we'd had more smarts and listened to our guts, because Warren Costello and Bill Page at Mushroom were very nurturing and truly believed in us. They encouraged us in everything we wanted to do, including our decision to cover a lot of different musical styles.

Doug's advice was: 'Do what you want with your music, and I'll handle the business.' He was a kinda hardball.

We hated going into the Albert Park office of Mushroom and Premier Artists (our booking agency) because we knew it meant an hour of intense negotiating from our camp, no matter what we were there to discuss. Every meeting was like running a marathon in water. It was hard work!

LINDA
End of the Sorrows
Doug was so busy at this point that he needed help managing his acts, and that help arrived in the form of Andrew Walker and

Michelle Buxton. Andrew and Michelle were together at the time, and they brought a lot of fun and lightness to the mix. They worked extremely hard as a team, and Andy was very thorough, which is exactly what you need in a manager. I remember Doug referring to himself as the 'big picture guy'. So Andy was the one who made the 'big picture' happen, while Michelle was our publicist and handled all the interviews and live performances for the Unspeakable Acts roster. She also handled publicity for a lot of fledgling comedy acts, who later became some of Australia's biggest stars. Michelle was always up for a wine and a laugh, and she was so lovely to both of us.

We were doing heaps of shows in this period with our band, which included Lucky, Joffa, Stuart 'Stewie' Speed or Steve Hadley, and Jex Saarelaht. When Vika took a solo, I'd run off stage for a quick ciggie in the band room, scull a shot of whiskey and then run back onstage to sing the next song. Not very professional, and if I'd kept that up, I wouldn't be singing now.

It was my job to collect the money after gigs, so I always made sure I wasn't so pissed that I couldn't count properly. As everyone else started to unwind, I'd be sitting in some seedy manager's office, counting out our hard-earned dosh. I liked to make the manager sit and wait for me to count our pay, to make sure they weren't short-changing us. Even though I was a quick counter, it used to drive these men crazy. They were busy and wanted to get back to running their clubs, but I wanted to keep them honest. I was propositioned a few times in these offices, but always made sure to keep the door wide open. If anyone tried to lock me in, I stuck my foot in the door.

Vika had more responsibilities than me. She oversaw all things musical, including directing rehearsals and choosing the set list. We had a good thing going and it worked.

We were finally starting to see a pathway into our solo career, so it was time to tell Joe we were going to leave the Black Sorrows. We knew that Pete, Wayne, Joffa and Hadley had all told Joe they were going to be leaving soon too. Because Joe had been so good to us and so incredibly supportive, we didn't want to make it hard for him, so we gave him one year's notice. He was upset but not too shocked. He had been expecting it.

In 1993, our last year with the Sorrows, we went on a massive national tour in support of the *Better Times* album. Joe wanted to capitalise on this as much as possible, so the tour was billed as the last blast of the original Sorrows line-up.

That final tour was bittersweet because, even though the band was falling apart behind the scenes, we still had that incredible magic on stage that we'd always had. That's not something you can fake. That final year's line-up was made up of Joe, Joffa, Pete, Steve, Wayne, Jen, Michael and us, and it was the best we'd ever had. The magic between Joe, Vika and me was always there on stage. We fed off each other, and it was spontaneous and unrehearsed. I was sad that our time with the Black Sorrows was coming to an end, but I was also proud of the way that Vika and I were leaving the band.

Our six years with the Black Sorrows had been the best years that any young singer could ever want or dream about. We were with great people and had been taken around the world many times over, doing what we loved, and it hadn't cost us a cent. That time with the band was the best apprenticeship anyone could have in the music industry. I feel very grateful that the music we all made together is still played today, and that people still love it. At the end of the day, that's what you strive for and why you do it.

Now it was time for us to focus on our own careers as a solo act, and we hoped our management team would be there to support us as much as possible. Doug's wife Ros was English, so he was always commuting between the UK and Scotland, juggling his acts and his young family. DAAS were very successful at Edinburgh Festival, so Doug spent half the year overseas, leaving Andrew and Michelle to run operations in Australia. Cracks started to show between him and Joe, and Joe eventually decided to part company with Doug, but kept Andrew and Michelle on as his managers. Andrew and Michelle started Buxton Walker and moved to their own office in Balaclava. They started up Head Records, with Joe and Stephen Cummings on their books.

Now Vika and I had a tough decision to make. Did we stay loyal to Doug, who we'd first signed with, or follow Joe to Andrew and Michelle? After all, they were the ones doing all the face-to-face hard yakka for us. Mum was in Tonga at the time, and I would have loved to call on her for an opinion, but we couldn't reach her. Our grandma had just passed away, and it wasn't fair to burden Mum with anything else. I think she would have told us to go with

Andrew and Michelle because she liked Michelle, but we ended up choosing Doug out of loyalty.

Telling Michelle and Andrew we weren't going with them was very difficult. We knew it would hurt them as much as it did us, and we both had knots in our stomachs as we delivered the news. I tried to be kind and diplomatic, but I made the mistake of referring to Andrew as an amazing 'administrator' when he was way more than that. He was a great manager. I could see that I'd offended him and immediately regretted my choice of word. Andy's face dropped and his eyes glazed over, and I knew I'd stuffed up. Going with Doug meant we were effectively severing ties with Joe as well as with Andrew and Michelle.

My wedding

I should have known he wasn't the man for me the moment I fell down the stairs at the Batchbox all those years ago and found myself face to face with his happy shoes. Being so fashion conscious I had thought to myself, why is he wearing slippers in public? Has he no real shoes?

Unfortunately I ignored the sign.

We had just left the Black Sorrows. Justin headed off to travel through Europe and I went over to meet him in Amsterdam. While I was there, he proposed.

'No,' I said. 'But if you're serious, take me to the Louvre in Paris and we'll see.'

We travelled to Paris with another friend but none of us got to go inside the Louvre because we couldn't afford the entry fee. I would have been able to pay for myself but didn't have enough money to pay for all three tickets. When I asked Justin to take me to the Louvre I meant inside, not delivered to the door! It felt like a failed promise and I felt really let down. Instead, we sat outside near the Pyramide du Louvre, eating baguettes, cheese and paté, and watching all the lucky people going into the world-famous museum. There was more than a little envy in my heart, and I made a vow that I'd return one day and go inside, and no one would stop me (I haven't yet). But he had half followed through with my request, so I accepted his proposal.

When we got home, Dad and Vik were not as excited about my engagement as I would have liked, but Mum was very happy and instantly took me shopping for a wedding dress. Money was tight, but I'm a bargain hunter from way back, so we went looking for a dress for under $500 at Mariana Hardwick. We both knew that finding a cheap dress in a shop like that was a long shot, but I managed to find a sample dress in a bargain part of the shop. The dress was browned from being tried on so much and it had weird sleeves, but the bodice fit me perfectly.

'I can fix it,' Mum said firmly, and I knew she could, so we bought it for $250.

I trusted her so much that I didn't even try the dress on until the day of my wedding. When she pulled it out of the bag that morning, I was shocked. Mum had worked her magic and it was a vision. She'd washed and dry-cleaned it, then taken off the sleeves and replaced them with beautiful spaghetti straps, which she'd embroidered two days before the wedding. It fitted perfectly and I was rapt. I still have the dress; it is a symbol of Mum's love for me. She spent so many hours perfecting it, and I hope my kids will wear it one day. If they do, I'll tell them to brag to all their friends that they are wearing a dress by the one and only Siniva Bull.

Joe chauffeured me to my wedding at the Grace Darling Hotel in his beautiful cream Thunderbird. Dad sat in the back with me, while Vika and Joe sat in the front. During the ceremony I laughed a little too loudly when it got to the part about 'for richer or for poorer', but my new husband didn't find it funny. My new mother-in-law was also unimpressed when it came to signing the certificate and I signed my name: Linda Bull. She had assumed I would be taking Justin's name, which I never had any intention of doing. But Dad looked chuffed that I'd chosen to carry on the family name. Bull was my name and my identity, and I felt strongly about holding on to it.

The Grace Darling was our second home, not only because it was owned and operated by Samantha Gowing, Vika's bestie from South Yarra, but also because we had done heaps of gigs there together. Samantha had owned and operated this iconic pub with her brother Chris since the ripe old age of twenty-four. I had always dreamed of getting married in the old stone church my great-grandfather had helped build in Doncaster, but my fiance was allergic to anything religious or church-related, so we asked

We were cutting our teeth in our own band, the Honeymooners, when the chance came along to temporarily join Joe Camilleri's band, the Black Sorrows. A six-week tour turned into six years as the band's popularity grew and grew. It was an amazing apprenticeship for us.

(*Above*) A promo shot for the Black Sorrows' album *Harley and Rose*, released in 1990. *Back row from left*: Wayne Burt, Peter 'Lucky' Luscombe, Jen Anderson, Richard Sega, Joe Camilleri. *Front row from left*: Jeff 'Joffa' Burstin, Linda and Vika. (*Credit: Tania Jovanovic*)

(*Left*) With our fearless leader, Joe Camilleri. (*Credit: Tania Jovanovic*)

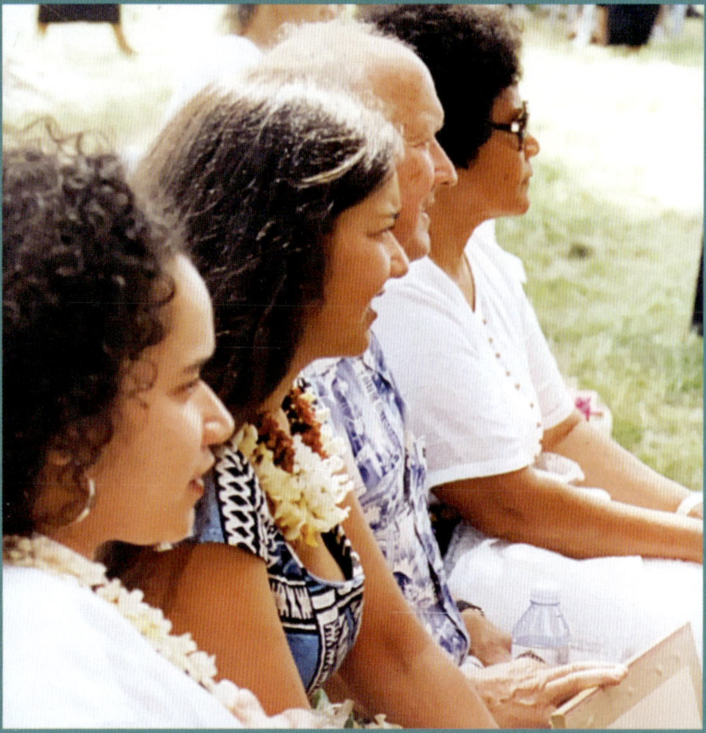

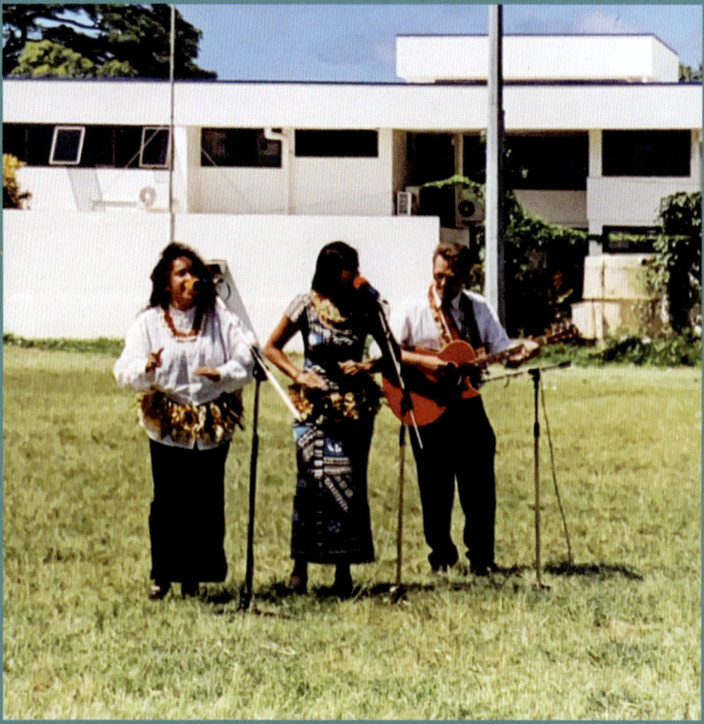

Tonga has always been a massive part of our lives, and we've enjoyed so many memorable trips there, including in 1995 when we had the honour of singing for King Tāufaʻāhau Tupou IV with Jeff Burstin (*opposite*).

(*Top left*) Watching the formalities with Mum and Dad. That performance was the only time our Tongan family, including our grandmother (*top, middle of the second row*), heard us sing. We also got to hang out with the famous Mosi Mosi Kava Club Choir (*bottom*), who featured on our track 'Grandpa's Song'.

(*Left*) With our producer and long-time collaborator Paul Kelly, making our debut album, *Vika and Linda*, in 1994.

(*Right*) 'I am a thorn between two roses,' said Nelson Mandela when this photo was taken. We got the chance to meet him during his lecturing tour with Rubin 'Hurricane' Carter in 2000. Our bass player Bill McDonald (*left*) and drummer Michael Barker (*right*) are in the background.

Iggy Pop to the rescue! Recording at Real World in the UK in 1994 with our knight in shining armour.

Flanking His Holiness the Dalai Lama, a big ray of sunshine. We met him as part of the *Mantra Mix* album project, a record put together by the Michaels – Gudinski (*left of Linda*) and Chugg (*right of Vika*) – to raise funds for Tibetan refugees in 1996.

(Credit: Stephen Oxenbury)    *(Credit: Tania Jovanovic)*

(Credit: Stephen Sweet)

We've always loved it when a photographer captures the energy of our live performances, although we've had some great studio photos taken over the years. *Top right* is our mum's favourite.

(*Top*) Cracking each other up at The Famous Spiegeltent in the 1990s. You could say that our priorities changed from the late 90s, and very happily so. (*Credit: Stephen Sweet*)

(*Middle*) A first birthday party for Vik and Watto's cute daughter, Mafi.

(*Left*) Linda's beautiful daughters, Nia (*left*) and Kiki (*right*). (*Credit: Anna Bertalli*)

Vika: During the recording of *Tell the Angels* (2004), a live gospel album, disaster struck when I lost my voice. It had come and gone before, but this was the first time it became clear I couldn't continue the way I was going if I wanted to keep singing. (*Credit: Stephen Sweet*)

Sam if we could use her beautiful pub instead.

We had a very tight budget for our wedding, but still managed to have three hundred and fifty guests, mainly because Mum did all the catering. She and at least twenty of my Tongan aunties took over the Grace Darling kitchen and made all the food. This is where Tongan people are amazing. They will help without any expectation of reward or payment, simply doing it because that's what Polynesian families do. They help one another. They were all in there, chopping, peeling, grating, stirring and laughing. I felt very loved.

We also saved a lot of money when Sam gave us free rein of her famous pub for the entire day. The Grace Darling is an historic establishment, right in the heart of Collingwood, and, being the die-hard Pies supporter he is, my dad was very happy to be there. I was stone-cold sober for the entire day, mainly thanks to Mum, who took a drink out of my hand every time I managed to get one, saying, 'Nobody likes a pissed bride.' Thank God she did because I would have hopped into it and forgotten the entire day.

I remember clearly that Vika sang the John Hiatt version of 'Have a Little Faith in Me', and my Tongan cousins did a traditional Tongan dance, then gave all the money the guests stuck on them to us for a wedding present. It was a lot of money, which was much appreciated because at that time I was flat broke. It was 1993, we had just left the Sorrows, and Vika and I had to reset. Without the surety of a regular income for the first time since I was nineteen, I had to be very careful. My new husband had recently returned from Europe and was trying to find work in bands. He was broke too, so we weren't exactly a match made in financial heaven.

There were a few casualties on my wedding day, but, thanks to Mum, I wasn't one of them. Wish I could say the same about my marriage.

VIKA
Our debut

Doug uprooted his young family and relocated back to Australia so he could properly manage us and DAAS. He took over a big office space in Brunswick Street and found an assistant in our good mate, Jenny Mac. To thank us for our loyalty, Doug made us his priority, but this made us feel a bit under pressure to make enough income to support his massive move. We didn't want his wife and kids going hungry while we lived out our rock fantasy life. Even though Linda and I didn't have kids of our own yet, we understood family life and knew there was a lot at stake. There were wages and bills to be paid, and we had to earn a lot of money to keep everyone happy.

We were working hard on building up a repertoire of new and old material and doing lots of shows on our own. We played three regular pubs that covered the golden triangle of St Kilda, Richmond and Fitzroy. Our regular Sunday night slot at the Espy front bar was always a great night, and our regular shows at the Cherry Tree in Richmond and the Royal Derby in Fitzroy went off.

Linda and I were getting a kick out of playing our new songs live. 'We've Started a Fire' went over as well, if not better, than the covers we were doing and that was a good sign. It was such an easy song to sing, so we kept them coming. The next song we wrote with PK was 'Ninety-Nine Years'. Playing these songs in our own shows gave us the confidence boost we needed.

We were also getting ready to record our debut album with Mushroom and gaining a crowd of our very own.

※

Linda and I had to focus on getting an album to Mushroom. Bill Page helped us a lot and rang a bunch of writers to help us organise some writing sessions and start gathering songs. It wasn't like we could go straight into the studio with a bunch of songs we'd been writing since we were teenagers. We had to start from scratch. We didn't have a clear direction or musical identity of our own either, which made it more difficult. We were backing singers for a famous band, that was all, so nobody knew what we were going to do. The world may have been our oyster, but it was also scary.

We put out the feelers and were flattered when people like Mark Seymour, Tim Finn, Stephen Cummings and Tim Rogers all offered us quality songs.

Once we'd gathered our songs, we went to Metropolis in South Melbourne to record demos with the legendary Ian 'Mack' McKenzie. We had worked with Mack at Platinum, but he'd left and opened his own studio. Mack was the recipient of the first

Sanyo Australia Music Award, in 1974, for 'Engineer of the Year' for Renée Geyer's *It's A Man's Man's World*. He was also the engineer for Joe Dolce 'Shaddap You Face' and Pseudo Echo's 'Funky Town', which went to number one around the world. Over the years, Mack had recorded and mixed a lot of famous records for bands including Pseudo Echo, Uncanny X-Men and Noiseworks. Mick Jagger even came in to work with him when he was in Australia on a solo tour. He'd sneak in late at night to do some mixing with Mack. We would all gather around in the morning, relishing every detail of the previous night's session. Mack told us how the backing singers came in one night.

'Hilarious,' Mack said. 'They all just sat there doing their knitting, then getting up and singing their bits.'

I thought, Oh my God, here are the coolest chicks in the world, working with Mick Jagger, and they knit! No fucking way. That was so inspiring for me to hear.

Mack was very generous, doing our demos for us and helping us get ready to record our debut album. Paul was going to produce. We had the dream team, a kick-arse band, a kick-arse production team and some great songs. I was also just starting a relationship with Watto, so things in my life were pretty exciting at that point, and my head was spinning.

When we started recording the album, Mark Seymour paid us a visit in the studio. He had a song for us and sat in Metropolis with his guitar and played us 'When Will You Fall for Me?' We were instantly hooked, but the bridge wasn't quite done. So the three of us sat there together and finished the bridge, then Linda and I went in and recorded the whole song. I still love the sound of that song.

Mum and Dad did all the catering for that record and came to the studio every night with a home-cooked meal for us. Mum always prepared a feast, laying it out on the table for everyone to share. Steve Hadley, in particular, looked forward to this ritual. It was all the little details, and the extra mile Mum always went. A beautiful tablecloth, cutlery wrapped in individual napkins (not paper, obviously), beautiful white plates and silverware to serve the food. Linda and I were used to this, of course, but for them it was a highlight of making this record. The band appreciated what my parents did so much, and we got such a kick out of seeing Mum and Dad in the studio, relaxing after a hard day preparing food, and enjoying a drink with the band.

The album initially had a laid-back country sound but as songs came in it started to take shape. It ended up being quite an eclectic mix of styles and it covered a lot of ground from the straight-ahead guitar rock of 'When Will You Fall for Me?' to the reggae and island feel of 'These Hands' and 'We've Started a Fire', which was the first song PK played us. We also had a New Orleans feel with 'Sacred Things' from Joe, and a beautiful, almost jazz ballad 'The Blue Hour' from Stephen Cummings. In my opinion, it didn't matter that the songs were written by others, or that they were such a mix, as long as they were sung by us.

Label head Warren Costello supported our song choices and the direction we chose for our first record. He was happy to let us do whatever we wanted and didn't try to mould us into the next soul-singing sensation, as Sony would have. He respected the fact that we had to find our sound and was willing to work through the process with us, no matter how long it took. He was a patient man but had his work cut out for him: we were hard to pigeonhole and our song choices were diverse, because we sing a lot of different styles.

We decided to self-title our debut album *Vika and Linda*, and Mushroom let us guide the Gauguin-inspired artwork for the front cover. This was a difficult cover to pull off pre-Photoshop, but the art department team at Mushroom, led by Pierre Baroni, Marni Aitken and Peter Barrett, did a great job. They understood that we were going for something that was a direct nod to our heritage and it felt good to be working with such lovely people. Linda was in her element because Gauguin was a favourite of the family's and our cover combined her love of painting, art history, photography, set design and costumes with music. She couldn't believe they actually let us do it because it wasn't exactly a rock'n'roll look. It was more arty. I mean, there were mangoes and frangipanis and we were wearing sarongs, for God's sake. But it worked a treat. Paul Kelly and his wife Kaarin loved it so much that they framed and hung it in their toilet for years. A good-looking cover was one thing, but the sound was what we wanted people to connect with.

When the album came out it had a lot of interest because people's questions were answered about what the two of us would sound like on our own. It was a great feeling to have the record company behind us, and even better when it went on to sell so well. Phew! What a relief! Triple J liked the first single 'When Will You Fall for Me?' and added it to their playlist immediately. I took this for granted, thinking, yeah, they bloody should add it because it's a great song! I didn't realise how hard it was to get a song added on that very trendy radio station back then.

LINDA

Show 'business'

The business side of music hasn't always interested me, but I had to learn more about it out of necessity. When we were in the Honeymooners we were making $100 each per show, but when we started with the Black Sorrows we took a $25 pay cut. The challenge for us in leaving the Sorrows was to not let that happen again. We both knew we could do it. Neither of us were interested in being massively famous, but we sure as hell didn't want to work for nothing. We believed in ourselves and were willing to work our arses off. So, to protect our future, we paid attention to the contracts we had to sign, and to all the talk going on in boardrooms about royalties, terms and copyright.

Dad was keeping an eye and ear on what was happening too. I had lots of helpful conversations with him. While we were with the Sorrows, I took note of the business dealings and Dad would ask me questions about what we'd signed and how much money we were keeping and earning. He was concerned we were being underpaid for doing the same amount of work as the others. My dad is a straight talker and doesn't like anyone who isn't.

He'd always say things like 'Keep yourself fit and don't drink too much because they don't just want you for your voice' or 'Don't be afraid to ask questions if you don't understand anything'. Dad wasn't a big-wig businessman or anything, but he'd paid off his houses by the time he was forty-five and retired at fifty-five, so he certainly wasn't stupid.

I wasn't so naive as to believe that being great singers would be enough for us to succeed. We needed to be smart about our future too. I didn't want us to become a casualty of the seedy side of the business and be used up and spat out by the time we were thirty. I wanted us to thrive. So in that last year with the Sorrows I had listened and asked as many questions as I could. I used to drive everyone crazy, but Vika got shitty the most because she was the closest to me. I wasn't driven by greed, but by a distaste for the inequitable side of the business, the one where the talent does all the work and the rich executives at the top keep all the money. I didn't want us to become a rock'n'roll cliché. I wanted success for us, and success to me meant longevity. I wasn't going to have a long career if I blindly signed the first thing that came my way.

I didn't have a single cell in my brain for business in the beginning and had no confidence to take part in a meeting, let alone negotiate with anyone. I learned quickly that you had to have your wits about you because sometimes important decisions had to be made on the spot. It seemed to me that in the music industry everybody wanted everything yesterday. Everyone wanted a signed agreement before an appearance. In the early days if we didn't understand anything, we'd follow our gut instinct and just cross it out and initial it. We didn't want to hold things up but this approach was not always popular.

The music industry is a dog-eat-dog, sink-or-swim kind of world. It's punishing because you've got to be tough to survive the lifestyle … and that's all before you've even stepped foot on stage. But Vika and I have always had each other, which has been our strength. It was harder for the big boys to take both of us on. It's not like we rallied together against them, but we were raised to stick together no matter what and relied heavily on our gut instinct and upbringing to get us through in those early days when we went out on our own. We didn't always get it right but whatever decision we made, we made it together. If we stuffed up, the blame lay with us.

VIKA

Me and my baby

John and I continued dating throughout my twenties, and all that time he had said he wasn't into having kids.

'Fine by me,' I said. I wasn't ready to have a kid either. John gave up drinking when he was thirty-one but I was still gigging, touring, partying and happily grooving along, doing my thing. Then I hit twenty-nine and fell pregnant.

Shit!

I knew John didn't want kids, but I was about to turn thirty and my clock was ticking. We were living together by then, so I walked into the house and found him in the kitchen making a cup of tea.

'I'm pregnant,' I blurted out.

John stared at me, shocked, trying to take it in, then said, 'Well, you know how I feel, but if you want to have a baby, Vik, then I'll stick by you.'

I thought about it and decided that I did want to have the baby. John was thirty-six and I was about to turn thirty, so I figured those were good ages to have a kid together.

Mum was visiting Tonga when I told her over the phone that I was pregnant.

'Oh no, Vika,' she said. 'Not you. You are too selfish. I'm coming home.'

I was angry and surprised by her response. I thought my mum would be over the moon to hear this news and I didn't like being told I was selfish.

When Mum got home, she came over, sat me down and gave me a big talking-to. She told me that my life was going to change in a very big way, and that raising a baby was going to be hard work, but I told her I didn't care and that I would be fine.

My labour was long – thirty-six hours, to be exact. We'd decided to have our baby in the birthing centre at the Royal Women's Hospital and I wanted a natural birth. We attended all the birthing classes leading up to the big day, and the only thing I reckon John got out of them was to make sure to pack snacks before coming to hospital. Mum and Dad were with us at home and when the time came to go to hospital, after about thirty hours, John was nowhere to be found. Mum eventually found him in the kitchen, packing snacks.

'What the bloody hell are you doing, John?' Mum said. 'Forget the snacks and get her to the hospital!'

It was pretty funny, I gotta say. I think John was nervous and it was his way of trying to help. It took my mother years to warm to John, and even though they can fight like cats and dogs, they get along great now. I think they're just too similar!

Mum and Linda came to the hospital too, and everyone at the hospital caught on quick that Mum was a midwife, so they pretty much left us to it. Mum coached me through the birth, which wasn't easy because the baby was posterior. I'd opted for a drug-free birth and the only thing that relieved my back pain was being in the bath. I hopped in and there I stayed for as long as I could. But I wasn't allowed to give birth in the bath, and when the time came for me to start pushing, I refused to get out.

'We've gotta get her out of the bath,' the midwives said to Mum. 'Can you help us out?'

Mum put on her stern Nurse/Mum voice. 'Vika, out! Get up and out of that bath! You are NOT giving birth in that bath!'

The voice worked. I got out and reluctantly returned to my room with Mum and Linda, where I paced back and forth, naked and in tremendous pain.

Everyone was wonderful in the delivery room. Mum talked me

through the whole thing, John was up at my head, holding my hand, while Linda stared straight up my vajayjay keister, waiting for my baby to appear. I nearly broke both of John's hands, but my beautiful baby girl, Mafi, was finally born at 5.55am on 22 June 1997.

'Oh, this one's been here before,' the midwife said, looking at her wide-open blue eyes.

We named our daughter, Mafi'iolani – Mafi being a Tongan word for strength, and after Mum's sister, Aunty Mafi, even though her full name was Fakatoumafi. Mum suggested that perhaps we could take the Mafi part of my aunty's name and combine it with 'iolani' as a nod to my mother's French grandmother.

As soon as our Mafi was placed in John's arms, he looked down at her and said, 'Why did I wait so long?'

I've never known a love like the one I feel for my baby girl, but motherhood didn't come naturally to me. When the midwife handed Mafi to me, I was so shocked that I handed her straight over to Mum. It was instinct because Mum had taken care of everything in my life.

'No,' Mum said, handing Mafi back to me. 'This is your baby, and you need to take care of her.'

Oh God, I thought. How on earth am I going to do this? This is going to be hard. I'll have to be strong, and I don't know if I am.

Everyone assumes that I'm tough, but I'm not, and certainly not after having my baby. When the doctor came in to test Mafi's hips, I thought she was going to break her legs, and I burst into tears. I couldn't stand the thought of anyone hurting her.

When I got back home, Mum and Dad stayed for a month to help John and me get into a routine because I had absolutely no clue. I needed someone to show me how to be a mum and, luckily, my mother was the best teacher in the world!

Firstly, Mum wouldn't let me leave the house for a whole month. She said it was a Tongan thing and was all about getting the baby strong and not exposing her to anyone in case she got sick. I think Mum was also worried because I got chickenpox from my cousin, who came to visit when I was one week old. Mum raised us by herself. She had no extended family here and Dad worked all day, so she understood how hard motherhood is and how bad it would be if Mafi got sick. So I stayed at home for one month, breastfeeding and learning how to look after a baby.

My baby girl was so cute, and I called her Butternut because her head was shaped like a butternut pumpkin. She used to laugh in her sleep, and I remember wondering how a two-week-old baby could be having fits of laughter in her dreams. I decided the midwife was right and that she must have been here before.

I was ravenous all the time, and Dad often went for a stroll up to the shops and returned with scones and custard tarts to satisfy my sweet tooth. I really appreciated these little things and loved having Mum and Dad around to help us. They cooked, cleaned, bathed Mafi and let me sleep, although I was so paranoid about SIDS I checked on her every hour and hardly slept for the first year.

A week after they left, Mum and Dad returned to find me on the couch in tears. I wasn't coping at all. The birthing classes hadn't prepared me for any of this, even though Mum had certainly warned me. She told me it would be hard work but, WOW, this was on another level.

As soon as Mum saw me crying on the couch with Mafi in my arms she jumped into action. Mum was worried that postnatal depression was setting in.

'Right, that's it!' she said. 'We're moving in!'

My mum loves babies. Babies and old people, that's it. She's not so fond of everyone in between. So, when it came time to helping with her baby granddaughter, Mum was in her element.

In the end, Mum and Dad didn't stay with us. John and I moved in with them instead, for a whole year. The five of us lived at Mum and Dad's two-bedroom Victorian place in Clifton Hill, where they'd moved after living in Box Hill for fourteen years, and where Linda and I had lived until she got married. Most nights there, Mafi slept with me and poor John slept on the floor. I loved having my baby close to me at night, and John never complained, not once. He and Mum clashed at times because Mum was used to being the boss and John wouldn't stand for being told what to do, but he realised that Mum was a kick-arse woman who could handle any situation. He was happy to have a caring family to help us look after his little one, because he didn't have a clue what he was doing either. He loves my parents and was so grateful for everything they did for us.

'This is my family now, Vik,' he said, 'and I want Mafi to have all the love and support in the world, which your family provides in bucketloads.'

John loves the Tongan people and, just like my father, he accepts the fact that 'You marry one Tongan, you marry the lot!'

Mum was always on top of any little thing that went wrong and was so devoted. When Mafi got sick, Mum sat up with her all night and taught me what to do. Dad had wanted to travel once he retired, and Mum was all for that, but their plans went out the window when the grandchildren started coming along and became their number one priority.

It was lovely watching the grandparent–grandchild relationship blossom. My parents and Mafi became very close, and I was more like the big sister. I was still struggling to come to terms with motherhood, but Mum acted like more of a guide and made sure I was in charge as much as possible.

Eventually I had to get back to work, so six weeks after Mafi was born, Linda and I went on tour around the top end of Australia and Mum and Dad came on the road with us as our nannies. It was great fun and Dad loved driving in the Tarago with the boys – Brett Kingman, Stewie Speed, John, and Jex Saarelaht – Mum, Mafi, Linda and me.

Linda liked having Mum and Dad on the road with us too

because she knew they calmed me down and let me rest so I wouldn't lose my voice. Having them there meant we could go back to work, so that made her happy.

But looking after a baby while performing and travelling was hard too. I was expressing, breastfeeding, getting up early to drive to the next town, performing and then doing it all again the next day. It was tough and I was tired all the time, but I've worked since I was fifteen and always made my own money, so getting back to work was important to me. I was exhausted and looked like a wreck. Thank God for Mum and Dad, who were there to help every step of the way.

John and Dad were fantastic with Mafi too, but I learned quickly that babies rely more heavily on their mums. John understood this and I think he sometimes felt kind of helpless and left out, but he always tried to help in his own way.

Working nights and taking care of a baby took its toll on my body and eventually my milk dried up. I felt lucky that I'd been able to breastfeed for three months, and I actually loved breastfeeding. It was a beautiful bonding experience, and I was eating better too because I knew that everything I put in my body affected my little one. I was very healthy and Mafi was growing big and strong, but I was so tired. If I had my time over, I would take the first year off and just concentrate on being a mum. That's my main regret. I was focused on getting back to work and singing for my supper, but John would happily have provided for us, as he always has. Still, we were living with Mum and Dad, learning how to be parents, touring and managing to keep it all together. We were very close and Mafi thrived.

Sometimes I had to leave Mafi behind with Mum and Dad, which I hated doing, but I wanted to make money so she could have whatever she needed. I missed her terribly but at least I knew she was safe with my parents. The longest stretch I was away from her was three weeks, when we travelled to a few different states around Australia. When we got back, Mum and Dad were waiting at the airport gate with Mafi in their arms and I was beside myself to see her again.

'I don't think you should do that again,' Dad whispered in my ear as he hugged me.

He was right, and from then on Mafi came everywhere with me. She was such a terrific kid to travel with. As she got older, Mafi learned to pack her bags the night before, so we'd be ready to leave first thing in the morning. I'd wake her at 5am sometimes and she'd immediately get up, get herself ready and be in the car ready to drive to the next town, or catch the next flight.

When she was three years old, Mafi went to Tonga with my mother for a month. I missed her desperately but wanted her to live with her Tongan family for a little while, as I had when I was a kid. Mafi was different when she came home from that trip. She had been treated like a princess while she was there, but she also got to see another way of life, a life that is much harder and poorer than here in Australia. The kids there aren't spoiled with material possessions like kids here, and I wanted Mafi to experience that too, and it definitely had a positive impact on her. She had much more perspective and gratitude for what she had and even the teachers noticed when she started school.

Being the daughter of two musicians made Mafi grow up fast. Her lifestyle was different to those of the other kids at school, because we were always travelling, playing different venues every night and staying in different hotels. I'd often pull her out of school to come on the road with me because I thought it would open her eyes to different ways of life, and I wanted to raise an independent kid who could take care of herself. She sure can and did! If Mafi ever had any gripe at school, she'd march herself straight into the principal's office and sort it out with him.

She's seen a lot and, even though I was thirty-one when I had her, I've grown up with her, because I still felt like a kid myself.

LINDA

Celebrity encounter

In 1995, Vika and I were travelling on Peter Gabriel's WOMAD (World of Music and Dance) tour in Spain and the UK when we were invited to record some songs at Peter Gabriel's studio. Peter had invited artists from all over the world to participate in his recording week, and most of us were artists on the WOMAD bill. It was a huge honour. He would set everything up and all we had to do was find a collaborative partner for a day. Someone who was outside our own band who either we could write a new song with or could join us on one of our own songs. It was very open and a useful way to get us to let our guards down and work with other people, as Neneh Cherry and Youssou N'Dour found on the great song '7 Seconds' in 1994.

Peter was incredibly generous and hospitable. All we had to do was pluck up the courage to approach someone, anyone. We thought of a few artists we could maybe approach, but Vika and I are both shy and we usually chickened out at the last minute. Time was running out and it looked like we could blow the opportunity.

The tour included a coveted spot at the Reading Festival, and we performed some gospel songs in one of the tents. As Vika took the lead on one of the songs, I ducked backstage to grab a drink and saw two strangers huddled on our couch having an intimate chat. It only took me a moment to realise that the two strangers were Johnny Depp and Iggy Pop! The space was tiny, the size of a Bunnings sausage sizzle tent, so I was a bit taken aback to say the least. They were immediately very sweet and apologetic about being in our tent, but I assured them I was fine with it. It was drizzling outside and they were cold, so before I went back out to finish off the set with Vik I said, as casually as I could, 'Sure, make yourselves at home!'

I walked back on stage and, as the crowd applauded Vika's performance, I whispered in her ear, 'You'll never believe who is backstage! Whatever you do, don't freak out when you see who is out there!'

Vik doesn't gush at the best of times, so when we headed

backstage after the gig and she walked smack-bang into the both of them, she held her cool. We all had a beer together, shared the backstage deli platter, and they were both lovely company. It's difficult in those situations not to be overwhelmed by the little voice inside your head that's on hyperdrive and screaming, *'Iggy Pop and Johnny Depp are standing here, Linda, and you're having a beer with them! What the actual fuck! How does the dork from Doncaster manage that?'* But I tried to ignore that screaming voice and just be myself, and not try to act cool because I was never gonna out-cool guys like Iggy and Johnny.

Iggy was very inquisitive and interested in what we were doing. We told him we were Peter Gabriel's guests and that we would be recording in his studio for a week. Here it was, our chance to ask Iggy Pop to collaborate with us. It was a golden opportunity that we couldn't, that we shouldn't, pass up. Our recording date was set for the next day, and we were stuck. We had nobody to collaborate with and were sweating over it. Before I could stop myself, I'd blurted this out to Iggy and he turned to me with those big, beautiful eyes and in his deep voice said, 'Well, how about me? I'll do it.'

Then I fainted.

Nah, only joking.

Vik and I both said, 'Are you kidding?'

He said he wasn't, and so the next day Vik and I found ourselves in the studio waiting nervously to see if he'd show. We both had a gut feeling that there was no way in hell he would … I mean, why would he? But then, at three o'clock on the dot, there he was, Iggy Pop himself, coming up the path. That beautiful man was good to his word, God love him. Not only that, but he'd brought along a couple of mates to watch and listen too. Mates that included Johnny Depp, Kate Moss and Vernon Reid. Gulp!

We told Iggy we had a song in mind, which needed a strong male voice to carry it off but wasn't much to learn.

'It's a song written by Paul Kelly called "I Know Where to Go to Feel Good",' we told him.

'What's it about?' he asked, not looking too interested.

'Masturbation,' we told him.

Now he seemed a tad more interested.

We sang it all the way through, with Iggy delivering the important line, 'I know where to go to feel good', whenever it came up in the song. We did one take then asked him to do another.

'I never do more than one,' he said. 'But I'll do it for you.'

Sweet man. He did a second take for us, nailed it, then left.

We'll never forget our experience with the legend that is Iggy Pop, or what he did for us that day.

VIKA
Stuffing up

Management and record companies are important parts of an artist's team. You've gotta be on the same page as them or have someone who can steer you in the right direction and give you good advice.

Over the years Linda and I have learned that you have to surround yourself with like-minded people. People who share your values and who want to see you succeed, but not at the expense of others. People who are kind, not aggressive or nasty. People who want to share in your success and who aren't greedy. People like our parents, two of the happiest, most contented people we know.

When Linda and I were doing our own gigs around town in the early days with the Honeymooners, we'd get our money and split it evenly between us and the band members. Easy! No problem! Fair's fair. I don't believe in screwing people over. If a promoter was gonna go broke, I was always happy to take a pay cut, but wasn't encouraged to do so. I was always told by management that the promoter had taken the punt and that's the way it goes, but I was never comfortable with that. I should have had more guts. I should have said, 'No, that's not how I want it to work. Can't we come to some other arrangement and all work together?' But I never did. For some reason, I was always made to feel like I was working for management, not the other way around. I was still very inexperienced and too gutless to say what I wanted. I also hate confrontation.

Linda and I needed guidance and good advice when we first decided to leave the Sorrows, but we didn't know as much then as we do now. The small amount of success we received in the Black Sorrows went to our heads a bit and we thought, yes indeed, we can record whatever music we want! But we were a little directionless. We should never have asked Doug to manage us. He was Joe's manager, so we should have said thank you, goodbye, and gone in search of someone else. Someone who was completely outside of the Sorrows' circle.

We had great success with our debut album in 1994 but we didn't follow it up with a similar-sounding record. The songs on our debut were very eclectic: there was rock, reggae, country, jazz and the thread tying it together was our voices. With our next album, *Princess Tabu*, in 1996, we went in another direction.

Paul Kelly got us off to a very good start with songwriting, and when it came time to record *Princess Tabu* we were just starting to hit our stride, both as singers and songwriters. Tim Finn helped us with this, as well as Paul. Every song was co-written by us. Doug helped us take our band to Tonga for inspiration for this second album, and Warren was all for the trip too. We did some recording in Tonga and the band got to experience island life so that they could hear, see, feel and try to capture the sound we were looking for on the album. *Princess Tabu* had a strong focus on our Polynesian heritage, both lyrically and musically.

But when our gospel album, *Two Wings*, came out in 1999, people were like, well, are they soul singers, country singers, gospel singers, rock singers or Tongan singers?

We needed help with direction and strong leadership. We had a record company that knew how to sell records and wanted success for us, but we were young and naive and made a lot of mistakes. We really needed someone who understood the creative side of the business, as well as the business side. Don't get me wrong, I'm all for artistic freedom, but sometimes you gotta take a bit of advice because I reckon we ended up slitting our own throats.

LINDA
Tapana

Vika and I decided that if we were gonna have kids, we'd plan it so that our babies were close together in age. That way we could keep working and take them both with us on the road. It was a good idea and Vik went first.

I was amazed at Vika's stamina during Mafi's birth. She had a thirty-six-hour labour on two Panadol, for fuck's sake! The second little Mafi came out, she opened those big blue eyes and looked at the world around her. It was a privilege to be there, and from that moment on I was clucky, but my story is a little different to Vika's.

When I got pregnant, at the end of 1997, I'd just taken time off to go on a holiday to Cuba and did absolutely nothing health- or fitness-wise to ready my body for the birth of my first little bubba. I regretted this nine months later. But I did quit smoking and drinking, and changed my diet by adding Special K cereal because it was rich in folate. That was it.

During my pregnancy, I had a recurring dream of what my baby would look like when she was born, and the angels got it right. She looked exactly as she did in my dream: light caramel skin, pale green eyes and beautiful. It made me think twice about ignoring my dreams.

I wanted to give her a Tongan name because I wanted it to have meaning and a connection to family. I had to ask Mum for permission, as naming rights in Tongan culture are important, and she helped me choose a name that had a history behind it, and it was melodically beautiful. The name was the same as our ancestral family island in Vava'u, and translates into English as 'lightning'. So it was decided. My baby girl's name would be Tapana. Tapi for short.

The historical story of my daughter's name is that a distant relative of ours, who also happened to be a cannibal, liked to sit on the top of the hill of Tapana and play tricks on wayward sailors to pass the time. He would lure them by shining a little piece of shell into the afternoon sun, which looked like lightning to the unsuspecting sailors. Once the curious sailors came his way, boom, there was his next meal.

Mum helped with Tapana's delivery, just as she did with Mafi's. I would have liked to have had Vika in the room with me, but Justin and Vika clashed and I knew he wouldn't want her there, so I didn't ask her. He got along with Mum, so she was always going to be there.

After the birth, I was lying there, legs spread and mess everywhere, when the surgeon recognised me and said, 'Oh, I love your music!'

I stared at her, sitting there between my legs, and thought, You've got to be kidding me.

'That's very nice, but can you please concentrate on putting my daughter back together?' Mum said, always the boss.

I had my share of struggles after the birth, but I didn't seem to push against the changes to my life as much as Vik did. I had the benefit of seeing first-hand what my sister went through after Mafi's birth, so I felt more prepared. I'm also a very different person to Vika, so my reaction was not to fight these changes, but let them be. As she had with Vika, Mum came to the rescue and helped out a lot in the first forty days after the birth, but she didn't move in as she had with my sister. Instead, she came over to our flat in Fitzroy every day to clean, cook and show me and my husband what to do. I loved *that* lockdown time with my new baby and Mum. I trust my mother so much when it comes to all things medical, and Tapi had terrible reflux, so I was grateful Mum was there to pull out all her tricks and tips. Apart from the reflux, our beautiful Tapi was a peaceful and quiet little baby, and I loved her with all my heart.

As she got older, Tapi's piercing green eyes drew a lot of unwanted attention and comments from strangers.

'Oh my God, your eyes!' they'd blurt out in the street.

It was becoming obvious that Tapi was shy by nature and this kind of attention made it worse. She started looking down so people couldn't see her eyes. I always had to remind her to look up and say thank you when people complimented her.

From a young age, Tapi could hold a full-blown conversation with any adult she trusted, and I believe this was because she was never in creche around other kids, but always with family and in the company of adults. In prep, she read a long passage from *Harry*

Potter and the Philosopher's Stone out loud to her classmates and stunned teacher. She barely looked down at the book the whole time and seemed to have learned it from memory. I had never forced reading on her, apart from the usual book at bedtime, but I clearly recall all the mums outside the classroom on that first day of prep asking me if my child could read.

'No, why?' I said. 'Should she be able to read?'

Needless to say, I was a little shocked when I found out just how well she could!

I loved being with Tapi, and missed her when I went out on tour, which was quite a bit when she was young. I loved simple things like walking to the milk bar for a giant jelly snake with her after kindy and answering her many questions. She would be on her tiny trike with me walking behind. She'd stop at every house to pick little flowers, which she'd gently place in the basket of her bike for me, our neighbour or Mum. She was always a very gentle child and very switched on.

Tapi had a pretty normal and happy upbringing, but there were a couple of things that left a mark on her childhood. One was illness, the other was divorce.

It was Boxing Day 2002, the summer before she was to start school. We were down at Phillip Island with the family when Tapi developed a very serious staph infection called Osteomyelitis and was rushed to the Children's Hospital in Melbourne, where we spent the next two weeks by her bedside.

Hospital is a lonely place, but we were all trying to make it feel like home for her. My parents visited every day, and every night Vika and Johnny brought her a homemade meal. This was a time when I really needed my family, and they were there every step of the way. My husband was only young when his father died after an operation, so Justin hates hospitals. He was all at sea when his little angel got sick. He didn't want to be in the hospital but didn't want to leave her either. I think this time aged him tremendously; it was his worst nightmare.

I was scared and worried about my child, but still had work commitments to uphold over those two weeks. Vika and I had been booked to do a show at the opening of the newly renovated Federation Square in Melbourne, but my head and heart weren't in it. The only place I wanted to be was at my little girl's bedside, but we couldn't cancel such a big show.

Vika and the band sound-checked without me, so I didn't have to turn up until right at the last minute. I got ready in the bathroom at the hospital, put my sarong and matching top in my bag, and drove straight to Fed Square, where a crowd of around seven thousand people were waiting to bring in the New Year.

Any parent who's been in hospital with a sick kid knows that you don't sleep at all while they're in there, so I was exhausted by the time I walked out on stage. But something happened – maybe it was a combination of adrenaline and sleep deprivation – but Vika and I put on the best show of our lives. I gave it my all, as did Vik, and the crowd sang at the top of their lungs when I did my best Freddy Mercury at Live Aid impression. I sang like it was my last show because I needed the release. I blew all my frustrations out at that magnificent crowd, and the energy they returned acted like a gigantic battery charge. It was just what I needed and a reminder of why I love my job so much.

As soon as we finished, I said goodbye to Vik and the band, and drove straight back to the hospital. The unreal situation I had found myself in only dawned on me when I woke up the next morning in the hospital next to my little Tapi, who was still very ill. It was a new year, and I was stiff and cold from sleeping on the fold-out hospital cot, but I was happy I could be there for Tapi and also for my sister and our band.

CHANGES: ACT II

VIKA

Stuffing up: the reprise

Things started spiralling downwards when Linda's husband became Doug's partner. It was around 2000 and Justin was finding it hard to transition out of being a musician into the business side of the industry. He knew what had gone down with our management woes, after we parted ways with Andrew and Michelle, and asked if he could help by assisting Doug. Justin and Doug got along well, and Andrew and Michelle had left a big void, so Doug agreed. Not only was this a bad match as far as I was concerned but we were also now paying a lot of commission: to Doug, Justin and to Premier Artists. Linda and I then had to pay the band out of what was left over.

Someone who saw what was going on and didn't like it was our father. He can sum a person up in about five minutes, and he should have managed us. Dad is good with money, fair and has always taken an interest in our financial affairs. I mean, the guy bought a house in Clifton Hill, on a public servant's salary. It was for him and Mum for their retirement. He said at one stage in our career that we were not likely to make a lot of money, because the likelihood of being successful in the popular music industry was very slim, for girls especially. Mum and Dad were living in Philip Island and the house was their city place, they let us live there when our career was just taking off.

Dad sat me down during that time to talk to me about what was going on.

'Vika, this is pretty silly,' he said. 'You're not making any money because you're paying commissions to two managers before your expenses. You're being bloody stupid, love!'

I knew he was right, but our new manager was Linda's husband. My sister had all the faith in the world in him and I didn't want to upset her. But I had a bad feeling about the whole thing. This was a guy who had a lot of bravado, but his main problem was that he was arrogant. This pissed me off. I should have had the guts to say, 'Listen buddy, you are representing me and Linda, so be nice because we're not arseholes!' But I didn't and we soon got a reputation for having a manager who was hard to deal with.

We should have been paying more attention but whenever I talked to Linda's husband about this stuff we always argued. He was a musician himself, but when he gave up the instrument and stepped into the management position, he sure changed his tune.

Many times, we employed a lawyer to read our contracts to cut through all the bullshit and save us some time, but Linda loves to read contracts too, so we'd go into their office and she would ask them to explain while I sat there watching the clock. I hate all that stuff, so thank God for Linda. My sister is very thorough. She'd take notes, go home and read the contract again, then get our managers on the phone the next day to reiterate what the lawyer said. After that, she'd have both me and our managers on the phone to talk it through for a couple of hours, before thinking through it some more and then finally signing.

I'd tell Mum and Dad that she's a pain in the fucking arse, and they'd say, 'She's always been like that, love. You know that!' So, you see, Linda's always got our back. If it was up to me, we'd probably be broke … and maybe in prison.

We were still doing lots of gigs around town to support our next record, *Live and Acoustic*, and then in 2001, just before the release of our album *Love Is Mighty Close*, we were 'let go' by our record company. We were a little shocked but mostly understood their reasons. It was the way we were told that pissed me off. Linda's husband came home from a meeting with the record company and quite matter-of-factly said, 'You've been dumped by the label.'

It didn't stop us, though. We borrowed $50,000 from our parents and stuck to our plan of going into the studio to make our gentler, country-style album, with Joffa producing. The album went on to receive an ARIA nomination for Best Adult Contemporary Album.

In 2003, we were looking around for a guitarist to play at the live gospel shows we had lined up at the Cornish Arms when we reconnected with a musician named Dion Hirini. We had first met Dion years earlier through Michael Barker from the Sorrows, who'd introduced us when Dion first arrived in Melbourne. But now it was my husband who introduced us again.

'You know,' John said, 'you really should get this fella to play with you because he's the real deal. He's got the feel, the funk and the groove going on.'

Funny that it was two drummers who suggested Dion to us. They knew exactly what we needed! We'd been playing with Joffa for so long at that point, but we felt like we needed a change. Linda had to call Joffa to let him know we were going to give Dion a crack at guitar. It was a very hard call to make because Joffa had been so loyal. We ended up playing with Dion because he could sing and harmonise so beautifully with us. The third Bull sister, we called him.

Dion was a popular fella, and everyone referred to him as BLX, pronounced Blex. He became a part of our band, and we loved the sound he added – he could harmonise with the two of us like no other. Dion was a Maori from Port Hedland and understood the Polynesian harmony thing Linda and I had going on. He had the Maori strum drown pat and was the perfect musician to accompany Linda and me. Dion played a lot by feel and didn't really play the same thing night after night. There were always slight changes. If we wanted him to learn a song, he'd never learn it note for note but did his version of it, giving it his own spin. Sometimes this drove us nuts, but we put up with it because we understood what a beautiful player he was, and when he was on fire, he stole the show. He would sometimes have off nights too, and that's when we'd wonder what the hell was up with him, but we never pulled him up on it because the nights he was on more than made up for those rare occasions.

I don't recall much about the business side after we left the Sorrows, except that we made a lot of mistakes. The only good decision we made was signing with Mushroom and not Sony. We are partly to blame for stuffing up our careers, as well as our management. I knew in my gut that Linda, her husband Justin, Doug and I were not a good match or a good team. We ended up dropping Doug as our manager. We told him face to face and it was another hard one. I think he was very upset with us, and he left Australia and returned to the UK soon after. Now we just had Linda's husband managing us. I thought it might be a good move, to keep it all in the family. WRONG!

After we parted ways with Doug and then got dumped by our record company, everything became a lot harder for Justin to manage, and he and I clashed big time. The only reason I tried to be nice was that he was married to my sister, but, geez, he made it hard for me. With him it was all about money. I know he was trying to make us money too, but money isn't the most important thing for me. I didn't get into this business to make money or be famous. I wanted to sing. I was so happy when singing for a living replaced my day job because I hated working behind a desk. I hated the ritual of getting up early, trying to decide what to wear, then walking to the tram in the freezing cold and taking public transport to a place where I sat on my arse for seven hours a day, five days a week. When I was finally able to quit, I rejoiced and shouted, 'Hallefuckinlujah!' I was gonna sing for a living and I didn't care if I had to live on baked beans to do it. Singing brought me more joy than money ever did.

Don't get me wrong – money is fantastic, but not at the expense of relationships Justin never had any discussion with Linda or me about fees or stuff like that. He just went hard. It was embarrassing and over the top at times and promoters were perplexed and astounded by the fees he'd sometimes quote. We lost a lot of gigs because he was too hard to deal with. The old bulldog approach of doing deals was phasing out and not as productive as it used to be. Basically, he was just too difficult to deal with, and Linda and I weren't in control of our careers when we should have been.

Around this time, Linda and I were given a really bad review in a street mag. It was a personal attack. The reviewer hated our guts and let us, and the public, know it. What upset me the most was that it wasn't constructive at all, just downright nasty. Also, this was a magazine I bought every fortnight to support those who were selling it, feeling like I was doing something good. But here they were being horrible to us. Linda's husband read the review and saw red. He got straight on the blower and tore the editor of the magazine a new one. I was still seething from the review when he told me he'd called up the editor and blasted her head off. Oh no, I thought. This isn't good.

I knew that he could be really fiery himself and so I got on the phone to apologise to the editor for his behaviour. I explained that he was upset because the review was so nasty, and she agreed but said they didn't believe in censoring their journalists, which is why it went to print. But she thanked me for the call and said she had indeed burst into tears when he was yelling at her. There you go. When two arrogant men meet – in this case the reviewer and our manager – the women have to clean up the mess!

We should have let it go but it was the worst review we have ever received. It was so bad that I had to have therapy and nearly quit singing over it. I had a beaut doctor in those days who I saw on a weekly basis for acupuncture, cupping and a good old-fashioned chitchat. At my session with Doctor Doug after the review came out, my body was a tense mess and as he started sticking needles into me, I burst into tears.

'What's up?' he asked.

I told him about the review and his advice was something I've never forgotten.

'Vika, in your business, people will say nasty things and try to cut you down,' he said. 'But the one thing they can't do is take away your talent.'

Goddamn, I thought. You're right! I wasn't going to let that bastard make me quit something I loved to do. Fuck him! I left that session a more enlightened person, so thank you, Doctor Doug!

I wasn't so enlightened that my feelings towards Linda's husband had changed, though.

LINDA

The spiral

Vika and Justin have always clashed, they've never really seen eye to eye, even in the early days when he was my boyfriend. Vika calls a spade a spade and is a sharp judge of character. When Justin was trying to transition away from being a musician and into management, he asked me if he could come on board our management team. At first Vika was open to the idea because she wanted to please me and we thought it might be better to keep it all in the family.

But their relationship got much worse when he became our manager. I cringe now thinking about the cliché I was becoming: singer managed by husband. I wasn't so naive as to think there wasn't a conflict of interest, but I hoped we could overcome that because we were all family. But, in my heart of hearts, I think I always knew it would end in tears.

After Justin had been managing us on his own for about five years, I knew Vika and I had a problem with a capital P because it just wasn't working. I could feel the tension between them, and that was the worst part. I was always the meat in the sandwich. But I was the one who got us into this situation, so I was the one who had to now find us a way out, especially as Vik had problems of her own.

VIKA

Voice angels

In 2004, Linda and I made a live gospel record, *Tell the Angels*, with our band. Dion Hirini was on guitar, Adam ACE Ventoura on bass, Bruce Haymes on piano and my hubby, Watto, on drums. We recorded it at the Cornish Arms on Sydney Road, Brunswick, and you can actually hear my voice going by the fourth song. You can hear the raspiness setting in and that I am struggling to reach the notes.

My voice had been getting more and more strained and by that stage I had lost all my top-end range. I could still sing, but not as well. By the end of the *Tell the Angels* recording, I had no voice left at all.

I hauled my arse to my GP in Clifton Hill, and she put me onto a terrific place called the Melbourne Voice Analysis Centre. That's where I met my lifesavers: speech therapist Debbie Phyland and surgeon Neil Vallance.

Debbie and Neil checked out my vocal cords with a camera that was attached to a thin flexible tube they shoved up my nose and down my throat. I didn't mind this, but the other method they used, which involved them holding my tongue and looking through my mouth with a camera attached to a cold metal thing, made me gag. They took a photo and inspected my cords to see what kind of damage I'd done and there it was, clear as day: a little lump, a polyp.

Debbie and Neil didn't send me for surgery straight away. Instead, they recommended voice rest and voice exercises, and sent me off to a fantastic singing teacher, Gary May, to learn proper singing technique. Gary understood the workings of the voice incredibly well. He's taught a lot of opera singers and musical theatre people over the years and knows all the tricks in the book.

Gary lives in a gorgeous apartment overlooking the city of Melbourne and has a beautiful grand piano. When I got there, he sat at the piano and played scales for me. I'd never heard scales sound so good, and it was a joy singing them with him. I liked Gary immediately, but I was very intimidated because he knew his shit. I was worried he'd think, Oh God, a rock singer! What am I going to do with this wreck? But after he heard me do scales, he told me I should have studied opera singing, but that it was too late and the damage had already been done. It's a shame because I would have loved to have sung opera. I always try and sing it around the house and my husband can't stand it.

I was always hoarse when I arrived at Gary's apartment, so he'd give me exercises to massage my vocal cords. By the end of my lesson with him, voila! Gary had worked his magic.

There was a big tour with Paul Kelly looming. Oh God, I thought. What am I gonna do? Team Gary, Debbie and Neil kicked into action. They were going to help me get through that tour with Gary's exercises, and drugs when I was desperate. I ended up taking steroids throughout the whole tour. I knew I was in serious trouble, but I wanted to tour with Paul, and I wanted to be able to sing. Touring was what I did, so I was going to do that tour no matter what.

I knew my voice was under par, but I thought that with help from my Voice Dream Team I'd get by. Just. When the tour started, Paul knew I was having trouble with my voice. I was only singing backing vocals, so it wasn't too taxing, but I did have to sing lead on one song. Paul had given me the song 'Everything's Turning to White' to sing and there were some nights when I was a bit under, so Paul knew something was up. 'Everything's Turning to White' is a song about four friends on a fishing trip who stumble upon a dead woman's body, then continue their fishing for three days before reporting it to the police. It isn't a hard song to sing and my job was to just sing the story, no belting necessary, but because of the problem with my cords, I was pitchy most nights and barely holding it together. It was a stressful situation.

That tour was a struggle. My throat was tight and I had the constant feeling that I needed to clear it, which is one of the worst things you can do. It's always best to swallow to clear the throat, not cough. During the day, I didn't talk at all as we travelled from place to place. I sat in the back of the Tarago in total silence, then started gentle warm-up exercises at around 4pm so I could get through Paul's notoriously long set.

I knew that taking steroids could be dangerous and that if I wasn't careful, I would come to rely on them. Steroids make you feel great and weird, and they give you a kind of rush. I'm the kind of girl who enjoys that sort of rush. I knew I could get addicted to them.

As soon as I got back from the tour, I went straight to see Neil and Debbie.

'Yep, there's a big fat nodule there,' they said once as they looked at my cords.

Neil said he could zap it off, but the whole idea of it scared me. I'd heard the story of what had happened to Julie Andrews after she had surgery. Her voice was so pure and strong, and the first voice I fell in love with as a kid. That beautiful voice was destroyed after she had the same surgery that Neil and Debbie were suggesting for me. When I'd heard what happened I was heartbroken for her. I understood how devastating it would be for a singer to lose their voice like that: like losing an arm or a leg. It would be for me, anyway.

But Neil assured me that all would be okay, and that after the surgery I would be singing like a teenager again. This was an exciting prospect, but Neil also warned me that the nodule could always come back so I had to keep up my exercises and look after myself after the surgery too.

I woke up after surgery to find John sitting beside me holding my hand. He took me home, and over the next month my whole family took care of me. I didn't speak a single word for that entire time because I had to give the cords time to heal. There was no way I was gonna mess up all of Neil's good work. Mafi was seven at the time and became my interpreter. She understood everything I needed, or wanted, by the simplest gesture or look. After the month was up, I started speech therapy with Debbie. What a gun that woman is. She got me back on track and, yes, true to Neil's word, I was back singing like my old eighteen-year-old self again. What a relief!

Now, I do my exercises every day. I warm up, I cool down and I don't drink alcohol at all before I sing. I make sure I hydrate, especially the day before a gig, and try not to smash my vocal cords too much when I'm singing the big notes. Of course, after a big sing I always come off stage a little hoarse but now I know how to fix it, and not with hot concoctions, but with rest and hydration. The more gigs I do, the more fit and strong my vocal cords get, and I love that about them. Once a belter, always a belter!

LINDA
Kiki

It was a long time between drinks as far as having babies went for me, and there's a seven-year age gap between my two daughters. As a kid I always dreamed of having six kids but having a second baby at thirty-eight was pushing it, so that was never going to happen. I was happy with the two, and, as Dad always says, 'There's too many people in the world anyway!'

I got pregnant in 2004. This was also when my daughter Tapi asked if we could start calling her by her middle name, Lavinia, because she was sick of people getting 'Tapi' wrong. Lavinia became 'Nia' for short.

I was four months along by the time Vika and I finished a long tour in 2004, opening for Kasey Chambers. Kasey and her best friend, Worm, were throwing their votes in for baby names, and their favourite was Little Stevie. I was very fond of the name Stevie for a girl, but thought I'd better check with Nia and Mafi what their ideas were too.

While I could still travel, Vika and I decided to take off with the kids to Hawaii for a holiday together. Justin and I had planned the trip, and because Vik was so tired after the tour with Kasey, I persuaded her to come along. Nia and Mafi eventually settled on the perfect names as we were all floating around the beautiful lagoon at Waikiki: Emmi after Emmylou Harris, who is one of my favourite singers, and Kiki after Waikiki Beach.

Emmi Kiki was a great choice, but a couple of months before she was born, I decided to change the name to Mana, which means 'power' in the Polynesian culture, and this is the name that ended up on her birth certificate.

Even though Mum liked the name, she thought it might be too powerful and was inviting trouble. Dad thought I must have been too high on pregnancy hormones to think straight, after naming one kid Tapana and the other kid Mana. Not just because they rhymed, but also because it meant I would have two kids whose names meant 'lightning' and 'power'. That was just a bit too 'superhero' for his taste.

'You'll regret it later,' he said.

I thought he had a good point, so I changed her birth certificate back to Emmi Kiki. Now we call her Kiki, and it suits her to a T.

When Kik was born in 2005, she looked like Dora the Explorer on steroids, with the chubbiest cheeks I'd ever seen on a baby. She was a cherub, for sure. When I'd carry her around in a sling, people in the street would bend over laughing at how cute she was with those cheeks. They were so big that they made her beautiful eyes disappear into her face. We soon learned that Kiki was also blessed with a personality that was the same size as those cheeks.

At school drop-off, she'd ride in the baby seat on the back of my bike and wave to everyone like she was the queen.

'I'm Kiki!' she'd shout at full volume, pointing to herself. 'Prep next year!'

She had so much confidence that it cracked me up. Kiki was so sure of herself, even at that young age, and was giving everyone early warning that they'd better be prepared.

Kiki didn't even know I was a singer until one day, when she was in kindergarten, she overheard a stranger in the street ask if I was still singing.

'Mum,' she asked when they walked away, 'what did they mean?'

'I'm a singer, sweetie,' I told her. 'With your Aunty Vik.'

Kiki went straight to kindy the next day and told her friends to invite their parents along to hear her mum and her aunty sing them all her favourite bedtime song, 'Rainbow Connection'.

The teacher Leanne called me to say that Kiki had organised it all, and told everyone, so I couldn't let her down. What choice did I have? I called Vik and Dion, and bless Dion's heart, he came to the rescue, learning the song in about twenty minutes. The three of us got together for a quick run-through and then performed it to a room full of parents and Kiki's classmates. Seeing Kiki's beaming proud face was a beautiful moment, and I was chuffed. She sang along with us, quietly and in a harmony that I had taught her, and it was right on the money.

Kiki has always been my little shadow. Wherever I am, she's never far behind, and I put this down to two things: workload and age gap. Kiki and I spent way more time together than Nia and I did. It makes me sad to say that but it's just the way it was. When Nia was little, I was away touring a lot more than I was when Kiki was born. Still, I tried hard to always be with my kids on their birthdays, and for every significant event in their lives. I worked around this by either bringing them with me, or flying home after shows, wherever I was, so we'd at least wake up in the same house together on their special day. If there was ever a clash, I'd try to move things around so I could be with them.

Luckily, I've only missed one of Kik's school plays and one of Nia's birthdays – her twenty-third – and I think that's a pretty good run. I'm proud of those stats. My main intention has been to not only tell them I love them, but show them as well.

Anybody who knows me well understands that family and my daughters are the most important thing in the world to me. I never wanted to be their best friend. I'm their mother, that's my role. They have their friends. I don't quiz them on every little thing they get up to, but if they choose to confide in me, I try to give them guidance without judgement. Sometimes I get it right and sometimes I get it wrong, but, regardless, the three of us have an extremely tight bond and they know that they come before anyone else.

Hoochie Coochie

In the doldrums is the best way to describe our career from around 2001 through to 2011.

Up until then I'd measured success by how busy I was. I thought I had to be busy all the time, whether that was touring, doing gigs or recording. That was my life for years and I never stopped, until I had no choice. When things began slowing down, and the gigs weren't as frequent, I felt like I was losing my grip on my singing career. I also started questioning my value in the industry, which I felt had a lot to do with my age and who I was, and this is when Vika and I decided to open a kids' clothing shop in North Fitzroy called Hoochie Coochie.

The initial idea for the shop came out of my desire to see if I could do something other than sing for a living. I was approaching forty, and it was looking like I'd better plan for my future away from the stage, especially since I now had two kids and a husband whose future was as uncertain as mine. I always thought I'd retire from singing by the age of forty anyway, because I assumed it would be all over by then. (What an idiot I am!)

It was while walking around Fitzroy with newborn Kiki that I started thinking about how there weren't any cool shops for baby clothes in the area. Maybe I could open a kids' clothes business myself, and maybe Vika could do it with me? I knew there was no way I could run a shop on my own with a four-month-old. Thankfully, Vik said yes so I began looking around, having decided that the shop should not only look beautiful but be in a great location.

I found a place close to the local school, medical centre, supermarket and park, right in the heart of North Fitzroy's bustling village. It was the perfect spot.

Two weeks later, Vik and I had the keys and, with absolutely no previous retail experience between us, started selling old stock and buying new. We soon discovered that I just had to learn how to open the till to make money. It wasn't rocket science. Somehow, I had a knack for selling stuff, and I also liked to shop, so it turned out to be a match made in heaven. I've always loved fashion and wanted to deck my new baby out in cool stuff, so I based my buying choices on that. Vik was not as into it as me. We took turns on the floor, and on buying trips finding stock. One thing I loved doing was decorating the windows. I didn't even know it had a special name and had never heard the term 'visual merchandising' before, but I was good at it and it satisfied my creative urges. I'd stay up all night fiddling with them until they were perfect. I always got a buzz when a kid stopped outside the window the next day and said, 'Look, Mummy, that's beautiful!'

I was a mum, a shop owner and a singer who wasn't doing that much singing. Vika and I were doing the odd show here and there, but we hadn't created anything new for ourselves since our album *Tell the Angels* in 2004. Creativity is the key to longevity because it keeps you interested and fulfilled, but my reality had changed and my singing career was in cruise mode.

So, in 2006, I made the decision to reduce how often I performed so I could focus on my kids. Juggling singing, running the shop and looking after the girls was getting too hard. There was also a lot of tension between Vika, my husband and me because he was still our manager at that point. We felt uninspired on a creative level, and our output slowly ground to a halt. The only way I could relieve all that pressure was to stop singing for a little while, and concentrate on the shop and my girls, which is exactly what I did.

VIKA

The monkey on my back

Alcohol has always been my drug of choice. I hate weed and speed and have never tried heroin, but cocaine is fun, and I've downed a couple of Es, done amyl on Razor's dance floor a few times and have done acid twice. I liked acid, especially when I found myself rolling around in the flowers at Treasury Gardens in East Melbourne at 6am, after a night out in Hardware Lane with my bestie Samantha. Gee, that was a trip! I remember the sun coming up and there we were, rolling in the yellow flowers, giggling our heads off, a couple of fucked-up hippies in East Melbourne. My parents would have been so proud.

I remember choking on my first and only bong. God, that was embarrassing. Snot shot outta my nose and I nearly choked to death, so then I tried smoking the stuff and got the giggles so bad that I drove everyone in the room nuts. Cocaine mainly seemed to sober me up when I was stupid drunk. Ecstasy made me feel warm and fuzzy. The first time I tried it was at the Wailers gig at the Palace in St Kilda, and we had such a great night, hugging and feeling those positive vibrations, that we went back for round two on their second night. But alcohol was always my thing. I loved the buzz it gave me, and being a shy girl by nature, I felt those reservations disappear.

I was fifteen the first time I got drunk. It was during a Tongan dinner dance, and I made my way around to all the empty tables and finished everyone's half-drunk drinks while they were on the dance floor. By the time I drunkenly staggered up to a table full of men to ask them all to dance, Mum had seen what was going on and dragged me away by the ear. She didn't tell me off, but I remember hearing her and Dad through the bedroom wall the next morning, discussing my bravado and foolishness, while I cringed with shame. Despite this, I kept up this embarrassing behaviour for years afterwards: drink, make a fool of myself, wake up with horrible dread, apologise and repeat.

When we were kids, Mum and Dad were constantly telling us that our skin was beautiful and that kids who said mean things were just jealous. But I never believed them. When you're young and all you ever hear from other kids is that you're different because you're brown-skinned, and you know boys don't ask you out because they're scared their friends will tease them, you can't help but feel ashamed. I think it was all those years of feeling embarrassed and ashamed just because I was brown-skinned that contributed to me falling in love with alcohol. Because when I drank, I suddenly felt confident enough to tell people to get stuffed. I'd still be hurting inside but the alcohol made me feel and act tougher than I really was.

There was another time, in our very early days with the Sorrows, when Linda and I went to the nightclub Inflation. I was pissed but wanted to drive home. Linda didn't want me to drive so she got in the car with me to supervise, worried that something would happen. Soon after leaving the club, we were pulled over by the police and I was breath-tested. I was way over the limit, so the cops put me in the back of a divvy van and took me to Russell Street Police Station at five in the morning. Linda says she remembers sitting in the visitor's room and hearing me sing in my cell, my voice echoing down the corridor. Apparently, a bunch of petty crims sitting in the hallway all started to clap and cheer, but I had nothing to be proud about that night.

Alcohol is also the reason I told Linda exactly how I felt about her husband. I don't remember what I said, but my sister didn't speak to me for two months afterwards.

It broke my heart.

LINDA

Bust-up

It was one weekend in 2006 when Vika and I and our kids all went down to stay with Mum and Dad at our family holiday home on Phillip Island. On our first night there, Vika got very drunk and started to let rip at Mum and me. First, she said she was angry and frustrated with Mum because of the tight reins she felt had held her in, and then she turned on me. Vika said she was pissed off with my 'pain in the arse' ways and said I was 'up myself'. She also finally let out her true feelings about my husband and made it very clear that she had no time or respect for him at all.

Everything my sister had been bottling up about all of us for so long came tumbling out that night in one fell swoop, and it was awful. Not only did her words hurt me deeply, but I was also very upset that my little Nia, only eight years old, heard every drunken word out of her angry aunty's mouth.

The next morning, Nia and I left Phillip Island and I didn't talk to Vika for two months. I was so hurt and saddened by her behaviour and what she had said to me. She tried to call me most days, but I refused to answer the phone. Her temper and angry words were still clear as day in my mind, and I didn't want to see or talk to her.

I know there's always a semblance of truth in words spoken in anger, but I wasn't ready to face the truth at that point, especially with what she'd said about Justin. Mum was heartbroken that we weren't speaking, but I needed space.

It was a pretty grim time. Kiki was still very young, so doing night gigs, waking up early with two kids, then working at the shop during the day was taking an extra toll on my marriage and wellbeing.

After the argument we didn't talk to each other or work

together for two months, because I did everything I could to avoid both. Vika would call me, but I wouldn't answer the phone. This was when I started to pull back from performing altogether because it was too difficult at work and it was too difficult at home. Vika was going out and doing her own gigs with the Hornets and taking odd jobs at catering companies and doing secretarial work to make ends meet. The relationship between Vika and Justin was strained too because I'd told him about our argument, and he knew how my sister felt about him.

If it wasn't for Mum, Vika and I probably still wouldn't be talking. But she pushed and pushed for us to talk, and eventually, two months after that horrible night at Phillip Island, Mum was at her wits' end. I was walking around Collingwood Children's Farm with my little Tapi when Mum called me.

'I want you to come over to talk with your sister,' she said in her stern mum voice.

I wasn't into the idea at all. Seeing and speaking to Vika was the last thing I wanted to do, and I think my sister felt the same way, but we did it for Mum.

I had needed time to let my feelings go, and park the hurt, before I saw her. It turns out that had been a good idea because after a break of two months we sorted things out very quickly once we were back in the same room together. It was pretty frosty at first, but when Vik apologised, I said sorry too, for not speaking to her. We realised that a husband wasn't worth the fight and that we were stronger than that. We were family and we cared about what our mum and dad thought. We were raised to be together, and to be better than that. Also, we missed each other.

The day we reconciled was a turning point for me. I knew that Vika had said some pretty horrible things, but I also knew that she was frustrated and had held a lot of her bad feelings in until she couldn't hold them back any longer. I understood this. Sometimes it's better to let your feelings out the moment you feel them, but that's not always possible, and then they get bottled up until the person explodes. Either way, you will get to hear the truth at some point, whether you want to hear it or not.

The fight with Vika made me realise how I was being pulled in different directions and losing some sense of myself. Most critically, though, I realised I was in a situation where the most important relationships in my life were in direct conflict. Something had to give. I needed a circuit breaker.

VIKA

The demon drink

My problem with alcohol is the reason my relationship with Linda broke down that night in Phillip Island. I'm not a naturally outgoing, loud or gregarious person. I'm quite shy and quiet, but when I drink I turn into another person. Dr Jekyll and Mr Hyde, that's me. I have a wild streak inside and the booze lets it out. When I'm sober, I will do anything to avoid confrontation, even if I'm really upset about something. I'll keep it bottled up inside until I have too many drinks and then, BOOM, the beast comes out and I let everyone know exactly what I think, which is what happened that night.

My family has been very patient with me. At certain times over the years, when the drink has taken over and I'm about to turn, I've even heard Linda say to my husband, 'Hold on, Johnny, we're in for a ride!'

Unfortunately, my daughter has also been on the same ride many times, as have my nieces, aunties, cousins, uncles and friends. But they've always forgiven me. Every time. I've battled with the regret I feel after the 'ride', and I hate the fact that I love alcohol.

I think our job is one of the only ones where you can have a drink before you start work. A bit of Dutch courage, perhaps? It takes the edge off, especially if you're nervous, which is natural when there are two thousand people expecting you to give them their money's worth and put on a great show. But drinking six nights a week to take the nerves away before a gig, then more booze after to relax, is not good for someone with alcoholic tendencies. There was always a rider backstage – white wine, red wine, beers, vodka, whiskey and mixers – every night, six nights a week, and let me tell you we drank every single drop. Dad warned me. He said, 'Be careful, girl, it catches up with you!'

He was right.

My relationship with my sister nearly broke down forever because of my drinking. That's when I knew something had to change. Linda isn't just my sister, she's my best friend, and has been the one constant in my life besides my parents. I don't remember my life without Linda. Mum and Dad brought my sister home from the hospital a short seventeen months after I arrived in this world, and from that moment on we were always together. In the beginning, she'd follow me around and copy everything I did, but I'm happy to say she's grown wiser over the years. I've always got her to do my dirty work and can't count the number of times I've pushed her to the front to do our bidding over the years – payment for gigs, negotiations with band members, making deals with management, she's done it all. Linda can talk her way into, and out of, anything, and I love that about her. I'm always happy to take a back seat and let Linda do the hard work, but God help anyone who screws her around, or treats my sister with disrespect. Then I'll march straight up to them and let them have it. No bloody fear.

So to know that I'd been the one to hurt her like that was horrible. I know drink is a problem for me, so I was extremely angry with myself for bottling up my feelings about her husband, only to get pissed and let them all out. How destructive! I should have had the guts a lot sooner to say, 'Listen, Linda, your husband is not good for our career because I just don't see how he and I are ever going to get along; we clash big time.'

Instead, I pretended everything was okay until I exploded, and then, BANG, my whole family was nearly torn apart. All because I was too afraid to speak up. I needed the demon drink to give me the courage to say something, and then it all came out in a much worse way than it should have.

I've only recently come to terms with my drinking. For years I was in denial, and it nearly destroyed all aspects of my life. I've been to AA (Alcoholics Anonymous) and NA (Narcotics Anonymous). The first NA meeting I attended was on the recommendation of a terrific therapist I was seeing. I went along reluctantly, thinking everyone would be fucked-up junkies who couldn't string two sentences together, but I discovered that they were some of the most coherent, funny and clever people I'd ever encountered.

I went to a few AA meetings but found that I couldn't go through with the twelve-step program. AA just wasn't for me, but I enjoyed listening to people's stories, even though their stories were a bit too close to home and hard to hear. But it was also a relief to know that I wasn't on my own. I wasn't the only one who acted like an idiot when they got horribly drunk, embarrassing themselves and being an utter nuisance. I loved how those programs were places where people could share.

I went to see a couple of therapists, and even though I enjoyed my visits with them, I found it too confronting to talk about myself for an hour. I knew what they were telling me made sense, but I couldn't go back. They told me that I'd relapse, and I did, because I couldn't stop. I loved the buzz that alcohol gave me, and the way drinking made me more relaxed in social situations. The fact that alcohol is always available in the business I'm in is great for a girl who never feels sure of herself. Great for a while anyway.

I can go for days – even weeks – without a drink, but once I start, well, I may as well go the whole way and really fuck myself up. This is something I've done many times. What's the saying? One's too many and a thousand's not enough? Well, that applies to me.

Hair of the dog always makes me feel better, or so I think, but, really, it's my destroyer because then I'll continue on for another day and do it all again. What a pain in the fucken arse I've been over the years. This is my new favourite saying: 'Pain in the fucken arse, that's me!'

I am slowly dealing with my demons because I know that my relationships matter more to me than alcohol, especially the one with my daughter. I want my kid to like me, and keep talking to me, and I'm only sorry it's taken me so long to grow up.

LINDA
Endings

By 2011, Vika had re-established her talents as a legal secretary and got work at a law firm, and I focused on running Hoochie Coochie and looking after my girls. The time I spent with them during this time was precious. I know now that had I been more successful during that period, I would have missed out on a special time in their lives – time I would never get back. In that respect, I'm grateful for my lack of direction over those years. Instead, I turned my energy onto my girls, which was a much better investment, and one I knew I would never regret.

Then I decided to leave my husband.

I was forty-three, with two kids, a shop and a singing career that had stalled, when I realised it was time to end my marriage. It wasn't just the financial risks he had taken or the escalating tensions between Vika and him at work, though they were stressful enough. I'd also learnt of his shocking betrayal – through friends, co workers and family – of me in our relationship, and that was the heartbreaking clincher for me. That was something I just couldn't live with, nor did I want my girls to grow up with a mother who would tolerate that treatment. So I left. I had to make this tough decision not only for my kids but also for myself. It took everything I had to get up and go. It was so terribly sad after twenty-three years together, but there was no other way.

My love life didn't turn out anything close to how I imagined it would. I know I wanted to find that same love and devotion my parents had for each other, and I've often wondered why the strong male figures I've had in my life didn't have more of an influence over the man I chose. Why didn't I choose a man like my dad?

After making the difficult decision to leave my husband, the next hardest thing was telling the girls. We knew that they would both be very upset, but I worried more about Nia, who was twelve years old and so would feel it much more. The timing couldn't have been worse for our eldest daughter. She was in the middle of Grade 6 and making the transition to high school. I never wanted to break my own daughter's heart, but when her father and I sat her down to tell her we were splitting up, I could see by the look on her face that this was exactly what we had just done. It felt like a hugely selfish move, hurting our beautiful girl and breaking up the family, but I could not be in that marriage any longer. Deep down I knew that I didn't love him anymore.

Once we told the girls, I knew I had to act swiftly to tidy up the financial side of things, which is a hard thing to do when you are so upset you can't see straight, but I had no choice. I wanted to keep my house, a house I had worked hard for, but that wasn't a realistic option because he had borrowed against it to fund his businesses, which went bust, and there was too much debt for me to handle on my own. As I was stressing about losing it, a good friend reminded me that it wasn't the house behind the photograph that was important, but the people inside it. Good point. My girls were my happiness, not the house.

I decided to sell up. My parents, my best friend from high school, EO and two other good friends, Polly and Bruce, all helped me get the house ready for sale. Vika and Johnny loaned me the money for a lawyer, and I got myself a good one. It was a very stressful time, but four months after I told my husband it was over, the house was sold, I had sorted out my finances and my kids and I were ready to move on to the next chapter.

Johnny and Dad got stuck into renovating the flat above Hoochie Coochie for me and the girls to live in, and they soon transformed a shitty old building into a beautiful home. It was so nice to move into such a lovely place after the shift in our circumstances. We'd gone from being a typical nuclear family, living in a beautifully renovated family home in a quiet street, to the three of us living above a rented shop on a busy main road. It was a huge adjustment for the kids to have to make, but they took it all in their stride and I believe it has only made them that much more resilient.

Staying in our North Fitzroy neighbourhood was a good move. We were still close to my family and friends, but I also had my independence. To be living above the place you work, as a single mum with two kids aged five and twelve, is very handy. There was no having to leave work early to tear around town, picking the kids up and dropping them off. They could just come home, dump their schoolbags and relax, while I kept working downstairs.

Nia studied hard, graduated from primary school, started at a new school and made new friends through all of this and she never once dropped the ball. She was incredible and, because she was old enough to prepare dinner and care for Kiki after school, she was a huge help to me. The three of us worked together as a team, which was ultimately a game changer for our relationships with each other. It's the reason we are all so close today – because we made it work when things were hard.

Apart from my amazing friends and customers, my beautiful dad wandered down to the shop to check on me every day. He'd buy four giant dim sims and two cappuccinos, then wait out the front of the shop until I was free to come out to drink my coffee, eat my two dim sims and talk with him. These talks helped me so much, but I'll never forget the taste combination of those dimmies and coffees. Ewww.

I was slowly discovering freedom on my own terms. Ending my marriage had been a hard decision to make, and even though it was a difficult time I knew I'd done the right thing. The only regret I had was hurting my children, but at least I was now raising my girls my way. The buck stopped with me, and now I just had to find a way to keep the bucks coming in!

CHANGES: ACT III

VIKA

My favourite singer

I was feeling a bit directionless in those years from 2006 to 2008 because Linda had decided to take a break from singing, so I stopped touring for a while and got back to doing some more regular, nine-to-five work. I thought having a day job and being home every night would give Mafi some stability, so I went back to secretary school to learn my way around a computer and get a job. While I was doing the course, I was also doing the odd solo gig here and there. One night I met a fella called John Wycherley at a gig in Sydney Road, Brunswick. John was a lawyer and a music lover. He'd shown up at our gigs every now and then over the years, and I eventually struck up a friendship with him.

John told me that he was a partner in a law firm called Moray and Agnew. I mentioned I was doing a refresher course and brushing up on skills so I could find a job and be at home with Mafi.

'When you've finished the course, come and see me,' he said.

And that's exactly what I did. On my last day of school, I rang

John, went into Moray and Agnew for an interview, and got myself a job. I started working five days a week but kept doing the odd singing gig here and there. There was no way I was ever going to permanently hang up my boots.

I enjoyed working at the law firm. There were really lovely people there, all the support staff and the lawyers, who helped me a lot. I'll forever be indebted to them, especially because they let me go on tour whenever someone called for a backing singer, then return to my job afterwards. I worked with a team in the personal injury area, and it was fascinating, but eventually I found the confines of working within office walls too restricting. I loved being home with Mafi, but my passion was singing. After two years working there, I knew that I had to leave and return to my first love.

I've never been a big fan of musical theatre, but around this time I got the call to join that world. This was a call I was never expecting, and one I had to think long and hard about because I was being offered the chance to be part of a show about my favourite singer, Etta James. Etta had only passed away three months earlier, in January 2012, and so when I heard there was going to be a show about her, the first thing I thought was, Jesus, the poor woman isn't even cold in her grave and everyone is already out to make a buck!

I'd auditioned for musicals in the past, including *The Lion King* and *We Will Rock You*, but had gone along very underprepared. I had no idea what was expected of me because I never went to one of those exciting performing arts schools where you learn how to sing, act and dance. My mum taught me to sing, but I had no clue how to act, so of course I never got any of those parts. But it never bothered me because I never wanted to be a musical theatre kind of singer. I wanted to be a rock'n'roll singer – raw, rough and ready. That's why I fell in love with Etta James, because she was all those things. Before I heard Etta, my idol had been Aretha (still is). But when I heard Etta, the earth fucken shook!

Etta was a great singing teacher, as all those black singers were. My singing teachers, apart from Mum, were Aretha, Etta and Ruth Brown. They were all on high rotation in my house. I'd sing along to those gals day and night, until I was blue in the face. I reckon I was born in the wrong era, because the stuff I was hearing on the radio back then was fantastic, but not as fantastic as those women, as far as I was concerned.

So, when I got the call to do *At Last: The Etta James Story*, my first instinct was, Oh God, a musical? No, not interested. But when they said it would just be me and a band, telling Etta's story and singing her songs, I gave it a bit more thought.

I knew it would be a big ask to have one person singing all those songs. Etta had a big career and could sing a lot of styles, like R&B, rock'n'roll, jazz, funk, blues, soul, gospel and country. Hells bells, whoever did this show was gonna get crucified! But after thinking long and hard about it, I decided I was up for the challenge.

Joe Camilleri is the man responsible for me getting that call. He was approached about being the musical director for the show and he said to the producers, 'You're gonna ask Vika to do this, aren't you?'

I don't think I'd even entered their brains before that, so thank you, Joe.

Once I'd decided to take on this massive task, I got started on the research, and there was a lot to do. I wasn't worried about the singing part of the show, except for jazz, because I knew a lot of her repertoire. But we had very different voices. Hers was richer, deeper, and told the story of a life lived. I can belt too, but my voice is higher and can be a little harsh on the ears. Also, my life was nowhere near as tough as hers. It was downright cushy in comparison!

I started to dig a little deeper into Etta's life. Linda bought me her autobiography, *Rage to Survive*, and it was a brilliant read. What a life! After reading that book, I understood why she could sing so well, and I fell even more in love with Etta James. I also watched lots of interviews and concerts on the internet because I'd never been lucky enough to see her sing live. I was fascinated by the twinkle I noticed in her eye when she was performing, and she seemed like really good fun, and very naughty. I could relate!

But how was I going to portray this woman? Etta was very sexual and would do the most outrageous things on stage. She was known for being an openly sexual performer, always was, and could make a grown man blush! I have heard stories from people who saw her live and told me that sometimes her performances were so sexual – tongue gestures, gyrating hips – that they didn't know where to look. There was no way I was gonna do that kind of stuff.

CHANGES: ACT III

No way! I wouldn't be able to carry that off! Etta had also been to hell and back. I watched an interview with her on YouTube and when the interviewer said she'd had a roller-coaster of a life, Etta said, 'You just gotta take it, fall down, get back up, brush yourself off and keep going, and I love the highs and the lows. I think that's put some fat on my head!'

BRILLIANT! I thought. Damn, this woman is super cool.

When I received the script, it was so thick that I nearly died. I can learn songs and lyrics no problem, but a whole script? Then I realised that all the lyrics to all the songs were in there too, and once I'd separated the songs from the actual dialogue, the script was a little less daunting. I was still nervous about the acting part, though. I'd never done anything like that in my life. I could ad lib on stage and talk to the audience, but this was different. I had to tell someone's life story, and not just anyone, but my favourite singer. It was going to be tough, and what made it even tougher was that she had only just passed away, and her children were still alive. Yeah, she had her demons, and some really shit times, but I wanted my performance to be a celebration of who she was, because she overcame all of that. She picked herself up, brushed herself off and kept doing what she loved, right up until she died.

Oh shit! I thought. What have I got myself into? I can't act, I've never narrated and this whole theatre thing is totally foreign to me. Do I sing the songs true to the originals, or give them my own spin? And how am I going to remember everything? I'd need an elephant-sized brain. I am *fucked*!

But then it occurred to me that this was theatre. It was very different to the rock'n'roll world. Here, I had directors to help me work on everything. They'd tell me what to do, where to stand and how to deliver the lines. This realisation instantly made me feel better, and when I met Tibor Gyapjas, the man who'd be onstage helping me tell the story, I felt even better about everything. Tibor is also a fantastic trumpet player, so he'd be playing in the band too, and what a lovely fella he is. A real lad. Tibor is an all-round good bloke who loves a laugh and loves to party and, damn, can he blow that horn! We clicked immediately.

Joe didn't end up being musical director after all, so John McAll, a fantastic pianist and brilliant musician, stepped in. Together, we hand-picked our musicians, and ended up with a fantastic band. I already had my rhythm section picked out, and John chose the horn players. In the end we had Watto, my husband, on drums; Chris Bekker on bass; Dion Hirini on guitar; Tibor on trumpet; Ben Gillespie on trombone and Remco Keijzer on saxophone. Remco was subsequently replaced by Anton Delecca, and sometimes we used other fill-in players on the saxophone if Anton wasn't available.

It was a great band that could play all styles of music, and what a luxury it was to have horns. I love a horn section, and like all Tongans, I love a brass band. Who doesn't? The only condition John had regarding the players was that he could have a laugh with them, and, my God, laugh we did for the next five years. John should be a comedian, and most nights I nearly pissed my pants, but when he played that piano, damn, he was a serious mutha!

It took twelve months from the time I was offered the role to opening night. I felt like that was a respectful amount of time since Etta's passing. I would have to get match fit, so I was glad to have that much time to learn the lines and the songs. I didn't want to stuff it up but knew I probably would the first couple of rehearsals.

Narrating is hard. Narrating as well as singing is harder. You go from singing to speaking, to singing again, and when you're doing Etta's material, most of the singing is very powerful. I can't act, so thank God I didn't have to. I just had to tell Etta's story. John Livings wrote the script. John is a very funny guy and he added his own sense of humour to lighten the story a little. Etta sure had some story to tell and doing that, as well as fitting in twenty-three songs, all in the space of an hour and forty-five minutes, is no easy task.

We sat down with the producers and agreed on what songs to sing. There were so many, so where to begin? Etta's career spanned over sixty years, so there was a lot of discussion. I had my favourites and tried to avoid the jazz part of her career, but it wasn't possible. One of Etta's mother's favourite singers was Billie Holiday, and Etta dedicated a record of Billie's songs to her mother, Dorothy. *Mystery Lady* won Etta a Grammy in 1995 for Best Jazz Vocal Album, so we had to include a couple of jazz songs. Those songs became m' favourites to sing in the whole show.

Once we'd decided on the songs, I spent a lot of time learni my lines. God, that was hard, because while I was singing the so

I was thinking about the next line I had to say. What a mindfuck! The producers enlisted some wonderful people to help me with the delivery of these lines, and even my good mate Julia Zemiro tried to help, but I'm just not a natural. That's when I realised how great actors are at what they do, and how natural they make it look. I was intimidated by the actors' talent, especially Julia, who is so switched on and funny. Mum helped me with my lines too, but we spent most of the time in fits of laughter because of her Tongan accent. Mum was eager to help, because after reading Etta's book twice, she was in love with her too.

I did a lot of work independently too, especially on the music side of things and learning the songs. I wasn't worried about the band because they were all guns. The first time we stepped into the rehearsal room and they played 'Tell Mama', I burst into tears because they were tough and that's exactly what was required. No messin' about. I'd decided to try to sing the songs as true to the original versions as possible, but Etta did a lot of different versions of some songs, and not all members of the band had learned the same versions. This was a little frustrating, but they were so good at what they did that it was never really a problem, again. Once the band had all the music down, there was a thing called the 'underscore', which was when someone played instruments while Tibor and I delivered the dialogue. I hated the underscore because it was so distracting. Sometimes, it was a tinker on the piano, or sometimes it was bass and a drum or guitar.

CHANGES: ACT III

'Fuck!' I said to John McAll one day. 'Do they really need to do that?'

'Yes, Vika, they do,' he said. 'Otherwise, you'll always be delivering your lines in silence, which will sound a little dull. This gives the story some dramatics. Some light and shade.'

John was always good at talking me round, and he always seemed to get his way. But that's because he was usually right.

While it took a good nine months to learn all the material, we didn't have much time rehearsing the show as a whole. Before we started our season at the Melbourne Athenaeum, the producers booked three warm-up shows at the Clocktower theatre in Essendon. Phew! I thought. That will give me a chance to stuff things up in front of a small audience before we do the show for real. No such luck because they sold out every single warm-up show. Damn!

There was no budget for costumes, so I had to buy my own and the producers didn't seem to mind what I wore. I'm not a fussy person, and as much as I've learned to embrace fashion over the years, I don't have the patience for it and I'm not good at it. Not like my sister. I'm a tracksuit kinda gal, so when it came to Etta's costumes, I thought I'd just buy a couple of wiggle dresses, like gals wore in the 50s. Not flowing, but tight, and that would do me. My outfit wasn't my priority, the singing was. Lookin back, I wish I'd taken more time to think about my costume know Linda would have.

Rehearsing is one thing but doing it live is another. The ne soul, and she studied them with more energy and passion than anything she ever had at school. That style of singing was already a part of her DNA when she was offered the chance to play Etta, but Vika was concerned that theatre was too foreign a world for her.

She was a nervous wreck about the script she had to memorise but worked incredibly hard for over a year to prepare for the show that would honour the memory of her favourite singer. And it paid off. I went along with the rest of our family to Vika's opening night at the Clocktower in Essendon in February 2013. In my completely unbiased sisterly opinion, Vika completely nailed that role and I was beyond proud of her.

The only drawback for me was knowing that when the rest of the world saw how good Vika was in theatre, she was going to be busy for a long time. The show had 'legs', as they say in the business, and I realised that I'd better find a way of making a living on my own for a little while. That little while turned out to be seven years. It was the first time since we started singing together that Vika and I would be apart. This was a confronting time for me because, although I understood this was important part of her development as a more rounded entertainer, without Vika, I thought I didn't have a singing career. My singing life came to a grinding halt. I was stagnant.

I admit there was a moment at the very beginning when I wondered why the producers of *At Last* hadn't thought of including me in the show somehow. I knew it would be good for Vik to take centre stage without her little sister tagging along for once, but the decision to exclude me was a big wake-up call. I realised that I'd better pull up my socks and start defining myself in my own way. In other words, I didn't want to be left behind. I perform best when I'm under pressure, and the pressure was coming from where it usually came from – within myself. So, after acknowledging, then parking, my damaged ego, I got busy going about my life, and trying to find out who I was outside of music.

With Vika out touring the world, I thanked God for my beloved Hoochie Coochie. If not for the shop, I would have been screwed financially. Vik was very generous, though, always coming back and spoiling my girls if they needed anything I couldn't buy them. Whenever Vika was back in town my girls would be high-fiving one another with excitement at what they might get, and she and I would do the odd singing gig together, either on our own or with Paul Kelly. He always had an eye out for us.

Meanwhile, I was loving my new neighbourhood. I soon realised that when we moved into the flat about Hoochie Coochie, we'd become part of a strip of shops with an amazing community. The owners and the staff at all the various shops were wonderful people, as well as the many colourful characters who lived in North Fitzroy back then. These people were to become an important part of our lives, because they all had a hand in raising my kids. One of them owned the cafe next door to us. His name was Ian.

The first time I saw Ian, he was helping Vika wind up the awning on our shop window. Ian is hard to miss, at six foot four in his preferred footwear of thongs, and he loves to laugh. It was this laugh that I heard even before seeing him that day. Ian has a laugh that would bounce off the walls of every shop in the village on a daily basis, before eventually reaching my ears in Hoochie Coochie. The sound of it made me smile. Ian had seen Vika and me sing years earlier and had wanted to meet me afterward, but his friend talked him out of it. So he already knew who I was when I walked into his cafe to introduce myself.

I liked him straight away. He was not only tall but handsome and had such kind eyes. His mountainous size reminded me of my Tongan cousins. He and his partner had just had a baby girl together and the cafe was their new business, so it was an exciting time for them all. When I first saw Amelie with her mum in front of the cafe, I felt happy to see new faces on the strip.

Ian and I found it very easy to talk and joke around with each other, so we quickly became friends. Like me, Ian could chat until the cows came home, so if the shop was quiet, or when he brought me a coffee, we would always talk. I was impressed by how hard he worked, and how quickly he turned that business around. It was also good for my business if his cafe did well and brought in a lot of customers.

There were a bunch of us in the neighbourhood who loved getting together to chat in the street after a long day on our feet. Being part of the North Fitzroy neighbourhood reminded me of the Botanic Drive Gang, and the way we'd all hang out together after school. As the kids grew, they got to know so many people, as well as customers, retailers and friendly passers-by. It was a great way for the kids to become involved in their community, and for me to meet people who were outside the music industry. I loved watching my girls' confidence growing as they chatted with strangers in the shop every day, or in the street outside.

Everyone in my strip knew I was going through a divorce, and they were so good to me. I was a mess and worn out by the stress of it all. My girls were home from school a lot because of the drama of the separation. Money was very tight, and it was hard. We went without a lot of the time. Some days it felt like I was just holding it together, but the kindness of my friends and staff kept me sane. Ian was especially kind. He would sit me down out front of the shop at various times during the day to make me stop, rest and take a breath. He'd hand me a coffee or a beer, and tell me some silly joke to make me laugh, which always fuelled me to get back in the shop and keep going. Considering Ian was going through his own problems at the time, he was incredibly sweet to me, but I didn't know anything about that then.

A year after my divorce, I learned that Ian had split from his partner. Too many beers and a couple of wines later, we ended up together and, halfway through that first night, he fell and somersaulted down my stairs. I heard the almighty fall and thought, Oh God, I'm going to find him lying at the bottom of the stairs, dead, with bones sticking out, and then I'm going to go to jail for killing him and my kids will have no mum for the next twenty years! Just my luck that I've killed the first guy I've brought home after being married for twenty-three years!

I rushed out to find him at the bottom of my death-defying staircase, rubbing his head, with blood gushing out of a gash the size of my hand. Luckily for Ian, he was pissed and so his rag doll fall saved him. I got him cleaned up and he went home nursing sixty-eight bruises and a sore ego.

That was our first date.

Nobody knew that we were seeing each other because I wanted to take it slowly for my kids' sake, as did he. But that all changed one day when my kids came home and found three-year-old Amelie sitting on the end of Kiki's bed, watching TV. Amelie was a gorgeous kid, with her curly hair and sad little eyes, and the three of us had fallen in love with her the moment we met her. Ian and I told the girls we were seeing each other, and Kiki and Amelie soon became inseparable, as did Ian and I.

We laughed a lot together and spent every Friday night hanging out with our kids. This became a ritual over the next eight years. Kiki and Amelie were as close as sisters, and even looked like siblings. It seemed like a weirdly easy blending of families, because now Kiki had Amelie. When I was too tired to cook, Ian would feed us, and he looked after Kiki a lot if I was away singing. He taught them how to ride skateboards, igniting a passion in them for cars, 80s and 90s hip hop, rugby league, AFL, the Big Bash, James Bond and Bunnings sausages. Ian went to every one of Kiki's school plays, as well as her graduation, and they were very close. They have a lot in common: they're both Pisces, outgoing and friendly, while Amelie and I are both Virgos and very alike. Ian genuinely loves my girls, and Kiki looked to him as a father.

After my divorce, alongside my own family, I have Ian to thank for being my bestfriend and support right when I needed it. Even now we talk talk every day, and I couldn't have gotten through all that without him.

VIKA

Marvin

It seemed that I was now the go-to gal for theatrical producers because soon after the first leg of the *Etta James Story* finished, I found myself learning the script and songs for *Let's Get It On: The Life and Music of Marvin Gaye*. I was brought on board to sing the parts of Tammi Terrell, Diana Ross and Kim Weston, who all did great duets with Marvin. I found out later that I stole the job from a terrific little Melbourne gal, who had a ripper voice but was more suited to a Carole King–type show. It was a pretty dodgy move by the producers, bringing me in to sing a couple of songs when the other girl was already doing them and singing all the parts, and we were both in the show for a couple of nights there until I took on the role. I know she was very upset at losing the part and felt bad about that, but I wasn't going to turn down such a great opportunity.

Once again, I had to learn dialogue and more songs, but was much less worried about that after having done the Etta James show for so long. I was now into the swing of all things theatre and

Linda: I was thrilled for Vika when her career blossomed into musical theatre. Here she's in London, touring the wonderful *At Last: The Etta James Story* with our late, great friend Dion Hirini.

Our renaissance in the 2010s came thanks to a couple of lifelines: SBS TV's *Rockwiz* and Paul Kelly, who has always supported us and been incredibly generous sharing the stage.

(*Right*) With Michael Franti and Julia Zemiro on the set of *Rockwiz*.

(*Below*) Our 'Rising Moon' moves at Riverstage, Brisbane, with Paul Kelly and band. (*Credit: Stephen Booth*)

(*Top*) Getting down to business with Frank Stivala (*left*), our agent, Lisa Palermo, and Joe Camilleri.

(*Middle*) Just a pic we love, taken in 2014 by our lifelong friend, photographer Tania Jovanovic.

(*Bottom*) In action at the Sidney Myer Music Bowl with Paul Kelly's Making Gravy show in 2019. (*Credit: Lisa Businovski*)

(*Above left*) The late, legendary Chris Wilson supported us from the beginning. We miss him dearly. (*Credit: Tania Jovanovic*)

(*Above right*) Backstage at the Sidney Myer Music Bowl, 2021, carrying on our matching-outfit tradition with our manager, Lisa. (*Credit: Lisa Businovski*)

(*Below*) Backstage with the gorgeous Kasey Chambers at Bluesfest.

(*Above*) Holding our notes and trying to hold it together in front of 100,000 people at the MCG for the AFL Grand Final in 2016. (*Credit: Julian Smith/AAP*)

(*Below*) A very happy day indeed with the A-team from Mushroom Records at the digital streaming launch of *'Akilotoa* in the depths of Melbourne's lockdown (with special permits), at Bakehouse Studios, June 2020. *From left*: Vika, Dean McLachlan, Lisa Palermo, Bill Page, Warren Costello, Linda. (*Credit: Tania Jovanovic*)

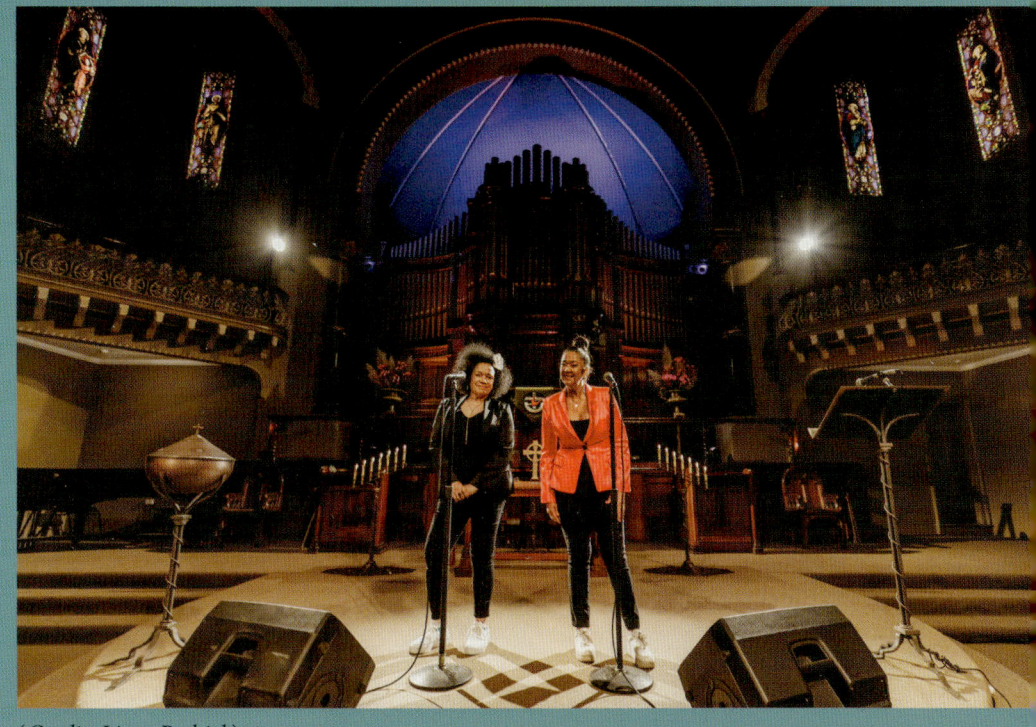

(Credit: Liam Pethick)

During the pandemic, our industry saviour in our hour of need was Michael Gudinski (*left*). It was his idea for us to film 'Jesus on the Mainline' at St Michael's Uniting Church in Melbourne for *The Sound* on ABC TV. Michael was another great man sadly lost too soon.

(Credit: Lisa Palermo)

Inducted into the Music Victoria Hall of Fame in 2019. Whoop! (Credit: Martin Philbey)

In 2020, social media became our new best friend. Who knew it could be so powerful?! Much to our surprise, we have had over eight million views for our parody song 'Iso City Limits', and we just loved hosting our Sunday Sing Songs as a way of staying connected with people during the lockdowns (and of keeping our own spirits up). (*Credit for images across this spread: Lisa Palermo*)

(*Left*) Celebrating our ARIA number one for our career anthology '*Akilotoa*, released in 2020 on the wave of our Sunday Sing Song sessions, and our first ever number-one record. The feedback we get about having helped to lift spirits during difficult times just means the world to us.

(*Below*) We released *The Wait*, our first original album in nearly two decades, in 2021 and it hit number two on the charts. Not bad for a couple of fifty-somethings, eh?

After a few more instances of life getting in the way, we eventually got to tour *The Wait*.

(*Above*) With our fabulous band, the Bullettes, before our headline show at Melbourne's Palais Theatre in August 2022. *Back row from left:* Lachlan O'Kane, Ben Edgar, Richard Bradbeer, Cameron Bruce, Ben Hauptmann. *Front row from left:* Vika, Susie Goble, Lisa Palermo, Hailey Cramer, Linda. (*Credit: Lisa Businovski*)

(*Left*) Backstage with the rock that is our family. (*Credit: Liam Pethick*)

We feel so lucky to have the support of all these people.

understood how these shows worked. I knew from reading Etta's book that Marvin sang backing vocals on some of her early stuff. They toured together in the early days, and Etta knew that he was moody, shy and had some troubles. I've always loved Marvin Gaye – the Prince of Motown and Prince of Soul – and knew he had a sad, tragic story, but I didn't realise just how messed up his father had made him.

As I read the script, I learned that although he was a very talented man, Marvin had many demons. It's strange how so many great singers have these 'been to hell and back' stories of trauma, and not all of them were able to make it out. It's heartbreaking, but I believe this pain and hardship are part of what makes them so great.

The show cast three different men to play Marvin for the duration of the run. Marvin is a hard sing and has a heavy story to tell, so it's not an easy role to play. Singing the show with three different leading men was tricky for me too because I had to find a different rhythm with each one. Some were better story-tellers than singers, and some were better singers than story-tellers.

The first time I did the show, it was alongside Bert LaBonté – a very talented Australian actor and singer. My role was to step in and start singing, and telling, Marvin's story. Bert and I rehearsed together quite a bit. He was brilliant and helped me so much with the delivery of my lines, which, as we all know, is not my strength.

The most interesting Marvin Gaye I met was when we did the show in Johannesburg. I was excited at the prospect of going to South Africa. I'd never dreamed I'd be lucky enough to visit the homeland of the great man Nelson Mandela. I was slightly apprehensive because some people had told me it wasn't the safest country to visit, but I was very excited too. Our flight was basically empty and I took this as a sign that South Africa might not be too high on people's holiday destination list. The only people on our plane were a few people returning home, me and the band, who included John McAll on piano, Travis Clarke on bass, Haydn Meggitt on drums and Josh Owen on guitar.

South Africa is a beautiful country, but as we drove through Hillbrow it was obvious it wasn't a safe area. I soon learned that Hillbrow is one of the most dangerous places to live on the planet, and the poverty there was heartbreaking to see.

When we arrived at the hotel in Johannesburg, I was advised not to venture off anywhere on my own. I was also told that I would be escorted to and from the theatre, even though it was only 100 metres from where we were staying. This ended up being very expensive because I had to make four trips to and from the theatre every day, and each walk cost me ten bucks in tips for my escort. I didn't have to tip but wanted to because they were doing me a favour and didn't make a hell of a lot of money.

South Africa was very cheap overall, including the alcohol, but I'd decided not to drink on this tour. I knew I'd been given an amazing opportunity and I didn't want to risk messing it up in any way, especially in front of a new audience, so no booze for me. I also had to be in the best voice possible. Good thing I made this decision because I was about to meet a fella who could sing the phone book and dance like Michael Jackson.

My leading man in South Africa was a Zulu man, Lloyd Cele, who was runner-up in the TV show *Idols South Africa*. Lloyd had been working on the script with the director for a couple of weeks before I arrived and was not shy in coming forward. He made some great suggestions for how to change the script for a South African audience so it would be more relatable. He was confident, lovely and a little puzzled as to why he would be doing this show with an Australian girl when there were probably plenty of well-known local girls who could sing these parts standing on their heads.

We performed the show at the Joburg Theatre and would be using some local horn players to fill out the band. These guys were amazing and a good hang.

The great thing about doing shows in different countries is experiencing different kinds of audiences. South African audiences are fun and wild, full of beautiful black faces and the best dressed people I've ever performed for. And they all have their iPads and iPhones out during the show, filming everything. At one of the shows, a woman sat right up the front and filmed the whole show on her iPad. I don't think she looked away from her screen once to watch what was happening right in front of her on stage. And noisy? Man, those people are not shy. They whooped, sang, danced and swooned over Lloyd throughout the whole show. I felt like a spare prick at a wedding because it was clear they were there for one thing, and one thing only – to hear

Lloyd Cele sing Marvin Gaye.

But the highlight of the whole trip was the night when Lloyd got a whole bunch of kids to jump up on stage and dance to 'Got to Give It Up'. About twenty of them got up and all started dancing the exact same moves. It was an extraordinary sight to behold. All those kids in sync with one another, not a single one of them out of step, doing moves like the electric slide, and they all had rhythm. It looked like they'd known these moves their whole lives, and it was so beautiful I cried.

I did the Marvin show for a few years, and sometimes the shows overlapped with the *Etta James Story*. In fact, I remember flying home from South Africa and immediately doing an Etta show. Once we were back in Oz, the lead role of Marvin Gaye went to Andrew De Silva, an amazing singer from a Melbourne group called CDB. Again, we all spent a week rehearsing with Andrew, and Australian audiences loved the show, but weren't nearly as passionate as those screaming South African girls!

LINDA
Phoenix rising

When I look back at that doldrums period in the early 2000s, I can see that it served both Vika and me well for different reasons. We both achieved significant milestones in our lives outside of our comfort zones, personally and professionally.

For me, it was a complete change in lifestyle, and I felt like I had shed my old skin and was starting again. I had a new home, a new job at the shop and different friends. I was travelling further and further away from my life as a singer. Seeing Vik out there doing it in those shows, and on her own, made me feel worse about how valid I was, but that doesn't mean I wasn't happy for her. I had made a choice to step back from singing, so I had to live with that decision and make the most of it.

I felt comforted by the fact that Vika and I always had such a strong bond, which meant we would never want to see the other fail. So, while I mainly watched on from the sidelines, whenever we did sing together at the occasional gig I still felt the same way I always did. Happy. There's never been any other job in my life where I've felt as happy as I am when I'm standing beside Vika and singing, and even during that period it felt so easy and right, like we hadn't quite finished what we'd set out to do. I think those doldrum periods are very important when you have long careers like ours because they make you stronger, and more confident that you can survive the down times.

In 2011 Paul Kelly threw us a lifeline (which I didn't even realise then that I needed and wanted). He was preparing to do a show called *Meet Me in the Middle of the Air* with pianist Paul Grabowsky. The show was going to be a reimagining of some of his most famous songs and would be led by the two Pauls, along with the Australian Art Orchestra. It would open at the Sydney Opera House, followed by two shows at Hamer Hall in Melbourne.

PK approached Vika and me and asked if we wanted to share

the lead vocals with him, as well as do backing vocals. I was not sure I was up to the challenge. I don't read music or play an instrument and, let's face it, it would be a big jump to go from running a little shop to singing onstage at the Opera House. Also, this gig would be different to what I was used to. It involved complicated chart arrangements, cues and heavyweight jazz musicians. I was nervous and not just because I felt a little rusty, but because of the scale of the show and the immense popularity of the two Pauls. But in the end I said yes, as did Vik, because I really missed singing. Also, it was PK. If he asked, we were never going to say no.

The prep for the *Meet Me in the Middle of the Air* shows was a test for me. I had to work all day, look after the girls, then stay up all night getting my head around the Grabowsky arrangements. What I found most difficult was trying to think of new ways to sing Paul's songs, because they were based around a biblical theme. I was given the job of singing mostly ballads, songs like the haunting 'My Way Is to You' and 'The Gift That Keeps on Giving'. They were my favourites. I felt pretty intimidated by the two Pauls, but had a crack anyway. Thank God I did because doing that show rekindled my passion for singing, and reminded me how much I had missed it. It was a turning point in my career.

Not long after this, PK asked us to join his band in a more permanent role, which meant loads more touring. Saying yes to Paul changed my course; I started to feel like I could see the path back to a regular working life in music again. Nia was used to seeing me disappear regularly, but Kiki, Ian and Amelie were not. It was hardest on Nia, who was thirteen at the time, and Ian, because they had to do the heavy lifting, like cooking and being there after school for six-year-old Kiki. Mum and Dad were in their mid-seventies by then but they were also onboard and helping out, so I wasn't worried about leaving the girls. I felt a bit guilty that my parents were still having to look after my kids when they could have been travelling the country in their caravan, but I was also happy because I knew my girls were in safe hands.

It was a hectic time, but I loved working with Vik and PK. I loved the camaraderie we shared with PK and everyone in the band – Bill McDonald, Ashley Naylor, Cameron Bruce, Peter Luscombe and Dan Kelly – as well as the crew. I had a massive soft spot for Greg Weaver, Paul's long-time tour manager and front-of-house sound engineer. All of us, band and crew, had a special connection right from the start, and it's a bond that is as beautiful and special to me now as it was eleven years ago.

Without my ex in the picture, my relationship with Vik was good, and during 2011 the phone started to ring again with offers for gigs. This time around we made the decision to manage ourselves because at that point there wasn't enough going on to justify paying someone. This made life a hell of a lot easier.

Jumping on board PK's ship reminded people in the industry that we were both lead and backing singers because Paul always graciously gave us a chance to show off both talents. He might have copped it from those who wanted to hear him, not us, singing his songs, but he stood firm, sharing his huge audience and stage with us. We will forever be grateful to Paul for his generosity and belief in us, then and always. He's one of the true, real friends in our lives.

Peter Luscombe, another true friend, asked us to join the RocKwiz Orchestra in 2013, which was another game changer. *RocKwiz* was a very successful music trivia TV show, hosted by Julia Zemiro and Brian Nankervis. Vika and I had both appeared on *RocKwiz* separately as guests over the years, and we adored the *RocKwiz* family. They were our type of people.

Saying yes to joining the *RocKwiz* band was a no brainer, and the weekly filming for TV was a new world for both of us and one we embraced wholeheartedly. Not only did we get to spend hours on end with both Julia and Brian, but we were given a front-row seat to a masterclass in 'How to be a professional actor, comedian and television presenter'. Those two made our lives on that show so easy and we laughed a lot! We were already huge fans of them both and I was soon in awe of the amount of work, focus and grit Julia put in to that job. She taught me that in order to make something look easy, you have to drill right down to the details, because when you are under pressure, all sorts of things can go wrong. If you're prepared, you stand a much better chance of everything going right. Whenever I think of professionalism when I'm on a job, I always think of Julia. She raised the bar on pre-game focus, and Vika and I learned so much from her. I loved that she was an intelligent, beautiful, kick-arse woman in control. Every time she walked out on that stage, she made the whole country swoon with admiration for her talent. Us included.

Then there's Brian. I mean, is it possible to squeeze an ounce more charisma into one man? One of the many things I love about Brian is how well he knows and is passionate about his music. His interest in music is genuine. He also knows how to switch it on and make good TV, which is priceless, but he's always been the same gorgeous man offstage too. Brian is a true gentleman and I've never once seen him lose his cool, even during times when we all wanted to scream. I loved watching him rev up the audience, and they loved him. His energy and love for *RocKwiz* were infectious, which was why he and Julia made such a good team. They both respected and adored their jobs, and always put the audience first. That's why *RocKwiz* worked. It was about music nerds from normal life, and they were the stars of the show. Julia, Brian, the band and crew were all there to make the panellists on the show the focus, not the other way round, and that's what appealed to me the most.

RocKwiz came along at a great time for us, because doing that show was a gruelling excavation of our roots as backing singers, and we needed that. My motto is: 'If you want to get good, get busy learning everything you can', and here we were, in our mid-forties, doing what we did in our mid-twenties, but this time it was in front of a TV audience. If we stuffed up, we stuffed up in front of a LOT of people, and we did stuff up a couple of times early on, so the pressure was on. Luckily, Vika and I are okay under pressure but, unfortunately, I'm very bad at hiding it. When I stuff up, you can see it all over my face. I either look straight at Vik, or pull a face or, worse, stop singing altogether. That's usually a dead giveaway, especially on TV.

We now found ourselves part of a new band too, led by James Black on piano and guitars, our old Black Sorrows compadre Peter Luscombe on drums, and Mark Ferrie (of the Models) on bass. Later on, after James Black left, Clio Renner and Ash Naylor joined the band, adding another spring in our step. Ashley can play any song you throw at him and his musical knowledge is incredible. They were a great unit and could pretty much play any song in any style, so they were a dream team. Every week, for three years, Vika and I rocked up to the Espy, our folders full of lyrics and songs to learn for that week's show. The songs covered a whole range of different genres, so we were constantly broadening our knowledge, and we got the chance to sing with some of the most respected singers around, both established and emerging. We had to sing everything and, depending on who the lead guest was, in any key. Sometimes we felt like our heads might explode with the sheer number of things we had to remember, but it was exactly what we needed to get our 'chops' back, and to fine-tune our backing vocal skills. As Julia had taught us, we were getting prepared.

This job was a huge jump for us because suddenly we had three massive lines of exposure to big audiences – *Etta*, PK and *RocKWiz*. TV is a strange beast. You can work your arse off for years in pubs and clubs, and think you're making headway, then someone will walk up to you in the street and say, 'Oh, I remember you! I love you guys! Are you still singing?' The same cannot be said for television. The moment your mug is on the telly, heaps of people see you, and I immediately noticed the jump in recognition when I was out in public. The 'What are you up to?' chitchat with locals in my supermarket took a turn. Suddenly, everyone knew what I was up to. It was weird, but that is the power of television.

I also started to notice that our crowds were increasing by a noticeable number. The penny soon dropped – it was because of Vik's Etta show. Punters who had loved her performance, and were curious about my sister, had started coming along to her own shows. All of her hard work was paying off, and we were both benefiting from it. Vika always said that if she did well, then we as a team did well, and she was right. I was incredibly appreciative of that.

The busier I got with my singing career, the harder it became to run the shop. Thank goodness for my loyal friends Georgie and Alison. They ran the shop for me, as did all the beautiful women who worked there, saving me and my business.

Dad was worried about me too, and concerned I was burning the candle at both ends, even though he had enough to worry about at that time. He had recently been diagnosed with cancer, which had shocked us all and hit Mum incredibly hard. When they got the news, Mum sat around the house for a week doing nothing, something she has never done before in her life. I could see her gathering her almighty willpower during that time. It was like she was psyching herself up to care for him.

Dad was his usual laid-back self about it all. He took the diagnosis in his stride and seemed resigned to the fact that it might get him. I remember him saying, 'Oh well, love. I've had a good run!'

But Mum basically said, 'You're not done yet!' and swung into nursing action.

While he was having chemotherapy, she put him to bed and in-home quarantine. If we wanted to see him, she made us all stand outside his bedroom window so we couldn't infect him with our 'mangy bugs', because 'God knows where we'd been!'

She brought every meal to him in bed on a tray, fattening him up, and forcing him to drink lots of water instead of his usual cordial and cups of tea. Dad is bald anyway, so losing his hair wasn't a problem, but Mum was taking such good care of him that his hair actually grew, and he had to have two haircuts, which gave us a good giggle during a very dark time. Vika and I are still cacking ourselves about that. Dad needing to get a haircut was unheard of, and also a very good sign. Six months later he was given a thumbs up from his doc. He'd beaten cancer!

But during those early days of his diagnosis, Dad pulled me aside one night after a long day of working in the shop, followed by a long night singing, and suggested it might be time to choose one or the other. He and Mum always knew when it was time to give me good advice, especially when times were tough.

I sat there and gave some serious thought to Dad's advice. As much as I loved my shop and community, I knew that singing was the life I really wanted. Singing was in my blood, and nothing gave me as much joy as when I was singing with Vika. I didn't want to waste any more time either. I was forty-four, and believed the clock was ticking on my career. In that moment, sitting quietly with my dad and looking into his beautiful face, which was showing signs of rigorous chemotherapy, I chose to go with my heart and sell the shop.

It was September 2016 and I'd had Hoochie Coochie for almost ten years to the day. I found the perfect new owner, Kirsti, which made me feel happier to let go of the leash. Dad always told me that when you remove or change one big thing in your life, that shift can have huge consequences. For me this shift in direction created space for the right opportunities to fall into place, as well as a very important person to come into our lives. Enter Lisa Palermo.

VIKA

Carole King

In 2017, I was asked to work with one of Australia's leading ladies, Debra Byrne, in a tribute show to Carole King's album *Tapestry*. I was starting to grow a little tired of doing the narrative-style concert by this point but singing onstage with Debra was an opportunity I didn't want to miss. During act one we performed the *Tapestry* album in order, from start to finish, and in act two we performed songs penned by Carole King and her partner Gerry Goffin, made famous by others. *Tapestry* was released when I was five years old, so I was too young for it to be the 'soundtrack of my youth', as I've heard many people say over the years. However, I did know every song on that record because years earlier I'd done a *Tapestry* show with Linda, Jenny Morris and Jodi Phillis. That was when I first discovered the brilliance of Carole King.

When you're involved in a show like *Tapestry*, you are given the chance to really explore the singer/songwriter's catalogue. Carole King is not just a great singer but a brilliant songwriter too. I discovered how many songs of hers I had loved without knowing she'd written them. Songs like: 'It Might as Well Rain Until September', 'Up on the Roof', 'One Fine Day', 'The Loco-motion', 'I'm Into Something Good' … the list goes on and on. I'd heard Aretha Franklin sing 'You Make Me Feel Like a Natural Woman' before I ever heard Carole sing it, and Aretha's version was always on high rotation. When I discovered that Carole King had written it, and that she'd sung it on *Tapestry*, it blew my mind. It's fascinating to see how different artists can take someone else's song and make it their own, as Aretha did with that one.

The producers of the show hired a very talented writer to interview Debra and me to find out why we liked the songs of Carole King, and the album *Tapestry*, so she could write dialogue for us to perform in between songs. Debra was a massive fan of Carole and so she had a lot to share, whereas I didn't have that much to say. I knew I liked singing her songs, and I was curious to know what had inspired Carole King to write them. I was interested in her personal story, so a more biographical type of script probably would have suited me better. But Debra wanted to share her own moving experiences with these songs, because they meant so much to her. She lived and breathed every lyric and every note of those songs and knew them like the back of her hand. In the end, we settled on a bit of both. In hindsight, I'm glad Debra wanted to go deeper and tell the audience what those songs meant to her, because it forced me to think harder about why I wanted to sing them too.

I was a little intimidated but absolutely loved working with Debra. She's such a pro and, although I thought I knew a lot about singing by that stage of my career, Debra certainly taught me some new tricks. My sound-check routine usually involved walking on stage, saying 'Check one, two' a couple of times, singing a song or two, getting the foldback operator to turn it up or down, and then off I went. But Debra takes her time with sound check so she can hear herself clearly and doesn't have to push. This is very smart because she never loses her voice. Debra gets her sound just right, with exactly the right amount of reverb, so when she hears herself in her foldback wedges she sounds sweet. I, on the other hand, sometimes prefer my foldback dry with no 'fairy dust', as we like to call it, because I think it helps me sing more in tune. But I learned from Debra that you can sound a whole lot better, and singing is easier for some reason, when you have a little reverb. What you're hearing is a lot more pleasant than when you hear yourself dry, which can be confronting, because you can hear every little bum note.

Debra has high standards and is very musical, so if you're a musician and you can't keep up, your head is on her chopping block! Debra's favourite musician on this tour was guitarist Dion

Hirini. Debra and Dion had a special connection because he played with so much feeling and they had a long history of playing together. Dion was different to a lot of musicians. He was very sensitive to the singer and never over-played; he always listened to what the singer was doing. He was a tasteful player too, and the notes he chose to play were always surprising and nothing short of genius. When Debra and Dion performed 'Up on the Roof' together each night, just the two of them, I sat there in awe and often in tears. It was Debra's story that they were performing, and Dion understood how much the song meant to her.

LINDA
The Palermo effect

We had just taken on our fabulous new manager Lisa Palermo, and were feeling excited to be entering a new phase of our careers. Before managing us, Lisa was the assistant for our trusted agent Frank Stivala. Frank, like Peter 'Lucky' Luscombe, has been there from day one and has stuck by us through thick and thin. After we left the Honeymooners and joined the Sorrows, he took us on as an independent group and became our agent, booking our gigs and negotiating our fees. When he booked us our first show we delivered his commission in cash, not knowing that this was not the norm. He just looked at us with his cheeky grin and said, 'Hey girls, you don't need to do this every time I book you a gig.' How silly we were!

We knew from working closely with Frank over the years that

Lisa was a classy lady. Even more than that, she was a strong and smart chick who sat quietly and worked solidly in the background for years, making our lives, and those of our band, easier. Lisa treated everybody with the same respect too, and we loved that. We watched as she managed some difficult artists without losing her cool, and navigated complex situations and itineraries that would make any well-balanced person run screaming to the closest psych clinic. Vika and I liked her style, which she had by the bucketload. She could write a far more interesting memoir than us, given the things she has seen and heard, but that would never happen. She's a vault and very tight-lipped, thank GOD, because no one with a loose tongue could do what she does.

When Lisa said yes to managing us, it felt like everything in our world, career-wise, would be better from that moment on, and a few weeks later the three of us found ourselves sitting around Vika's kitchen bench having our weekly meeting. We were still in the 'getting to know you' phase as artists and manager, and it can take a while to get into a particular rhythm, but Vika and I knew we were in good hands.

That day, Lisa worked her way through the list of things for us to discuss, and when we were almost done, she said, as casual as anything, 'Oh, and one last thing. You've been asked to sing the national anthem at this year's Grand Final in a couple of months.'

'No,' was Vika's immediate reaction, while I – a VFL Junior Supporter and long-time footy fan – had to take a moment and sit down. I was like, 'What!?' It was a lot to take in.

Poor Lisa stared at her two stunned singers for a moment, then said, 'Well, you take your time and think about it, but an answer tomorrow would be good.'

That was a typical Lisa response. Think, but don't think too long or you'll miss your chance. I could tell Lisa was shocked by our reactions, but she played it down.

Lisa watched on as Vika and I had our usual argy-bargy, only chiming in every now and then with wise advice. Vika came up with the idea of singing it acapella and I agreed. There would be no safety net, and it would be live to millions of people, but we knew that was our strength. That was how we started. The two of us singing together in our shared bedroom, then at church in front of the Tongans (the toughest audiences of them all), then on the pub rock circuit, trying to be heard over noisy punters blowing smoke in our faces. We also thought of the slap back hazard – the sound delay you get in large venues that makes it almost impossible to keep time – of singing in the enormous MCG and agreed this would be a deal-breaker. If the AFL refused to let us sing acapella, we wouldn't do it.

Lisa swung into action, and to our amazement the AFL agreed. What a leap of faith!

We were sworn to secrecy as we started preparing for the biggest gig of our lives. I mean, this was the Grand Final! I'd watched every single one since I was a kid and suddenly there we were, secretly posing with a footy at the AFL Headquarters boardroom for photographers and doing a kick-to-kick on the MCG with Vance

Joy and the Living End, for goodness sake. It was surreal.

In the week of the game, Channel 7's morning show, *Sunrise*, did a long dramatic lead-up to the announcement of who would be singing the national anthem at the Grand Final. When they revealed the artists as 'Vika and Linda Bull', Kochie, the show's conservative male host, said, 'Huh? Who are they? I mean where's Joe Camilleri? Is he going to be there?'

Watching it at home, I was crushed and embarrassed, but thank God his co-host, Samantha Armytage, went on to say nice things about us, because I was about to throw the remote at his face. But even though his ignorant comments lit a fire in me to prove him wrong, a seed of doubt had been planted.

Hell, if he doesn't know who we are and he's in the media, what about the rest of Australia?

Fuck him, I thought. But also, we'd better not stuff this one up.

It wasn't just mainstream Australian media we were copping it from either. A close friend of mine gave me a serve over the phone for singing the anthem in the first place, telling me we should go into the middle of the MCG and stand in silence, holding our fists up in defiance.

'I can't do that because I've already told my mum we're singing and I don't want to disappoint her,' I told him. 'I have to do it now.'

Then he hung up on me.

I'd already spoken to some senior elders, who had all given us their blessing, so that was enough for me. But I was still very nervous about backlash, and the night before the biggest performance of my life I cried my eyes out to Ian. My boyfriend kindly and sweetly talked me off the ledge, saying he'd knock the socks off anyone who dared criticise us.

'You go and do what you do best,' he said. 'And that's to sing.'

The 2016 Grand Final was between the Sydney Swans and the Bulldogs, and Vika and I had to be at the MCG very early that day. Considering that neither of us had got much sleep, we were remarkably calm, which had a lot to do with Lisa. She calmed our farm just by being her, and we were so grateful to have her there with us.

Getting into the MCG on Grand Final day is like trying to get into Fort Knox. There are passes and IDs galore, and if they'd had retina-scan technology, I reckon they would have pulled that out too. That kind of security adds to your anxiety levels. Once we were through to the inner sanctum of the MCG, we were taken up to our own room to prepare, away from the other artists, Sting, Vance Joy and the Living End, who were involved with half-time and pre-match performances. This was a good move because our room was miles away from any noise or distraction. We were able to warm up, rehearse and have a champagne each to calm our nerves. Lisa was our rock throughout it all.

Meanwhile, Nia was at the Gasometer pub in Fitzroy with her friends, trying her hardest not to vomit from nerves, and Ian was inhaling beers with his mates, panicked and worried. I didn't find all this out until later, of course. I can't imagine what our parents were going through, except that they were probably praying we didn't embarrass ourselves in front of the nation. We knew the combined audience of the Grand Final was in the millions, so we were just a little bit toey.

But I kept reminding myself that we were used to TV cameras and big crowds, to large venues like the MCG, and, most of all, we were used to pressure. We got this, I thought. We've had enough practice over the years! If we can't carry this off, we may as well pack up our bags and go home! I didn't care that the majority of that massive audience wouldn't know who we were. All we had to think about was sticking to the melody and not getting too fancy. 'Sing it in tune and get the hell outta there so the footy fans can get what they came for!' I told myself.

As the clock ticked over, we were given the nod, and someone walked us down to the bowels of the building and into a holding pen. This was when my pulse started to race. Shit was getting real now. There were people everywhere, and then I heard the roar of the enormous crowd, all cheering as the past footy players were driven around the ground. It was the same routine I'd seen on TV every year for as long as I could remember, but when you're standing that close to the action the sound of one hundred thousand excited footy fanatics is deafening.

I could see our favourite – Bob Murphy, the captain of the Bulldogs – in the periphery, pacing, and that made me even more nervous for him and us.

Finally, the moment arrived, and as we walked out onto the ground I looked over at Vik, who was humming our starting note to herself so we would be in the right key.

'Whatever happens, let's enjoy this moment,' I said to my sister. 'Take a sec to take this in because it's amazing.'

She nodded and together we did exactly that. We held hands, looked around the ground at the players and the crowd, and took one hell of a deep breath.

If you watch the video of that performance, you can hear us humming the note to each other just before we launch into the national anthem.

A massive crowd like that emits a unique kind of energy. We'd experienced this energy when we played to big crowds in Europe with the Sorrows, and with Paul Kelly, so we had that advantage. We relied on that experience that day, as well as being by each other's sides, as we started to sing.

Standing in the middle of that ground, feeling that energy surrounding us and hearing the crowd singing along, then cheer us when it was over, is a feeling I'll never, ever forget. It hit me like a hammer to my heart, and something shifted inside me for the better that day. We did our job to the best of our ability, and it felt damn good. It didn't pay to think about the number of people who were watching. All I needed to care about was my family, because that's all that matters. They are the only ones who will always tell me the truth, good or bad, and they were all happy, as was Lisa, so I was relieved.

As the game started, we were whisked away to the airport to catch a flight to the Gold Coast to open for Kasey Chambers that night. As we sat watching the TV in the Virgin Lounge at Melbourne airport, I screamed my lungs out for the Bulldogs, who eventually took the trophy after a battle of mammoth proportions. They were all champions that day. It's the best Grand Final I've ever seen, and I'm so proud that we were part of it.

After all the excitement of the Grand Final, life returned to normal. One minute you're singing for millions of footy fans in what was undoubtedly the biggest audience of our lives, and the next it's back to the normal routine of school drop-offs, play dates and cleaning shit up.

We went back to touring with PK, and with *RocKwiz*, and Vika went back to touring with *Etta*. Our own shows were booking bigger rooms. We started taking on different projects too, and through 2016, 2017 and 2018 our calendars were full and varied. Every week we seemed to be learning a different set of songs and sometimes I didn't know if I was Arthur or Martha!

Vika did the Carole King show, as well as the Marvin Gaye show both here and in South Africa. I was asked to join the Aussie band ARC on their Beatles' Abbey Road show, which travelled all over the country. In 2018, my dear friend and mentor, renowned blues singer Chris Wilson, asked me to do the songs of Willie Nelson with him in a show called *Stardust*. Chris sadly passed away before the show opened. I didn't know if the show should go ahead without him but another of my good mates, Sime Nugent, stepped in, and we carried on with the show for Chris. He had the kindest heart, and even when he was very ill, Chris and his beautiful wife, Sarah, continued to have the good grace to egg me on. That kind of support is something I won't ever forget, and I love them very much.

Vika and I also went to Brazil with CW Stoneking, and performed at festivals around Australia and New Zealand, as well as singing on a few more hugely successful records, including Paul Kelly's *Life Is Fine*, which (unbelievably) turned out to be his first ever number one album.

In October 2018, while Vika was in the UK with the Etta show, I decided to get the ball rolling on a new album. After a fifteen-year break, we were welcomed back to the Mushroom Group when we signed another record deal under the leadership of Michael Gudinski and Warren Costello. Back with our trusted team, alongside Dean McLachlan and Bill Page. I got together with songwriters to begin gathering songs. This process requires patience and clarity because when you ask someone to write you a song you can't expect them to drop everything and deliver it straight away, even though this is exactly what Kasey Chambers did.

A week or so after we asked her if she'd write us some songs, Kasey sent five songs through, three of which we went on to record. God, we love her. The first song, 'Raise Your Hand', which she co-wrote with Brandon Dodd, was the one that got things moving. That song set the tone for the rest of the record, which was very much a 'speak up and be counted' kind of vibe. It was direct in its message and approach, not unlike the way we were feeling at the time.

The songs started coming in over the next two years, and we'd go through them all during our monthly meetings to decide if a song spoke to us, if we could convincingly deliver it, if we were drawn to melody first and lyrics second. It's simple, really. If we don't understand what we're singing about, then we'd ask the songwriter to explain – even though we hate doing that because it's kind of rude – and then either tweak the lyrics or leave it on the bench. We received songs from all over the place, written by all sorts of people, both unknown and legendary, and we could hardly believe how lucky we were.

Things slowly started taking shape. As per our usual process, Vika and I sat down and decided who would sing which parts of the song, and, weirdly, it ended up being an even split, with a couple of duets thrown in. This is a process that never usually causes problems, unless there's a song we both want to sing, and this happened with a song written by Glenn Richards from Augie March called 'Pigface and Calendula'. I couldn't give in to Vik just because she wanted it; I had to prove I could do it.

As we were getting the album together, Vik and I, with Lisa's encouragement and involvement, were suddenly willing to try more things and put ourselves out there. It was paying off too. Better to try and fail than to never try at all was our new attitude. Never in my wildest dreams did I think I'd be busier at fifty than I was when I was twenty.

In 2019, we did a run of shows at Memo Music Hall in St Kilda every Sunday afternoon. During these shows, we'd test out the songs people had written for our new album. These sessions were a hoot and were packed every week, which shocked the shit out of both of us. Soon after this, our mate Julia Zemiro, who was artistic director of the 2019 Adelaide Cabaret Festival, asked if Vika and I could write a show to debut at the festival. Both Julia and Lisa encouraged us to turn everything we had learned while telling other people's stories into a show of our own. We came up with a name for the show – *Between Two Shores* – and set about writing it.

I was so nervous because it was up to us to choose all the material and to write the script, which was a huge task and something we'd never done before. But if we were going to tell our story through songs, we agreed that they had to mean something. The songs had to be true to our journey as singers, showing how we either paved the way or changed our course, and we worked very hard to make sure it was right.

Every week we'd perch ourselves around Vika's kitchen bench, writing down ideas and choosing songs that triggered memories from our path as singers. We'd bounce these ideas off one another and Lisa, until we had a story. We also pulled songs out of Vika's Etta James show, out of *Stardust*, from our time with the Sorrows; we used songs we'd written with Paul Kelly, and songs sung in Tongan. But the best fun I had was when we were writing the TV show medley. It was surprisingly easy because Vika and I can still remember every single TV theme song and ad we learned and loved as kids. The hardest part was choosing what to leave out of that medley. It ended up being the part of the show that got the biggest belly laugh from the crowd.

After its success at the festival, we were invited to perform at all the major concert hall venues around the country. We were so nervous when we performed *Between Two Shores* at the Arts Centre in Melbourne. We knew that if the audience hated it, we'd find out straight away. Thankfully this didn't happen. The audiences seemed to love it and the shows in Melbourne went really well. I loved every minute of performing that show with my sister and truly believed things for us wouldn't get better than this.

And they suddenly got a lot worse. For everyone.

Next stop was the Sydney Opera House, followed by the Brisbane Powerhouse. One night at the Powerhouse, after I'd done my usual pre-show nervous wee and was zipping up my outfit … BOOM! The power went off. There I was, standing in a totally dark bathroom in the Powerhouse, wondering what the hell had happened.

There had been a power outage at the Powerhouse – the very place that, historically, was meant to generate it – and our poor audience had to leave in the bucketing rain. The last time we had cancelled a show was twenty-five years earlier and it was also due to heavy rain. I'm superstitious on a crippling level and couldn't help feeling like this night and the cancellation of our show was a bad omen. I believe that bad luck comes in threes, but after that night in early 2020, bad luck didn't come in threes, it came in thirty-threes. What was to come surprised everybody. Devastating bushfires, COVID-19, loss of income, despair, loneliness, isolation, frustration, fear, curfews, courage, kindness, sacrifice and the death of loved ones. It felt like we were all being tested on a completely different level, and the way Vika and I dealt with it would be not only deeply personal, but also very public.

VIKA

Offstage and online

Linda and I had never really used the internet before coronavirus came along. We had a Facebook page but never interacted with it or used it in any way. We had nice people looking after the page for us, but we were hopeless with a capital H because it just didn't interest us. I avoided social media for years. Neither of us cared much about promoting ourselves that way. Sometimes I'd see people and they'd know so much about what others were doing, and I was intrigued. How did they know all of this?

'Facebook!' they'd say.

A friend of ours suggested Linda and I film one of our gigs and put it up on Facebook to try to make a bit of money.

'You can charge people to see it,' he told us.

But I thought it all sounded too hard and complicated for my small brain to handle.

'Who would wanna watch that?' I asked. 'It would be pretty boring.'

I thought it was all too time-consuming. Now, I want to say thanks to those people for putting up with Linda and me and our slow brains. They were trying to kick us up the arse and get us onboard with evolving technology and the new ways of the world. It took us years before we caught on, which was thanks to Lisa.

When COVID-19 hit, we lost all our gigs, like every other artist in the world, and were gutted. Then Lisa had an idea.

'How about you perform a song, girls?' she said. 'You can put it on social media as a way of giving back to everyone. You can go live, check in with everyone and do one song.'

We found out later that she almost didn't suggest it, knowing how much Linda and I 'loved' social media, but we jumped at her suggestion.

'Good idea, Lisa!' we said.

'Great! When do you want to do it?' she asked.

'Tomorrow!'

We called up Dion straight away. 'Hey, D, you wanna come play "Up Above My Head" by Sister Rosetta Tharpe for us to post live on Facebook and Instagram?'

Dion thought it was a terrific idea. 'No worries, gals,' he said. 'See you tomorrow morning!'

We'd be filming it on a Sunday morning, so we thought, 'Gospel song! Perfect!'

Dion arrived early the next day, all dressed up and wearing his signature bowler hat, and we ran the song. Linda and I knew the song very well because we'd been singing it together for years, and it was one of our most-loved songs by one of our favourite singers. The lyrics are, 'Up above my head, I hear music in the air. Up above my head, I see trouble in the air, but I really do believe there is a heaven somewhere.'

Right words, right song.

We filmed it on my front porch, and it was heaps of fun and made us feel good too, and afterwards we just got on with our day. We were new at this whole thing and didn't understand the power of social media – we thought maybe a couple of people would watch it, like our family back home in Tonga, and that would be it. We didn't worry about what we were wearing, or the background. We only hoped we wouldn't stuff up the technology side of it, which later on we sometimes did. Well, what an eye-opener. A whole truckload of people watched!

We were shocked and kind of embarrassed, too, for being a couple of old-school fools. We decided to do it again the following week, but this time we'd pay attention to our background and what we wore, because even though people enjoyed the singing, there were also some comments about our house and our clothes. It was just a few little comments, and most were positive, but it made us realise how closely people were watching. We decided we'd better change things up a bit to keep people interested. Every week after that, we filmed in a different location of the house, and did different songs. It was always gospel, but with special guests too. Dion did the first one in person but after that it was all done remotely. Our mates would film and record themselves at home, then send the video to us and we'd put them up on our computer screen and sing along with them. Our little Bose bluetooth speaker and our laptop became our new best friends. This was all new to us. We weren't used to being apart and so we had to use technology to bring us together, something I thought I would never embrace but ended up really enjoying because it was so challenging.

We changed location to Linda's house and were joined by either Cameron Bruce on piano or Ben Hauptmann or Dion on guitar, and one time my husband on drums. At one point we brought in Paul Kelly for a duet; another time, Diesel; and even Kiki sang backing vocals on one of our songs. Nia and Lisa filmed every single one, for Instagram and Facebook, at 11am every Sunday.

John suggested we call these performances the Sunday Sing Song, and we did them for six weeks. It became a real production by the end. We'd spend all week preparing for the filming on Sunday, and it was a very good thing to do during lockdown. It kept us busy and gave us something to look forward to every week. Social media became our best friend and it changed our lives completely.

After each Sing Song, we spent a couple of hours discussing what song we should do the following week. We tried to keep them as uplifting as possible, because we had all found ourselves in this unique and worrying situation with COVID-19.

After that, we dived right in. Once the first few Sing Songs went out, Linda had an idea to do a parody of 'Nutbush City Limits', which we called 'Iso City Limits'. When they started calling the virus COVID-19, Linda had the lyrics, 'It's COVID number 19, the people keep the city clean' in her head, so she called me up and suggested we do it. My first reaction was 'Why?'

'Just for fun,' Linda said.

She'd written it with her two kids around the dining table the week before, and they based the lyrics on which ones got the loudest laugh. She'd had a lot of fun coming up with replacement lines and said she and the girls were cacking themselves. After a bit more badgering I said yes. By then I was so bored being locked inside my house that I needed to do something. I went over to Linda's, we tweaked the lyrics a bit, Kiki set up the camera and we went for it.

We sent the video to Lisa and she put it up for us. And BANG!

One million views in the first couple of hours ... then two ... then three ... then four ... then five ... then six!

Holy shit, what is going on? we thought. It was unbelievable, and ironic, that two chicks who knew pretty much nothing about social media had managed to go viral two weeks after they started. Our dad was sitting on the porch scratching his head. This new attention had a big effect on our Sing Song audience. One helped the other. It felt surreal that right when our industry was shutting down, we were getting the most attention we had ever received. What made it all worthwhile was the fact that it seemed to be bringing a little relief to those who were finding the pandemic talk, endless news conferences and lockdowns hard to take. That period of Sing Songs is one of our proudest achievements because, right when we needed it most, our love of music in its most basic form, two voices and one instrument, came to the rescue. It was our go-to medicine and had a very healing effect on all of us.

We were on the Red Hot Summer tour in March 2021, with

Jimmy Barnes, the Hoodoo Gurus, Jon Stevens, Diesel and the Living End, when we received the news that our beloved friend, Dion Hirini, had passed away. That day, Jimmy and Jane Barnes turned up on the side of the stage to watch our show, and this meant the world to us. It was another five hours before they were due to play, and their support during that sad time was the lift we needed when all we wanted to do was collapse into a heap and cry. They are both very special people.

Dion had died suddenly. He was driving home from Keep the Circle Unbroken, a gig in the country, and was almost home when his heart stopped and he passed away. In the weeks before he died, we knew that Dion wasn't well. We still did local gigs together, but we asked another guitar player to come on the road with us because we knew touring might take its toll on him. Linda and I loved Dion so much and were devastated when we heard the news. We had worked with him for twenty years, and often referred to him as the third Bull sister. The last time we performed with Dion was during a show that Michael Gudinski had organised for the people of Mallacoota after the devastating bushfires.

He was quirky and clever and we loved having him on the road with us because he was such a good driver and could always get us to wherever we needed to go, and always without a map! He had that Polynesian sense of direction, and sometimes we could have sworn he was navigating by the stars. Dion was a quiet fella, never rowdy except after he'd had a few, but he was a great drunk and we had a lot of laughs, like belly-ache laughing all night long.

He was a great giggler, especially when Linda and I hit bum notes. He thought it was a riot and couldn't control his giggles. Anyone would think Dion had heard the best joke of his life when we sang off-key. It was pretty funny, I gotta say.

Over the years, we travelled together a lot, and one of Dion's favourite things to do was get up at dawn to walk, explore and take beautiful photos, most of which he put on Instagram. Just before he died, I noticed that he'd started posting a lot of photos, and I wonder if Dion knew he wasn't long for this earth and wanted to capture every moment and place that he could. We could see that his health was getting progressively worse. He was coughing a lot more than usual and Linda and I were very concerned, but it never stopped him from giving his all when he played.

At Dion's funeral, they placed his signature bowler hat on his coffin, which I'm sure he would have loved. Linda and I miss our brother terribly. He was a funny bloke with a heart of gold, and what a talent. You know how the saying goes … only the good die young.

RIP BLX.

LINDA

The Wait

Recording *The Wait* was probably one of the most enjoyable experiences we've ever had in the studio. It felt like it had taken us forever to get there, so we weren't gonna muck around. We had been working closely with producer Cameron Bruce over the years, both in PK's band and as our musical director for our theatre shows like *Between Two Shores* and *Stardust*. He had also produced *Sunday (The Gospel According to Iso)*, throughout the never-ending lockdowns in the COVID-19 pandemic, so we wanted him involved with *The Wait*. He worked his arse off producing that record with Steven Schram, always willing to try anything in order to get the best result, which would test our patience but that's exactly what you want and need. Because, after all, records stay around forever. There is no way that *The Wait* would have sounded as good without him and Steven. No way.

I love being part of an album from the very beginning, whether it's mine or not. I love the writing process, making up harmony parts – either in a support role as a backing singer or as lead – recording the songs, doing the promotional stuff up to its release and then touring. The whole process is so satisfying every step of the way, and then it's an incredible feeling to have the audience sing parts that you created back at you. For so many years, Vika and I were witness to other people's incredible success, so we weren't strangers to that feeling you have when there's momentum behind something. When it works it makes me so proud and happy, and this album *worked*.

Whenever anybody in the media asks me why it took us nineteen years to make our 2021 record, my answer is, 'We were busy doing other things.'

I can't easily explain what happened to us during COVID-19 because, although it was a triumphant time for us career-wise, it was a time of terrible loss and heartache for others and that made me feel a deep level of guilt. COVID-19 hit Vika harder than it hit me, and I noticed that she started retreating more throughout it. My sister was already a bit of a loner and the longer it went on, the more she seemed to pull away. I thought to myself, Hello, I think she's a bit depressed, which is a feeling I don't think she'd ever experienced before. Not to my knowledge anyway. It was also the first time we'd been separated from each other for longer periods of time, and it was hard because I missed her. I was worried she'd retreat further into her shell, so I started to mimic our normal show-day routine. At night, I'd call her just before what would have been show time, to talk about whatever. Then, later, after show time, I'd call again, and we'd chat like we always do after a gig. It seemed to help.

The only other way I felt like we could overcome the feelings we were having was to create more. I have always been a creative person, so continuing to sing – even though there was no audience in front of us – was one way to scratch the creative itch. Sing Song did that for us, and the far-reaching upside was that I could sense that the music was uplifting the flattening spirits of our audience. There was very little backlash online and I learned later that this was unusual for the kind of reach we were getting.

During the first year of numerous lockdowns in Melbourne, Vika and I threw ourselves into work. While the ball had started rolling on *The Wait*, there were already plans in the making to release an anthology. Together with our trusted team at Bloodlines, led by Warren Costello, we selected songs that spanned a specific time of our careers, specifically from 1994 to 2006. Towards the end of 2020, *'Akilotoa* was released.

It seemed as if our beautiful fans had been waiting for a new release from us because it went really well, debuting at number one on the ARIA charts. We became the first female vocal duo to ever do that. Warren was so excited that he tore the number one off his fencepost and brought it into the studio so we could pose with a number. That was an incredible feeling. The happiness on the faces of Warren, Lisa and everyone involved was all I needed. I never ever thought something like this would happen to us. In the back of my mind, I believed our careers were winding down, not up!

Next thing we knew the dreaded lockdown kept getting extended, so there we were – hogtied and hamstrung again. Back to the drawing board we went for another round of Sing Songs, but this time we'd been working on a gospel album too. We planned to release it as soon as we were freed from our houses, as a way of putting a full stop on it all.

We worked away remotely with Cameron Bruce, who played all the instruments and recorded them on backing track. He sent them to us and we ran into the studio with producer/engineer John Castle, and sang all the songs as fast as we could. Most of the vocal tracks on *Sunday (The Gospel According to Iso)* are first takes because of the Melbourne lockdown laws. It went to number two on the ARIA charts, pipped at the post by Marilyn Manson, which was quite ironic to me as the styles of music are polar opposites. I would have loved to see our gospel album take down a heavy metal shock-rock artist like him.

VIKA
A fresh start

On 28 January 2022 I finally decided to get rid of the monkey on my back once and for all and quit drinking for good. It hasn't been easy, but I was tired of it all. Tired of the hangovers, the remorse, the stupid arguments, my family being disappointed in me and of looking like shit. I don't like myself when I drink, and I was hating myself more and more. I wanna be a dignified, bona fide old lady who will age gracefully. I don't wanna be a burden on the system and end up in hospital because of my own doing, and I was certainly heading down that path. It was time to change, time to grow up. But this wasn't easy for a girl who had been hitting it since she was seventeen years old.

I hate the fact that alcohol has become so much a part of our culture and our industry. It is always flowing freely backstage at gigs, and if it isn't there, boy, do people kick up a stink about it. I used to be one of those people. My drinking got progressively worse, and it started to catch up to me.

Then lockdown hit. Oh no!

Linda and I started the Sunday Sing Song and that saved our lives. It gave us something to look forward to every week, something to work towards. Something to keep us busy. But all of a sudden we found ourselves in this very odd situation. What would we do with our evenings now? No gigs, no travel and we couldn't even see the family.

Okay, let's drink!

By Victoria's sixth lockdown, drink I had and did. I think I tried to kill myself with booze some nights. Not on purpose, but it sure felt like it the next day. If I wasn't going to end up in hospital with COVID-19, I probably would have ended up in there on the waiting list for a liver transplant.

Everyone has their journey. Mine was that of a binge drinker. I didn't drink every day but when I did drink, I couldn't stop. If you want to give up drinking, then when you are ready you will. It's not easy, because it's so much fun to drink sometimes, but waking up with no hangover and no remorse is truly a fantastic feeling.

I tried AA but it wasn't for me, and I tried to quit on my own but I couldn't do it. I saw a couple of fantastic therapists and tried many times to stop but nothing worked. Then I found an app that suited me right down to the ground. Now, I visit it every morning and do my daily tasks, and it has helped me immensely. It has helped me on my alcohol-free journey, which in this business is very hard because the temptation is always there. I have no other option but to quit because I am not going to stop singing. I have no choice. I want to keep singing, and I can't remove myself from an industry where alcohol is always around and on offer.

These days I take it one day at a time. I wake up every morning and say to myself, 'Today I am not going to drink.'

I am grateful for so many things and I have come so close many times to losing it all but I am not going to throw it all away because I love getting pissed. It's not worth it.

I am still wild at my core, always have been. Quiet, but with a wild streak, and in the past I have done whatever I wanted to do and never worried about the consequences. Linda dots every i and crosses every t, but I can't be bothered with the detail. I just get in there and get it done. In the beginning, Linda would follow me around and copy everything I did because I was the eldest, but over the years, she has grown wiser. I'm so happy she decided to quit university and come sing with me, because she's always had my back and we've had a blast together. I knew we'd be a great team. Not only can we harmonise well but our differences make it work.

EPILOGUE

LINDA

After wrapping up the first draft of this book, Vika and I were awarded an OAM. If you'd told me that the chunky kid on the basketball team/the only dark kid in the class/the primary school times-table dork would end up doing something in life that was good enough to recieve this honour, I would have laughed at the idea. A lot of other people probably would have too, my nasty kindergarten teacher at the top of the list. But Mr Hobby, my Grade 6 teacher, and Miss Sutton, my high school principal, might be grinning. Vika and I are overjoyed that our parents are here to witness the two of us being recognised for our work in a notoriously tough industry. Our mother can't believe it, and Dad is still sitting on the porch scratching his head in wonder.

    Most of the people mentioned in this book have seen something in me that I wasn't aware of, both good and bad. I've done my best to listen but haven't always succeeded. Vika and I didn't set out looking for awards. I didn't even want to be a singer when I started out in the world as an adult. I was soft, and not tough enough to survive. Vika was the one who made me tough, and the one who has stuck by me the longest. Yes, we're different. We shit each other up the wall, we argue and complain about each other, and I think that's normal for sisters. But at the end of the day, don't you dare criticise her or hurt her in any way or I'll go you.

We're a team.

But the thing that gives us both the most happiness is seeing our children out there in the world, pursuing their own dreams and achieving their own goals. One thing we know for sure is that none of them are interested in following in our footsteps. Mafi is a nurse (like our mum), Nia is studying law (like Mum wanted me to do) and Kiki … well, anything is possible.

When Mafi and Nia told Mum what they wanted to do, our mother punched the air.

'Why did you do that?' Vika asked.

'I finally got my wish!' Mum said. 'A nurse and a lawyer in the family!'

Professionally, the last couple of years have been an intense time of growth. For Vika and me, it was the perfect storm, and now the thing I get stopped in the street for most is Sing Song. We got back to basics, with Dad's words, 'Just be yourselves', ringing in my ears. We relied on all those years of training and practice to do what we love to do best, and that is to harmonise together. We did it as simply and as genuinely as we could and let it loose on a globally captive audience. Letting our guards down, and letting the audience into our private homes, was confronting at first because showbiz is so much about smoke and mirrors. What if people didn't like what they saw? But we trusted our gut because it felt right at the time.

And our message was heard.

Once we opened our mouths, we couldn't stop. We still can't stop, and I'm enjoying the feeling that the faster I roll, the further I can go. Who knows what's going to happen next? That's what I love about singing. Every day is a different adventure and life is never dull. I've made it this far, so why stop now?

I love that I get to work with Lisa, our sister from another mister, and our talented band every day, doing the thing I enjoy most.

And all of it with Vika, my sister and my best friend.

VIKA

In June 2022, three days before we were scheduled to finally begin our The Wait tour, which had been postponed due to COVID restrictions, we hit another bump in the road.

I was feeling a bit green around the gills, and had been for a while, but I ignored all the signs. At the urging of Mafi, I begrudgingly made an appointment with my fantastic Doctor, Samantha Wilson, who immediately sent me to the Epworth Hospital to get checked out, which luckily was just up the road from the rehearsal studio.

I thought, yeah, they'll check it out, give me some pills and send me on my merry way. It had been almost a year since *The Wait* had been released and nothing was going to stop me touring this new record that I loved so much, with a bunch of kick-arse musicians I absolutely adored. That is until I had an x-ray and my big spunk of a doctor Mark Steven told me that I was going to undergo surgery immediately. I mentioned that I had a tour starting in a couple of days and could he perhaps please put it off for a couple of weeks. He grabbed me by the arm and very sternly but wisely said, 'Health first, wealth second, Vika,' and with that the team kicked into action and rectified my situation immediately.

I really want to thank those wonderful doctors and nurses who looked after me, especially Dr Steven and Dr Pendlebury, and Mafi for forcing me to get checked out.

While my health was being dealt with, Team Vika and Linda, helmed by our fearless leader, Lisa Palermo, kicked into serious action and rearranged the whole thing in two days. All of this happened while I was blissed out under general aesthetic – my second-favourite drug. As it turned out, the gods were smiling upon us and we only had to postpone for another couple of months – thank God, because I didn't want to tour a new record in 2023 that had been released in 2021. Linda and I are very grateful to have such a wonderful group of people who work with us, people who get shit done!

Finally, in August 2022, The Wait tour got off the ground. It was our first headline tour and our first time headlining at the Palais in St Kilda, Melbourne – an iconic venue next to Luna Park with the beautiful St Kilda Beach as it's backdrop. The Palais holds around 2000 people, and we have performed in it many times over the years singing backing vocals for various bands and doing the supports for the big acts, but never as the headliners. To see our names in lights out the front of The Palais was a weird feeling. I couldn't look at it because I couldn't quite believe it. All these years I have considered myself a singer – not a backing singer, not a lead singer, just a singer – but to be finally able to perform in a venue where 2000 people are happy to part with their hard-earned cash to come and hear you sing with your sister and shit-hot band was something I will never ever take for granted and something I will never ever forget.

I'm so lucky to be on this journey with Linda, who has been by my side since I was seventeen months old. We were brought up to look after one another, take care of each other. Mum was always drumming that into us. She wanted her little family to be close and she worked bloody hard to keep the four of us together. Linda has always had my back even when I have monumentally screwed up. My little sister taking care of me, watching out for me, defending me.

The life we chose hasn't been easy but it sure has been fun. We have had a lot of memorable moments and met a hell of a lot of nice people along the way who have encouraged and supported us. I wanna thank all those people and all of our fabulous fans who have come to our shows and listened to us sing – it has meant the world to me. To be able to survive in this business with my little sister by my side has been a dream come true.

ACKNOWLEDGEMENTS

Vika and Linda would like to thank …

Lisa Palermo, our most trusted and dynamic manager. Behind the scenes we are not a duo, we are a trio! Thank you for being the third sister and for your loyalty and passionate leadership. You always have our best interests at heart and we thank the universe that we found each other. We would not have finished this book if not for your unwavering determination that we could do it and not only that, do it ourselves! We have *No Bull* because of you.

Martin Hughes and the team from Affirm Press for approaching us in the first place and convincing us that we had a story to tell. Martin, your brutal honesty, sense of humour and no-nonsense approach is what has made this experience so enjoyable for us.

Joanna Murray Smith for her expert early advice on how to get started and stay focussed.

Fiona Harris, our hilarious 'book doctor', for looking at everything we'd written (you poor thing) and for whipping *No Bull* into shape.

Warren Costello for thirty years of friendship, both in and out of the music business, and for showing two young girls how to behave in an industry that is notoriously tough. We will miss you.

Dean McLachlan – we couldn't have asked for a better successor to Waz, you always have a kind and gentle ear and we couldn't feel in safer hands than yours.

Samantha Gowing, Peter 'Lucky' Luscombe, Kerri McKenzie, Kerri Simpson, Peter 'EO' Stephens, John Watson and Tanya Wright for having better memories than ours and for being our invaluable and reliable fact checkers.

Our parents, Austen and Siniva Bull, for your infinite support and encouragement of us every step of the way, every day. We are so grateful to you both for allowing us the freedom from a young age to go for it and to follow our dreams.

From Vika – thank you John and Mafi Watson, my two hot heads! I love you.

From Linda – thank you Nia and Kiki, my beautiful girls, you are the best daughters I could wish for. We are a great team and I love you always.